Rusty's Story

Carol Gino

aah-ha! Books© Inc.
New York

RUSTY'S STORY

REVISED EDITION
Published by aah-ha! Books, Inc.
http://www.starwater.com

Grateful acknowledgment is extended for permission to reprint the following:
Extract from "The Cocktail Party" from COLLECTED POEMS,
1909-1962 by T.S. Eliot, copyright 1936 by Harcourt Brace Jovanovich, Inc., copyright 1963,
1964 by T.S. Eliot. Reprinted by permission of Harcourt Brace Jovanovich, Inc. in the United
States and the Philippines. Reprinted by permission of Faber and Faber Publishers in Canada.
Extract from THE EPILEPSY FACT BOOK, "Psychomotor Seizures" and
"Partial Seizures with Complex Symptons", © 1977 by Harry Sands and Frances Minters. F.A.
Davis Company. Reprinted by permission.
Line from THE MAN OF LA MANCHA, ©1968 Andrew Scott Inc. and Helena Music Corp.
Music by Mitch Leigh and words by Joe Darion. Reprinted by permission.

For information address: aah-ha! Books, Inc.
12 Virginia Court, Amityville, NY 11701
(516) 598-8842

aah-ha! Books are published by aah-ha! Inc.
Its trademark, consisting of the words aah-ha! Books and logo,
is registered in U.S. Patent and Trademark Office
Library of Congress Catalog Card #96-095309

ISBN 1-889853-19-4
ISBN 0-553-25351-1

PRINTED IN THE UNITED STATES OF AMERICA

0   2   4   6   8   9   7   5   3   1

THE WORDS KEPT POURING OUT–UNTIL FINALLY CAROL COULDN'T BEAR TO HEAR ANY MORE.

It was dawn when I stopped Rusty from finishing her story. Through the window, the world outside the nursing home was in a rosy gray haze. I was crying.

"I'm so sorry," I mumbled between sniffles.

"For what?" Rusty asked.

As a nurse, one of the oaths I had sworn, one of the things I had promised was to do no harm. I was a true believer in Medicine. We could bring dead men back to life by pumping on their chests; we could relieve pain with a shot or a pill; we could make the blind see again, with cataract surgery and corneal transplants. And now as I listened to Rusty's story, I felt like some medieval nun who had joined the Church because of her belief in good and God and had just heard about the Inquisition. My faith had been challenged.

For Rusty

and the phoenix bird in all of us

CHAPTER 1

I didn't always love being a woman.

"Rites of Passage" used to make me think of animal skins hanging on tepee walls, hot rocks burning red in the center of a small circle of painted Indians, and a lot of chanting. But that's not how it was for me.

My first spark of womanhood came as I was standing on the hood of Jim's black Camaro in the middle of the Japanese tea garden in San Francisco, screaming hysterically, "I wouldn't marry you if my life depended on it."

It was a gorgeous day. Jim was tall, blond and handsome and we had just spent a month together deciding to get married–and, suddenly, I knew I just couldn't do it. I liked him too much to marry him.

Suddenly it occurred to me that I had always needed men not particularly to love, care and share with, but to jump off into Life. They were a safe haven–a solid shore from which to begin the big swim.

The beginning of the Rite of Passage.

I wanted to be a woman, a real woman. I wanted to give and live as a woman–not off a man.

And the most valuable thing about a Rite of Passage is that it does test your endurance, it does take you beyond yourself, but it doesn't do it without taking a searing iron to the center of your heart.

Still, I had an edge. The hidden talisman I held was nursing.

Salvation Nursing Home. The last place in the world I expected to begin any kind of initiation–or to be run down by a stretcher. But that's exactly what was happening. I heard the frantic voices and the fast spinning grind of wheels behind me as I walked the long white corridor and I instinctively jumped back against the wall. Still, the stretcher flew past so fast and so close that it almost knocked me over. On it was something that looked like a heap of dirty old rags and sounded like an old woman. "Oh God! Oh God! Help me ..." she screamed in a shrill hoarse voice. The sweet acrid smell of stale urine, dried feces and alcohol left on the wind immediately helped me understand this wasn't your run-of-the-mill old lady.

Up ahead, the two young ambulance techs stopped the stretcher in front of the nurses' station. I saw a woman dressed in white, obviously the nurse in charge, step toward them. "Rusty!" she hollered as soon as she saw what they had, and then, even louder, "Rusty! Stop what you're doing and come now."

A girl dressed in a green nursing assistant's uniform stepped out from one of the rooms in front of me. Something in her stance let me know she was the one the nurse had been calling. Rusty. She was attractive with blond short hair which fell in place perfectly. I figured she was about twenty. Her uniform was immaculate, obviously pressed carefully, and her white shoes were not only polished but buffed to a high shine. She was thin, her arms muscular, not in the way a man's are, but as though she had worked hard. She wore her watch low on her wrist on a thick leather band, the face turned in. She began to walk quickly toward what was now a real commotion.

The ambulance techs were trying with all their strength to hold the old woman down on the stretcher. Like Houdini, she had managed to loosen the straps that had held her. "Let me out of here, you crappers!" the old woman screamed. Rusty and I now ran toward them. Up close, the old woman was a terrifying sight. Her tangled mass of knotted gray hair stood straight out from her scalp and you could barely distinguish her features because of the caked and cracking dirt all over her face. Her arms and hands swung fast and hard as though she held a machete and anyone who came near was certain to be slashed by the yellowed nails that had grown so long they'd curled around her fingers and turned into bone. The nurse stood far back in the nurses' station. Very unpleasant looking. The name on her badge was "Mrs. Frick" and she was the head nurse on the unit. "Rusty!" she shouted again, though the girl was now standing next to me at the foot of the stretcher. "Calm Mama down. We have to get her admitted." Her dreary brown hair was severely pulled back. Her skin was a drab olive and she wore no lipstick to try to change the downward half-moon of her thin-lipped mouth. She stared icily at me and then impatiently waved me away.

The old woman looked at Mrs. Frick and her withered face contorted. "I'm not your mama, you witch! I'm Marta Sprite, a grown woman who has just been kidnapped." With that she began cursing and scratching while trying to hoist herself up. She looked as though she was getting ready to jump off the stretcher and bolt.

"Move away from her," Rusty said to all of us, and voice was soft but firm. Both techs, still trying to grab for the old woman's arms, looked up questioningly. Mrs. Frick nodded and they moved away. Marta, caught off guard stopped for just a moment, and Rusty walked up to her, hands at her side. But as soon as she got close, the old woman's hand shot out. One of her long claws ripped at Rusty's cheek. Rusty didn't move.

"What's wrong with you, Mama?" Mrs. Frick asked, exasperated, from behind the desk. She had to shout to get through the din of the old woman's screaming and thrashing. Marta was still hitting out hard.

Rusty had slowly and carefully raised her arm and held it up in front of her, a lion tamer now, as the old woman slashed again. "Don't call her Mama," Rusty said softly to Mrs. Frick. Her eyes stayed riveted on the old woman. "Her name's Marta and she told you she's been brought here against her will." Marta was watching Rusty suspiciously but she stopped struggling and slashing. Rusty's cheek was bleeding and there were several long scratches on her arm.

"The old bitch is crazy as a coot," one of the white-coated techs whispered loud enough for all of us to hear. "She's a damn old baglady whose house looks like a filthy pig sty."

Mrs. Frick looked as though she finally understood, but Rusty looked angry. "You know nothing about her," she said, "or about her life." She turned to Mrs. Frick, and added, "I think they can go now.

We can manage with Marta." Marta was lying quietly on the stretcher for the moment but I didn't know how Rusty could be so sure that the old woman wouldn't immediately erupt again. "Can you walk, Marta?" Rusty asked.

The other tech shook his head. "The old fool almost broke her leg. Been laying in shit, pardon me, on the floor of her place for days until one of the neighbors called. She won't let us take her to a hospital emergency room for X-rays. Best we could do is wrap it tight."

As though it was a challenge, Marta immediately sat up and threw her legs over the side. Mrs. Frick looked ready to call in the troops again. Rusty quickly moved forward to steady Marta. One of her legs was in an Ace bandage, the foot at the end of it crusted with dirt and the same thick yellow nails as on her fingers, again grown so long that they had curled around her toes.

"I'm getting down and walking," Marta announced. "Any of you jerks try to stop me and I'll let you have it again."

"Let me help you," Rusty said softly to the old woman. "Put your arm around my shoulders and don't lean on your bad leg. Frick, can you get us a walker?" Rusty asked. "And tell me which room is Mrs. Sprite's . . . if she decides to stay?" Then as Marta reached for Rusty, she added, "The guys can go. We're okay."

To my surprise Mrs. Frick, though she didn't look pleased, dismissed them. She immediately called for one of the other aides to get her a walker, and handed it to Rusty. Back on her feet, Marta looked no less grubby but much less angry. I was left standing at the nurses' station when Mrs. Frick followed them down the hall. I watched them go and plunked down on one of the small metal chairs. Then I hesitantly took a deep breath through my wrinkled nose and tried to absorb some of the atmosphere.

From the time I was a little kid, I'd always had a lot of curiosity and a great imagination. Like an actress, I could study a role, a person, and actually feel what it was like to *be* them. That's why I was here now. I was going to practice being an old lady.

I had decided not to remarry. I had given up the happily forever after with the prince again; the chance to grow old in bliss and comfort, to sit together on matching rocking chairs on the front porch of a big house. And I had chosen instead a life *alone* which held only treacherous territory and desperate loneliness, especially for a woman like me who was arrogant enough to think she could get through life unattached. That was the gospel according to my mom, who I swear believes that of all the evils to befall woman, being unmarried is the worst. Especially when you get *older*. So I was certain that without the porch and the man, there was only the nursing home.

The big trouble with confronting old ladyhood was that I really hated the idea that so many old people, like old cars, were discarded and were placed in junk-yards, separate from the rest of life. So I hated nursing homes. I was afraid of them. But I always ran toward things I was afraid of because I had been taught never to run away. For the six years I'd been divorced and been a nurse I had worked in medical surgical hospitals doing blood-and-guts nursing. Running *toward* and battling sickness and death–until I was no longer afraid in the same way. Now it was time to face old age head-on; to feel my own tomorrow's wrinkles and touch my own gray hair. To come to terms with the alternative I'd chosen. The fact that I was twenty-eight didn't deter me. I knew it was only a matter of time.

I waited at the nurses' station for about five minutes. When neither Mrs. Frick nor Rusty came back to the desk, I scanned the standing rack of metal charts, trying to find a clue to my patient, Mr. Gragone. The only thing I knew about him was what Mrs. Brian from the nurses' registry had told me when she had called the night before. He was seventy years old; had diabetes and Parkinson's disease. Penny was his night nurse and I knew she'd be waiting impatiently for me to relieve her. She and I had been roommates for a while and had graduated from nursing school together, we were good friends. When I found Mr. Gragone's room number on the meal-order list, I decided to wander around in search of him.

Now, the rubber soles of my white shoes squeaked as I passed the small semi-private rooms jutting outward from the bright white hallway. Inside these rooms, I could see nursing assistants dressed in pale green nylon uniforms pushing and pulling frail white-haired patients into their day clothes. Occasionally one of the old people moaned or cried out. There was no other sound.

When I came to the end of the hallway, from inside a room I

could hear a gentle voice I recognized as Rusty's saying, "C'mon, Louisa, let's fix your hair like the picture." Certain she would still be with Marta, I was surprised.

At the doorway, I looked in. Sure enough it was Rusty. Sitting upright on the bed in front of her was a skinny old woman with long wavy white hair. Rusty was combing it carefully.

I watched as the woman frowned and squinted her dark eyes. Then, without warning, she lifted her hand and with bony fingers dug deeply into Rusty's side.

"Louisa," Rusty said, quickly holding tight to the old woman's hand, "you know I'd never hit an old lady wearing glasses. You're not playing fair."

"I ain't wearing glasses," Louisa snapped.

"All the more reason not to do that again," Rusty teased her.

I laughed. Who ever thought of nursing homes as combat zones? Not me–but my first day was proof I was wrong. Yet, it didn't seem to upset Rusty at all. She bent down in front of the old woman and asked quietly, "What's wrong, Louisa? Did I hurt you?"

The old woman gritted her yellowed teeth, a pale old cat, and snarled, "I hate it in here."

"Well, it's not exactly a picnic for me when you take hunks of my body to show your unhappiness," Rusty explained. "Let's both make the best of it, okay? Now, what can I do to help you?" she asked patiently, still holding the old woman's hand. Louisa refused to answer and promptly began to kick her heels frantically against the lowered side rails, making a terrible racket.

Dear Lord, I prayed, if I survive life long enough to be a withered old lady who hasn't yet learned to be charming or even nice, could you please plant a flower like this young girl in whatever abominable weed garden I wind up?

"Can I help *you?*" I finally asked Rusty, smiling. She looked up quickly but she shook her head "No" and warned with her eyes to stay away. By this time the woman was pointing again and again to an antique framed picture, which was perched on her bedside table. Rusty nodded as though she understood the old woman, and then handed her the picture. Louisa, quiet now, stared at it while the young aide began slowly to braid her long hair.

"Who are you looking for?" Rusty asked me.

"I'm Mr. Gragone's private-duty nurse," I told her. "And Mrs. Frick never got back to the station."

"She's probably in with Marta," Rusty explained. And when, at that moment, both of us heard Marta start shouting and cursing again, Rusty said, with a deadpan expression, "Yes, that's where she is." The way she said it made me laugh. Then she added, "If you can wait a minute until I can get Louisa into her wheelchair, we'll ask her to move over and I'll give you a lift down to his room.

She was pretty funny. I nodded.

"This is a new nurse, Louisa," Rusty said as she introduced us.

"My name's Carol," I said. I smiled at them.

Louisa was lost in her picture.

"Mine's Barbara Russell, but everyone calls me Rusty." She had almost finished braiding Louisa's hair.

I was touched by the way the girl treated Louisa–she had an obvious affection for her–and I was impressed by how she had handled Marta. She seemed genuinely to care for them. It was only then I realized that few of the other aides I had worked with in the years before really talked to old people. They had washed them and dressed them like dolls, as though they were things, not people. They hadn't yelled or treated them badly, but somehow the feeling that they were real human beings was missing. Now, as I watched Rusty, I made up my mind that I would try never to take care of a person whose consciousness had been altered by senility or coma without remembering to really listen and speak to them.

Rusty helped Louisa into a geri-chair, a high-back blue vinyl chair with a white plastic tray across the front, and wheeled her toward the dining room.

At the end of the hall, Rusty pointed. "Mr. Gragone's room is down that way. It's the one with the white Cadillac parked in front of it."

"I think you're a nut," I said, laughing again. She had my cheek muscles sore from smiling and I hadn't even known her for an hour. At the end of the far hall, I opened the white-painted wooden door by its creaky gold handle and quietly let myself in. Penny was slumped in the vinyl high-back chair dozing behind a book. And Mr.

Gragone was asleep. So I sat in the far corner of the room and waited. Penny's shiny brown hair was a mess and her usually bright complexion seemed pale and washed out. She had chewed the lipstick off her full bottom lip and for the first time I noticed the many small lines around her closed eyes. Two weeks before, her ninety-year-old father had gotten very sick with uremia, and rather than put him in the hospital, she had been caring for him at home and working as well. It was taking its toll on her.

When Penny's book dropped, startling her, I teased, "How was your night?"

She smiled, a guilty self-conscious smile, as she rubbed her eyes with the back of her hand. Then, as she spoke, she tried to smooth the wrinkles out of her uniform. "Fine," she whispered, "except that every time I got close enough to the poor thing to make his bed or wash him, he woke up, grabbed my breasts and pinched me. I didn't want to hurt his feelings but it sure was making me uncomfortable."

"I probably would have given him a left hook," I said, laughing. "How has his urine sugar been running?" I asked.

She handed me the urine fractional board, a record we kept after we tested his urine, and I looked at it carefully. Penny gave me report as she slowly collected her books and knitting to put in the large green mesh shopping bag she carried. I noticed her shoulders were stooped as she walked out the door. I felt bad for her.

After she left, I stood at the side of the bed and looked at Mr. Gragone. His thick white hair, smooth dark skin and full face made him look younger than seventy. He was still broad and muscular. When I saw his eyelashes flicker, I knew he was awake. "Hey, Dominic," I whispered. "Good morning." When he didn't react, I shook his shoulder gently. He kept his eyes closed. I looked at my watch. It was only eight-forty-five. I could let him rest awhile longer. Penny had washed him and changed his sheets so there was nothing left for me to do but wait until it was time to feed him breakfast. In the meantime, I would get his chart.

As I walked back toward the nurses' station, I could see a row of at least ten old people parked in geri-chairs along the wall. Some had their heads down on the trays, some had their ears covered, some had their eyes closed. They reminded me of white marble monkeys.

See no evil. . .hear no evil. . . speak no evil.

Suddenly, with the sound of the breakfast cart arriving on the floor, as though a spell had broken, the white marble monkeys came to life. They began to rock, mumble and wail. Mrs. Frick shouted, "Rusty!" and instantly the young aide appeared.

Rusty, like a practiced mother of ten, walked along the row of patients placing bibs under each chin. She fixed and replaced bows on the old women's hair and pushed the fallen glasses back up on the old men's noses so they could see again. All the time, she teased and soothed. When the breakfast cart reached the nurses' station, she handed out the silver. The patients banged their forks and spoons on plastic trays. The noise was deafening so early in the morning, but Rusty moved from one to another, handing out breakfast trays, and never looked annoyed. She cut up bacon, picked shells off watery eggs, poured milk from containers onto cold cereal.

"Careful, Howie," she said as she mixed some Sanka in one old man's cup, "don't burn yourself. It's hot." And those who were too weak or senile to remember to eat, she fed. "Hey, Anna," she said, "here's some oatmeal. Your favorite cereal." She spooned the thin dripping cereal into the old woman's toothless mouth with her left hand, while she wiped Howie's chin with her right. Anna spit out the oatmeal and Howie and Joe choked on their bacon. And Rusty fed and wiped, soothed and smoothed.

I stood admiring. There's a certain kind of talent, or maybe it's art, when someone does something so well, that there's no mistaking it. I've seen it with dancers who had something special; the way they moved with the music made them seem a part of it. I've heard it in singers; a voice that reaches for and captures notes that the rest of us can only dream about. I saw it in a carpenter once, his hammer wielded with such precision it seemed attached to his arm. And I watched it now in Rusty.

Mr. Gragone was still asleep when I got back into his room with the chart so I sat again, reading and thinking. There was something about Rusty that nagged at me, something I couldn't put my finger on. It was more than just the way she cared for the patients, even though I was always on the lookout for people who did nursing the way I thought it should be done. It was more like the constant humming of a tune for which the title remains just out of reach–a quality about her that affected me, and left me feeling that I *knew* her, or had met her before.

Mr. Gragone woke up. He began to squirm and move around. So I rolled the top of his bed up. Like a rag doll, he slid over toward the side. I tried to straighten him out but he was listless and heavy to move. And each time I tried, I could feel his deliberate resistance. Crap! I thought, this man may drive me mad. Finally I managed to prop him up with a pillow under each arm and pull up the side rails before I left to get his breakfast tray.

By the time I came back, he seemed to be fast asleep again. I shook him by the shoulders and his heavy-lidded eyes opened halfway and then slammed shut instantly. He was obviously not pleased that I was there and had no intention of co-operating with me. Then I saw his eyes flicker and knew he was pretending. Something about that tickled me. He was being a brat, a fresh kid. I couldn't help it, I laughed. "Hey, Mr. Gragone," I said, "Dominic, I know you're kidding. You can keep your eyes closed if you want, but you have to open your mouth and swallow. You've had insulin this morning and if you don't eat something, you'll pass out."

His eyes flickered a few more times but he kept his lips tightly shut. "Dominic," I said softly, "if you don't eat, they'll have to put in an IV so you get your nourishment from a bottle." My worn threat didn't move him. Eyes flickering, mouth zippered, he resisted. I spoke to him for another half-hour, trying to convince him. Several times I tried shoveling in some applesauce, with no success. He just let it slide out. Finally I gave up trying to reason with him.

Convinced at the time that the end justified the means, I said, "Okay, Dominic, that's it. Open season." I grabbed his nose and held the nostrils shut tight between my fingers. When he gasped for air, I fed him applesauce. He spit it at me. When I grabbed his nose again, he grabbed my breast and twisted. I jumped back.

As I stood and stared at him, I began to wonder just why I wanted to help him–why was I so determined to help him? But then, that's just how I am. Once I start something, it's just too hard for me to give up. I needed a new approach. "Okay, Dominic," I said. "Truce. If you want to get well, it's up to you and I'm willing to help you. If you don't, that's also up to you."

I sat down in the chair and wiped the applesauce off my face, hair and uniform with a towel. Nothing in nursing school had prepared me for a situation like this. On hospital wards, it was all trial and error. In school, you have a perfect patient who's dying to help you help him get well. I took a deep breath. Thank God I had children of my own and had learned some fancy footwork or I'd be lost, I thought.

After several minutes, I leaned my head back against the chair. Mr. Gragone, his eyes still closed, looked sad. And now I felt very guilty about holding his nose. And very defeated. I usually didn't have to stoop to that kind of tactic. How the hell am I going to get him to eat? I wondered.

As a last resort, I tried some simple human kindness and Dominic weakened. "Would you like me to call the kitchen and order a scrambled-egg sandwich? You really should eat something so you can get out of this place and get home." He nodded and I left to order another breakfast for him.

When I returned, Dominic was trying to reach his glasses, which were on top of the bedside table. As he did, he knocked over the water pitcher. With a shaking hand he picked up the paper cups on the table and threw them at the wall across from me. "Dammit ... dammit!" he shouted, as he held one hand with the other to keep it from shaking. His tremors got much worse when he was upset.

I dried his glasses and put them on him. "Dominic," I said, "the doctor just ordered a new medicine that should help to stop the shaking from your Parkinson's. It's called L-dopa." But whenever I spoke, he just got angrier.

We managed the next few hours only because by some stroke of luck the diet kitchen had noodles for lunch. Dominic gobbled them down, mumbling in Italian the whole time, but eating at least.

Then I left for lunch. But as I walked the hall toward the cafeteria, I could hear Marta screaming still. And when I passed her room, dishes and towels and plastic flatware flew through the doorway. "I dare any of you wardens to come in here," she screamed. "I'll kill any of you who try." Then I heard the clank of the steel bedpan as it hit the tile bathroom floor. Finally Mrs. Frick came running out.

"She's a madwoman," Mrs. Frick said. Several of the aides were standing outside Marta's room now. "Where's Rusty?" the nurse asked them.

Lana, another young aide, answered, "She's down with Howie. He's crying again because he thinks his wife is cheating on him."

"Jesus," Mrs. Frick said, annoyed. "Go get her and tell her to stop wasting her time. This woman needs to be cleaned up before she infests the entire patient population with the stuff that's growing in her hair and on her body."

I waited to see if I could help, but before I could ask, Rusty was walking toward the desk and Mrs. Frick was reprimanding her. "Rusty," she said, "that man's wife is eighty years old. Why are you indulging him in his craziness when there's work to be done?"

Rusty frowned, but when she answered, her voice was even. "Frick, he doesn't see his wife as an old woman. He sees her as she was when they were young. So he's jealous. And it's painful for him. And that pain's as real as if they were young. He only needs to be reassured, and I don't think that's a waste of my time."

"I don't think it's wise to humor him the way you do," Mrs. Frick insisted. "Half the time he forgets she exists, he's so senile."

"But the other half, when he remembers she does, he's jealous and it causes him pain," Rusty countered. When Mrs. Frick huffed with annoyance, Rusty added, "We should all be as lucky as she is, to be loved that much–even half the time."

"I want that woman scrubbed," Mrs. Frick said as she pointed toward the door of Marta's room, "before you go home tonight."

Rusty hesitated for only a minute before she said, "Okay. Let me finish with Anna and Joe. If I can't get her done during the shift, I'll stay later." When she turned toward me, she winked. "The money's too good to pass up."

Again, I wondered about her. Mrs. Frick obviously depended on her and seemed to respect her, yet Rusty had taken an extra heavy load and even offered to stay late if she had to when Mrs. Frick muscled her. As she started down the hall, I stopped her. "Rusty," I said, "do you want me to help you with Marta?"

She smiled. "Thanks. I'd appreciate that if you can stay a few minutes when you're finished with Dominic. We can do her fast after Frick goes home."

I listened to Marta shout and watched as a roll of toilet paper flew out her door into the hall. Then I laughed and asked, "Fast? How do you figure that?"

Rusty said, "I have an idea. Stay, if you want, and see."

After lunch I went back to Mr. Gragone. Even through his closed door, I could hear Marta screaming all afternoon. And Dominic wasn't too much better. We had another cup-throwing scene when he tried to hold his coffee and spilled it because he started shaking again. "Dammit ... dammit!" he kept shouting in frustrated Italian-accented English. By the end of the shift, I was wearing a uniform covered in applesauce, tea, Sanka and orange juice. I vowed that by the following day I would learn to duck more effectively. I was thrilled to see Penny when she arrived early to relieve me.

I had almost forgotten my offer to help until I walked past Marta's room and heard Rusty's voice. The door was partly open so I peeked in. Rusty was standing against a far wall and as I watched, Marta took a greedy drink from a metal camper's flask. When Rusty saw me, she waved me inside and told me to close the door.

Marta was drunk. I mean hopelessly, obviously drunk.

"What's going on?" I asked Rusty as I walked up next to her.

"Marta's getting drunk," she said matter-of-factly.

"Aren't you afraid you're going to get killed—or at least fired?" I asked.

Rusty shrugged. "Couldn't do much about it."

"Where did she get it?" I asked.

"She had the flask hidden in her underpants," Rusty said, eyes twinkling. "Would you have gone after it?"

I laughed. But then Rusty looked at me seriously, and added, "That poor woman still has to be bathed and her clothes are glued to her by the scabs from the sores on her body. From tomorrow on she's going to be forced to stay stone-cold sober, and for a woman like her, in a place like this, it'll be hell. Standing guard for her while she ties one on for the last time seemed to be the kindest thing to do."

Just then someone began to push open the door and both Rusty and I threw our backs against it. "Can't come in just yet," Rusty called in a forced professional voice. I had to cover my mouth to keep from laughing out loud. Suddenly Marta started to sing.

"What's going on?" the voice from behind the door asked.

"Don't worry about it, Sanchez," Rusty answered. "I'm just try-ing to bathe the new admission." Rusty whispered to me, "She's the evening nurse. She's really okay. But there's no sense getting any-one else involved, in case there's trouble." I nodded.

Marta started to curse again. And the door handle began to wig-gle as Sanchez asked again, "Need help, Rusty?"

"No, we're fine, really," Rusty said.

"Okay," the nurse said, and we could hear her footsteps as she began to walk away. "Just call if you need anything."

"Sure will," Rusty answered back.

"What now?" I asked Rusty as I walked closer to the bed and looked at Marta. In the middle of her last curse, she had just stopped short and passed out.

"I'll get the basin and you can get some towels from under her night table," Rusty said. "Together, we'll get her done in half the time."

After we got everything ready, Rusty stood on one side of the bed and I stood on the other. Then together we both lowered the sheet. "Breathe through your mouth, so you can't smell as well," Rusty urged. But she hadn't needed to tell me that. I had been breathing through my mouth, except when I laughed, since I'd come into the room.

Marta was a mess. Up close, I could see that she was wearing two cotton dresses and a sweater. "Cashmere?" I said to Rusty, sur-prised as I touched Marta's sleeve.

"The flask is silver," Rusty said, as though that explained it.

The dresses and the sweater were just for starters. Several pairs of nylon stockings covered the top of Marta's leg which was wrapped in the Ace bandage, and several more were in various stages of deterioration on her other leg. Rusty and I working together tried peeling her stocking off. But skin had grown over the parts of the nylon which had eaten its way into her skin. In other places on her heavy thighs, blisters broke and bled.

Rusty said, "We'll never get her slips or her dresses off this way."

"Let's rip them or cut them off," I said. But when Rusty tried, we both could see that wouldn't work. So much liquid had spilled on the cloth, both from inside and outside, that it felt like cardboard and was strong as steel.

God! she really smelled awful. "Do you smell gangrene?" I asked Rusty.

She closed her mouth for a minute and took a quick sniff through her nose. "Bet she's got maggots," Rusty said. "The only person I knew who smelled like this had maggots."

"Yuck," I said, and then immediately felt guilty in case Marta had heard and I had hurt her feelings. "Who had maggots?" I asked Rusty. "I mean, where were you working then?"

Rusty didn't answer and something in her expression and her quick hand movements as she tried to remove Marta's sweater warned me not to pursue it. After a couple of minutes of uncomfortable silence, with the sound of Marta's snoring making it even more obvious, I said, "I'm sorry. I didn't mean to pry."

Rusty looked up then and smiled at me. "It's okay. It's my problem, not yours. I'd just rather not talk about it now."

"Sure," I said, "I understand." But I didn't really because there had been nothing in my life I thought important enough to keep secret.

"Marta should have a bath," Rusty said thoughtfully.

"She'll never walk in her condition," I answered.

"We'll have to use a Hoyer lift, to get her out of bed" Rusty explained, looking down at Marta, "and put her in a bathtub. We'll have to soak her clothes off and try to get her clean. Are you in a rush to get home?" she asked.

"I need to be home by five," I told her. "In time for my son Jeremy to be dropped off from kindergarten."

Rusty asked, "Do you have any other kids?"

"Yep," I said. "A girl. Lynn, eight."

"You don't look that old," she said as she walked toward the door. Then she added, "I'll go get the lift."

The Hoyer lift always reminded me of an elephant hammock. It's a big chrome dolly with a plastic sling hanging from large steel chains.

The whole room almost rattled when Rusty wheeled it in, but Marta never woke up. "You sure she'll be all right?" I asked, assuming that Rusty would know.

"She must have been drinking for years at home, to carry a flask in her underwear," Rusty said. "And if she survived there, it's likely she'll come out of it here."

I'm seldom squeamish, but I was really careful not to lean Marta against me when I turned her on her side as Rusty slid the plastic hammock under her. When we turned her toward Rusty, I pulled the plastic smooth, then we let her roll onto her back. Once the plastic hammock was hooked, top and bottom, by the heavy chains, Rusty stomped on the pedal of the hydraulic lift and the plastic rose off the bed. Rusty held the chrome bar of the lift while I swung the hammock off the bed. Hanging there, Marta looked like a dead mackerel waiting to be weighed.

CHAPTER 2

After supper I took my kids for a walk. Jeremy ran and jumped along the street while Lynn walked slowly next to me, hands folded behind her back. It had been a beautiful day and now the night was warm but humid.

"How come no birds are singing?" Lynn asked.

"Maybe they all flew south," I teased.

She gave me her tolerant look. "Mom," she said, "I was being serious. You know birds fly south in the winter, not in the beginning of summer."

I reached over and tousled her long dark hair. I smiled at her seriousness. "Forgive me, my child." I said. "It was my attempt at humor. The real reason the birds aren't singing is . . . I honestly don't know." Then I noticed that everything seemed very still. Not a leaf moved. "Maybe it's going to storm," I added.

Lynn seemed satisfied but Jeremy turned around and started a heavy-footed march toward us, his small hands held up against his head. He was making faces like a monster. "They're probably hiding," he growled with mock menace.

"Get out of here, you little creep," Lynn said, and swatted him.

A small black-and-white colt lived around the corner from our house, and often in the evenings we went to visit him and brought some sugar cubes or carrots.

Tonight, as we walked up to the fence and held out our hands, the young horse seemed skittish. He licked the sugar cube from Lynn's hand but ignored Jeremy's waving carrot and quickly trotted into his shed. Jeremy was crushed.

"Don't worry," Lynn reassured him with big-sister wisdom, "he still likes you. Maybe he just hates carrots today."

Jeremy flung his carrot between the bars of the wooden fence onto the ground as we turned to go. "Will you sleep in my room tonight, Lynn," he asked in his squeaky plaintive voice, "and tell me a story?"

Lynn's shoulders sagged under the burden of her younger brother's need, but when I looked at her face, I could see she was pleased to be so important to him. "Okay," she said, putting her arm around his shoulders, "but after this you'll have to get used to sleeping alone."

That night after the kids were in bed, the storm broke, with lightning and thunder so loud that the house literally shook. I tried to listen to music but the static interfered and I couldn't watch TV because the sound kept crackling and I was afraid the set would blow up.

Finally I grabbed a book and went upstairs to bed.

As the sky rumbled and rolled like some primitive god's hungry belly and lightning sliced through the black night, I felt scared as a child and very alone. There were certainly benefits to being a single independent woman, but lying in a cold bed by myself on a stormy night wasn't one of them. I looked at my watch. Midnight. And suddenly, outside my window, I heard a crack so loud and close that I instinctively covered my head.

The sky, in short shocks of bright white, pushed its way through my thin voile curtains and the rain hammered ferociously on the window panes. I sat up in bed and grabbed for the phone. My hands were shaking as I dialed.

After a few rings, Creede picked up. Creede was a friend of mine from England and different from me in every way. She was tall with reddish hair, while I was short with dark hair. Her whole presentation was cool and logical, while mine was hot and emotional. And so we got along.

"Creede," I said with panicky voice into the phone, "the willow tree outside is going to fall on the house."

"It's a lovely night out, isn't it?" she answered, ignoring my terror. "We've needed this rain for the plants and grass."

"Creede, didn't you hear me?" I asked. "The willow tree–"

"Is not," she said in a cool measured tone, "going to fall onto your house."

"How can you be so sure?" I asked.

"How can you be so sure it *will?*" she asked. "Think about it, Carol," she continued. "That tree is at least a hundred years old. In that hundred years, there must have been thousands of storms, with lightning. If in all that time it didn't fall, why tonight?"

"So then, you're sure?" I repeated. As I looked outside, I could see the tree's huge branches swaying in a wild and frantic dance. "It's a very big tree," I added.

"Well, in that case," Creede said quietly, "if it does fall on the house, you'll have nothing to worry about."

"Don't be funny," I said, but I laughed.

"I'm not," she said. "There are some things you'll have to trust to fate, or you'll be in a panic all the time."

When Creede came over from England as a domestic, she had no idea what the future would bring. But she said she always trusted fate and her life had worked out well. That was ten years before, and now Creede worked at night as an aide in a rehabilitation hospital. She was tough but wonderful with her patients and they responded well. She had been saving her money to open a flower shop. That had always been her dream. And she knew she would have it someday. In the meantime, she thought of herself as an artist who was taking time out to help people. I thought of her as a good friend.

"Creede," I asked then, "do you really like living alone?"

"Love it," she answered simply. "No one else to consider, to have to bother with, no one to account to, and plenty of time to paint, write poetry and run on the beach."

"I've decided I hate it," I told her. "I feel as though I live in a void."

Though I had been divorced for almost six years at the time, I had never before been in this position. I had either lived at home with my parents, gone to school, had Penny as a roommate for a few years and filled up much of the remaining three years with Jim. And even when a relationship doesn't feed your heart, it does take up time and fill in space. But now Jim was gone and even Penny was spending so much time with her dad, I hardly even got to see her.

"What about the kids," Creede asked, "and work?"

"Hmm. Not enough," I said quietly, "even though it should be. Maybe I'll go back to school."

"Sounds fine," Creede said, "but how will that solve your need not to live alone? Maybe you should find yourself another man to share your life."

With that, I almost choked. "Uh-uh. Absolutely not. You know that nice men, good guys, want to marry, and I don't fit the job description."

"What's that?" she asked curiously.

"You know, Creede," I said. "The kind of woman who can be a slave and love it. And not need recognition for her contributions."

Creede cut in, "All marriages or relationships aren't like that."

"Well, anyway," I added, "no ship can have two captains, and you know how competitive I am."

"There are other kinds of men," Creede reminded me. "The kind who'll appreciate your intelligence, sense of humor and originality. And forgive or accept what you're not."

"Yes, I guess so," I conceded. "The kind of man who's exciting, independent and loves freedom. You mean that kind of man?"

"That's what I mean."

"Well," I admitted, "the only problem with that is, I'm afraid of them. I'm bored with the known but frightened by the unknown."

"I can't help you," Creede said, "because you're not being logical."

She was right. But what did that have to do with anything?

Finally, after several minutes caught between the hammering of raindrops and Creede's silence, I asked, "What about another roommate? Another female, I mean?"

Before Jim, I had enjoyed living with Penny. We had shared the responsibility of the house and the children. And it was fun to have an adult to talk to over dinner, to tell about the troubles or fun of the day.

"Who have you got in mind?" Creede asked cautiously.

"Not you," I laughed. "I couldn't stand your constant logic or your pathological need for privacy."

She was obviously so relieved that she ignored my teasing and answered, "It's something to think about. You could give it a whirl."

The vibration from the sound of thunder knocked over the small crystal butterfly that I kept on my dresser, and when the lightning cracked this time, I thought it had split the house in two. Then I heard fire sirens.

"Creede," I asked, panicky again, "promise this tree isn't going to fall?"

"I promise," she said, laughing. Then she hung up.

Still I couldn't sleep. So I lay awake thinking. Why was I afraid? What was I afraid of?

One of the reasons I had always liked working at night in a hospital was that I didn't like being alone at home. Here with the loud constant day noises silenced by the dark, each and every small noise became a threat. I usually spend a good part of the night sitting stiffly in bed waiting. I was afraid of being killed or attacked.

Of course, working at the hospital could never be considered safe–especially with the kinds of patients I took care of. I could have caught encephalitis, meningitis, hepatitis and a number of other insidious diseases. They could have sneaked right into my body while I wasn't looking. They *could* have killed me. It occurred to me that when the threat became a real possibility, I wasn't that scared. Besides, I never figured anything bad would happen. I'd never heard a story about Jesus healing the sick and catching anything they had. I had read about Father Damien coming down with leprosy, but then I just figured that was one illness I should try to steer clear of. I finally realized how irrational I was being so I pulled the covers up to my neck and tried to fall asleep. But my heart was still beating fast. In the back of my mind, my search for a roommate had already begun.

As I arrived at work the next morning I heard Marta even before I got onto the ward. "Goddamn idiots!" she screamed. "I'll have you all fired."

On my way to Dominic's room, I bumped into Rusty.

"What's going on?" I asked her.

"She's relatively sober now," Rusty said, laughing. "And she hates every minute of it."

The afternoon before, when we had finally gotten Marta into the tub, she was so drunk she never woke up until Rusty began to wash her hair. We had to soak her clothes off; blisters had formed in some places, and in others, sores. She had flea and tick bites all over her body . . . and scattered circles of ringworm and impetigo all over her chest and belly. There were also small round scars on both her thighs and hips. I suspected they were old needle marks from a former drug habit. Rusty agreed. After Rusty washed her hair and still couldn't get some of the junk and goo out of the matted mess, we found lice, so Rusty had to cut Marta's hair. Marta hit at us constantly after that, and though I was ready to strangle her, Rusty said she understood how Marta felt.

"I think she's a little bit crazy," I had said.

Rusty disagreed. "I think she's acting okay for the situation," she said.

"How do you figure that?"

"Well, think of being in a strange place with someone you don't know bathing you, touching your most intimate parts, and then cutting off your hair without your consent," Rusty said. "Being without clothes makes you feel very vulnerable and defenseless. Why should she trust us? She says she doesn't even want to be here."

"Well, how did she get here?" I asked. "I mean with nursing-home beds in such demand, how come they accepted her?"

"Her family insisted," Rusty said. "And it's their nursing home."
I was puzzled. "You mean they own it?"

Rusty nodded. "And from now on Marta's supposed to be treated as a VIP," she said. When I raised my eyebrows Rusty explained, "She's a doctor."

I whistled. "What the hell happened to her?"

"Nobody really knows," Rusty said, "and she isn't volunteering any information."

Change of shift was the only time I got to see Penny, and getting report from her on Mr. Gragone was becoming the high point of my day. In the morning after she left, I tried to match wits with Dominic and give him a reason to eat. But right before my eyes he was becoming more and more resistant and depressed. He was in Salvation because his family couldn't convince him to eat, which would shoot his diabetes out of control and spin him into a coma. Then he'd have to be rushed to an emergency room of a local general hospital for a glucose infusion. Finally, his doctor placed him in a nursing home until his blood sugar could be regulated. When he had complained constantly that he'd been ignored by the staff, his family called a private-duty registry and hired me. They felt so guilty about not keeping him home that they would do anything to keep him happy. And fighting with me, though it didn't keep him happy, did keep him busy. Still, it seemed to me that the more I was willing to do for him, the less he was willing to do for himself. After three days, he even refused to turn over in bed by himself and he kept his eyes shut most of the time.

It took me until the following week to get used to Salvation's setup and routine. Mrs. Frick, from what I could see, was basically sadistic. Anytime an old person complained, she seemed to take it as a personal insult. She'd yell at them, then roughly give them what they wanted. The other two aides on the floor, Lana and Sherry, seemed slow but conscientious. Rusty always did most of the work. While each of the other aides dressed four patients, Rusty dressed eight. And whenever one of the patients called "Nurse," Rusty dropped whatever she was doing and ran to help before Mrs. Frick could get there.

Marta let no one near her except Rusty, and the rest of the staff was more than willing to avoid her because of her behavior and because they were afraid of crossing her and her family. I stopped by to see her a few times, but as soon as she saw the door opening she got furious and irrational. Once or twice, there was no noise and I peeked in to see her out cold with her back toward me.

At this time, the carousel of my life was spinning slowly as I kept jumping on and off different ponies. Mother, friend, lover, nurse. But no matter how hard I tried, I could never quite reach the gold ring of contentment.

Jim had spent so much time with us in the last years that we had practically been living together. I had gotten used to his being able to watch the kids at night if I had to work, I had begun to depend on his doing the grocery shopping. Though we couldn't agree on some of the most important life moves each of us wanted to make, he was a very good person. And though our relationship wasn't really satisfying, we were tied together pretty tightly. That's why he had decided to move three thousand miles away. So each of us could begin again. But it was difficult.

He called a few times from California, and each time it was the same. He wanted me to reconsider getting married. "I can't, Jim," I'd say. "I don't know exactly what I want, except maybe to try being a free woman for a while."

"You call having to bust your tail to make a living for you and the kids being free?" he scoffed. "That's pure illusion."

"Maybe you're right," I agreed.

But of one thing I was certain. I didn't want to ride the marriage pony again. Not after I'd been thrown. Even though it had been many years since then, I could still feel the bruises. And though "lover" was a pretty, gentle pony at the beginning, he had grown into a slow and plodding animal whose pace was different from mine. So I dropped the reins and held my breath as I jumped off.

"Find yourself someone who really wants to share your life, Jim," I said softly. "You have a lot to offer. It's just that I can't accept it."

The only constant in my life for all the years was nursing. No matter how harrowing and painful my regular life was, as soon as I walked onto a hospital floor dressed in a white uniform, I felt like Cinderella at the ball. It was the one place I could be totally me. The place I could be as smart, as kind, as giving, and as real as I was capable of being. My patients and I had an understanding past words; we needed each other; we healed each other; and neither of us judged the other. There was no mask, no pretense, we were just human beings who because of circumstance had to learn to trust each other and so were allowed to really touch each other. And I had gotten used to that kind of closeness. Regular relationships compared to those special ones were like trying to talk to someone through a glass barrier or trying to touch through a wire-mesh divider.

But that kind of special contact had its disadvantages. I had resigned from one of the large teaching hospitals just a few months before. I had to stop nursing in the burn unit because it caused me just too much pain. Every time I had to hurt someone to help him, I suffered too.

Now I was reconsidering which area of nursing I wanted to pursue; whenever I did that, I took care of patients as a private-duty nurse, in order to feel with my hands again, instead of machines, and have the time to remember why I had gone into nursing to begin with. But nothing can be all things to anyone–even nursing.

Each night I came home and tried to fill time with my kids and other productive endeavors. I read, watched TV, listened to classical music, took the kids out to eat, to the movies, to an amusement park. I did everything everyone else seemed to enjoy and it didn't help. It just felt as though I was marking time, marching in place. I wanted a blueprint. Like the Connect the Dots cards that little kid's used. From 1 you draw a straight line to 2, from there you advance to 3. When you've followed the instructions, you've got a complete picture. I was waiting for fate to hand me an invitation on a Live by Number card. At least that way I'd know what I was supposed to do next.

One morning while I was trying to change Dominic's bed, he was being especially uncooperative. He pushed himself onto his back each time I turned him on his side to change his sheet. I had visions of tying him to the side rail of the bed with a gauze lasso. I was about to let him win, and forget about fixing his bed, when Rusty appeared in the doorway and asked, "Want some help holding him over?"

Gratitude forced my mouth into a wide smile. "I'd love some, if you have a minute," I told her.

"I have fifteen," she said, walking toward the side of Mr. Gragone's bed. "I'm on my break."

I was about to protest but by that time Rusty had already pulled Dominic over on his side and was holding him tight against the side rail with two strong arms wrapped around him.

I quickly washed his back and buttocks, and as I was beginning to remove the bottom sheet, I saw Dominic put his right arm between the bars, reach around and grab hard onto Rusty's behind.

Without a change of expression, Rusty reached back removed Dominic's hand and said softly, "Congratulations, I'm glad to see you're still alive."

Then very deliberately she turned him onto his back, lowered the side rail and sat down next to him. In a quiet even-toned voice with perfect diction she told him, "Dominic, I know how angry you are about your sickness. And I know how frightened you are." Dominic refused to look at her and so she took his chin and gently turned his face until their eyes met, a lover's gesture, when she added, "I know because I've been as sick as you, many times. And as angry. Now, you don't have to listen when I tell you that the anger is good, is fine, if you use it properly. Stop fighting Carol, stop fighting your family and start fighting to get well." She patted his cheek and stood up. "You can do it, Dominic. Look at me."

Dominic didn't say anything, but under his flickering eyelashes, I could see tears.

Then Rusty stood up and without any more trouble we finished fixing Dominic's bed.

"Thank you," I said to Rusty as she was leaving. "Sorry we blew your coffee break."

She waved my apology aside and asked, "See you at lunch?"

And so Rusty and I began to eat lunch together.

When I asked if what she had told Dominic was true, she said, "Why would I lie?" But she offered nothing more.

CHAPTER 3

I was sitting alongside Dominic's bed. Dominic was sulking. "I don't wanna no company," he had said when I told him he was going to have a roommate. The new admission had to be put in Dominic's room because all the other beds on the floor were filled.

Rusty wheeled the patient in. He was wearing a baseball cap, a little man made even smaller by arthritis. Sitting in the wheelchair, he looked as though someone had sewn an invisible thread through his chin to his knees and then pulled it tight. When he looked toward me, I smiled and waved. His head moved up like a turkey's and he smiled too. Then with great difficulty he managed to lift his arm and wave back. I couldn't tell how old he was but his hair was still dark, and though his skin was wrinkled, his blue eyes looked wonderfully clear.

"This is Lenny, Carol," Rusty said as she helped raise the old man out of the chair and onto the side of the bed. He sat there primly and folded his hands in his lap. "He's a famous baseball star," she added.

Lenny blushed. "You'll embarrass me, young lady," he said, "if you keep on."

Rusty reached down and put Lenny's suitcase on his bed. Then as she unpacked, she found a large picture. "Look, Carol," she said, holding it up to show me. The picture was of the young Lenny and a group of his baseball friends standing together with their arms around each other. Lenny was in the center holding a trophy which proclaimed him "Most Valuable Player."

"Congratulations, Lenny," I said.

Dominic kept his eyes closed but I could hear him mumbling unpleasantly under his breath.

"Thank you, ma'am," Lenny said, struggling to raise his head again. He had a soft, almost musical voice. "In the old days I was able to hold my own with any team. He said it in a humble rather than boastful way.

"I'm sure you still can," Rusty said with a perfectly straight face. "You just have to find a team to play with."

Lenny held up his hand and said, "No, young lady. Not anymore. Not with these hands." Lenny's hand was rolled almost into a fist, held fast by his arthritis.

Rusty took his hand in both of hers and tried gently to pry open his fingers. Lenny winced involuntarily but allowed it. She had managed to get his hand half open.

"Enough for a baseball," she announced.

Lenny looked at it carefully. "I think you're right young lady," he said smiling. "But it won't stay that way. As soon as you let those fingers go, they'll curl as though I'm trying to hide something in my hand."

Rusty let go. Lenny was right. Back to a fist.

Rusty looked thoughtful. "How much pain does it cause when I do that?" she asked as he opened his hand again.

"Some," Lenny answered. "But it would be worth it if I could hold a baseball again."

"You've got it," Rusty said. "That's what we'll work on from now on."

Dominic was watching all that was going on. When he thought no one was looking, I saw him wipe a tear from his eye. I wondered what was going on with him.

Later, when the lunch tray came, I lifted the cooling silver cover from the plate on Mr. Gragone's overbed table. I stared down at three colored mountains floating in a murky river of juice. Pureed food. Yuck! My nose wrinkled. The little orange mountain must be carrots, I thought, or squash. The dark green was probably peas or maybe beans or anyone's guess. But there was no mistaking the mound of wormy-looking brown stuff. That was obviously some portion of a dead animal.

Dominic's eyes were shut tight again. I took a deep breath, walked over and put my hand on his shoulder.

"Lunch time, Dominic," I whispered.

His eyelids flickered but stayed closed. "You have to eat, Dominic," I told him, for the six hundredth time that week, "or you'll get really sick. You've had insulin." No luck! After another fifteen minutes of begging, pleading and cajoling, I put a glop of the green goop on the spoon and tried to push it past his lips. And before I could jump out of the way, Dominic again spit and I was covered with green freckles.

"Okay," I moaned, defeated, as I slumped down onto the chair next to his bed. "You win. I can't fight with you if you don't want to get well." And then I added, "But if I'm going to let you die right in front of me, I'm sort of an accomplice, you know? Could I know why you don't want to live?"

Big jump, I admitted to myself; maybe he didn't want to die, maybe he just hated green goop. But he hadn't even opened his eyes to see what it was. If something else was bothering him, I wanted to know. And now that I had probably scared him to death, he'd have to tell me.

But he tightened his lips and lay unmoving for what seemed like decades. So, finally, feeling bad for him, I stood up and ran my hand over his thick white curly hair.

"Is there any way I can help?" I asked softly.

Dominic opened his eyes. Clear light gray eyes with yellow flecks, shiny with tears.

I walked down to the foot of the bed, grabbed the handle and rolled him into a higher sitting position. Then as I started back toward him, he began to cry. "Imma hate that food," he shouted in a heavy accent, reaching out and shoving the tray off the table and onto the floor with one sweep of his shaking arm. "Imma want fried eggs and bacon. My wife maka me food Imma like," and without stopping, still crying, "An' Imma not a baby, I wanna eata myself."

One little bolt of lightning and I quickly understood. The whole Italian culture revolves around the ritual of eating. Dominic, now that he was diagnosed as having diabetes, would have to watch everything he ate. The pasta, the spaghetti, the wine. The three-course family dinner each Sunday, the special holiday food loaded with fats and carbohydrates. Dominic's wife saying, "Eat... eat," because she loved him. And if he did, it could do him in. What a disaster! That's when I realized that diabetes to an Italian is like a limp to a dancer.

❖❖ ❖❖ ❖❖

Rusty and I were sitting at a small table in the cafeteria, having lunch, when she asked, "Can you stop at my house tonight and check my mother? She's been sick with a cold for over a week, she has emphysema, and I'm afraid she's developing pneumonia." I knew she was asking me just to make sure because I was the one with the formal education and the nursing credentials.

"What about a doctor?" I asked, taking a bite of rubbery hamburger. "She might need a chest X ray and blood work."

"She'll never consent to see one," Rusty said, shaking her head. "She thinks they killed my father with weird treatments."

"How long ago did he die?" I asked, trying to chop apart, with a plastic spoon, a sugar cube that was lying in the bottom of my cup of cold tea.

"Hard to say exactly," Rusty answered. For several moments she stared past me out the large plate-glass windows into Salvation's trim green backyard. Several withered old people in wheelchairs, wearing white hospital gowns, dotted the lawn like stone statues. I wondered if the reason that old people were always so pale was that their long exposure to life had faded them.

"What did he die of?" I asked.

"Broken heart, broken dreams. Life, I think," Rusty said sympathetically. "He was like most of the people here."

"Old, you mean?" I asked.

"That," Rusty answered quietly, "and beat. In the last few years he had lived much more in his memories and dreams than in real life. He didn't, as I see it, die suddenly. He'd been dying for a long time. Six months ago he just gave in and stopped breathing."

I was surprised by how grown-up Rusty seemed, so calm and accepting. If my father had "stopped breathing" just six months before, I probably would have rolled over with my feet in the air, like a dead dog, and stayed that way for years. But then, I was Italian and my father had been the only constant, protective male in my life. Which, by the way, was both a plus and a minus.

"Were you close?" I asked. "Did you like him?"

Rusty laughed softly. "He was a gentle man, not terribly effective, and he taught me all I know about egg candling." She looked at me seriously when she added, "I felt sorry for him." Then she pushed her chair away from the table, got up and began to walk out of the room. I quickly followed her.

"Rusty?" I called, and she stopped. "I can come home with you after work. My kids are at my parents' house for the weekend."

"Thanks," she said, and she walked down the hall toward Louisa, who was motioning frantically for help as she slid sideways again in her geri-chair.

Rusty helped her to sit straight as I went back to Mr. Gragone. The afternoon went better than it ever had. Mrs. Gragone came early to visit Dominic and said she would stay until night. I talked to the dietitian and asked her to start working with Mrs. Gragone on Dominic's diet. Then I suggested Mrs. Gragone be allowed to cook food and bring it to Dominic for at least one meal a day. When I told him, he smiled for the first time. Over the weekend his children would come and so I was off until Monday.

That afternoon before I went home, I decided to stop in to see how Marta was doing. Her door was closed and I didn't hear any noise. I thought she might be sleeping so I tiptoed in. Marta lay asleep on her side, her back toward me, but from the snoring and the smell in the room I was certain she had been drinking again. Where could she have gotten liquor? I wondered.

Just then Rusty came in and I quickly pulled her into bathroom.

"Somebody's been sneaking in liquor for her to drink," I whispered. "There's no way she could have stashed enough to last her this long."

Rusty lowered her head and rubbed her forehead. Something in her expression made me ask, "You're not getting it for her, are you?" Rusty nodded.

"I don't understand," I said, annoyed. "I know it's none of my business, but why would you jeopardize your job just so she can drink?"

"Are you going to tell anyone?" she asked, ignoring my question.

"Of course not," I said. "I'm not talking morality; I'm talking intelligence. I just want to know why."

"She asked," Rusty said simply.

I breathed out hard. I knew there had to be more. "That's no reason," I said.

"You have to hear her tell it, and then you'll understand," Rusty said.

Suddenly Marta called, "Rusty? Who's in here with us?" She sounded angry but not at all confused.

Rusty didn't answer. "It's me, Marta," I said, coming out of the bathroom.

Marta looked wonderful. Her newly cut salt-and-pepper hair framed her face, which was no longer distorted by anger, fear and dirt. Even with the strong smell of liquor in the room, she didn't seem at all drunk. I was surprised she was so alert, but by the look in her sharp gray eyes, there was no mistaking that. And, stripped of her rags, even in a hospital gown, it was apparent she was thinner and younger than she had appeared. Maybe fifty-five. She was actually quite a pretty woman, with no resemblance to the bag lady we had admitted, except for the long talons still on the ends of her fingers.

"Carol," she said with a very firm voice, "come over and stand here." I was surprised she knew my name.

"Listen to what I have to say before you do anything," she said. She was sitting up in bed and Rusty was arranging the pillows behind her.

"I'm not going to do anything," I reassured her. "It's really not my business."

"That's never stopped anyone else from causing me trouble," she said. Then, "I am an alcoholic. I was drinking the rubbing alcohol as well as the mouthwash. I am also a doctor. You are a nurse. And so that should explain everything."

"Wait one minute," I said. "I'm not sure I get the whole picture. Now I understand why Rusty got liquor for you, but I'm still not clear on why you continue to drink. Are you afraid of withdrawal, of the DT's?"

"Of course," she said, "but more important, the doctor my family has hired is twenty years older than I am. He's been the family's doctor for years. He will immediately try to transfer me to a psychiatric hospital for detoxification. The family will then see that I am committed so that I can no longer cause them trouble or embarrassment."

"She's right," Rusty said strongly.

I didn't believe she could know that for sure. I looked at her and then looked at Marta. "There must be an alternative," I said, realizing that it wasn't as simple as I had thought. "Rusty is putting herself and her job on the line for you. How long can that go on?"

Marta looked upset. "Look, I'd like to get out of here. I'd even like to stop drinking. But I know the danger. There's a fifteen-percent mortality rate for untreated alcohol withdrawal. To ease withdrawal, I'll need tranquilizers. And if I ask for tranquilizers, that doctor will use the excuse to transfer me right over to a hospital, or they'll give me some medication which will alter my perception and leave me in their control."

Rusty said, "She's right again, Carol."

"How can you know that?" I asked. "How can you be so sure?"

"I do know," Rusty insisted. And the way that she said it blew a little siren in my head. There was something going on that I didn't know about. Then Rusty turned toward Marta, and asked, "Marta, can you still write prescriptions?"

Marta nodded and said, "But I have no prescription pads here and the pharmacy won't fill them for me anyway."

"That's easy," Rusty said. "There's always a prescription pad in the desk at the nurses' station."

"Is that legal?" I asked.

"I thought you weren't talking morality," Rusty said

"Legality is different from morality," I said.

"I'm not sure you're right," Rusty countered. "Legality seems to me to be an imposed morality."

Marta looked troubled. "What's wrong, Marta? Is something still bothering you?" I asked.

Rusty walked up to the bed and said, "I'll stay with you if you're frightened."

Marta immediately looked relieved. Then she looked at me. "If I can keep my wits about me, I can get my lawyer to release some money," she said. "I'll pay you as a private-duty nurse, if you'll stay as well. It may take two of you. . . and if they know I have my own nurse, the rest of the staff will stay away."

"Okay," I said, "I'll stay too. But not because of money. And if you have money, why did you live like that?"

"You're being presumptuous," Marta said harshly, "and it's none of your business." Then she caught herself and her voice lowered. She spoke like a doctor. "From the time of the last drink, withdrawal begins between twelve and thirty-six hours. Then the acute stage, the period of real danger, lasts from twelve to twenty-four hours. In that time, I'll need some help."

I tried to reassure her. "I've taken care of people who've gone through withdrawal."

Rusty said, "So have I."

Marta seemed to relax a bit. "I haven't decided yet that this is what I'm going to do. But as long as you're both willing to help, I've at least got a reasonable choice." Then as Marta automatically rearranged her sheets, she added, "I'd like both of you to stay for at least thirty-six hours. I'll let you know when, so that you can reschedule your time."

Rusty and I agreed, and when we left, Marta seemed to be resting much more comfortably.

On the way to our cars, I asked, "Are you going to keep bringing her the stuff to drink?"

"For a little while," Rusty said. "Rubbing alcohol makes her very irrational, and it will kill her if she keeps drinking it." Then we both jumped into our cars to go to Rusty's house.

The house was a small Cape Cod past its prime, disheveled as an old woman in a torn housedress. Faded green paint peeled off pitted shingles and wild grass grew scattered in clumps on dusty brown earth that once had been lawn.

I was glad that Rusty and I had taken separate cars so she couldn't see the surprise I felt as I pulled into the driveway. I never would have pictured this her home. Except for the curtains on the windows, the place looked abandoned.

Rusty scaled the front stoop and I followed her into the living room. Inside, the same feeling of sparseness pervaded. It was easy to see that the people who lived here were immaculately clean and desperately poor. The wooden floors had been scrubbed clean so often that the wax and finish were gone. One green flowered couch, covered by hand with hesitant stitching showing, lined the far wall. The only window was framed with two tattered panels of the same green flowered material as the sofa. Across the room, one side of an overstuffed deep purple chair rested heavily on a cinder block which was barely concealed by the slipcovers threadbare skirt. In the corner next to that chair was a delicate old mahogany table and on that table was the only lamp in the room, a cracked white porcelain jug topped by a tobacco-stained linen shade.

Rusty looked embarrassed. "When my mother first saw this house she said, 'This furniture will have to go'. " Rusty shrugged and smiled. "But not while we live here, I guess, because that was seven years ago and she hasn't mentioned it since." Then, "C'mon," she said cheerfully, waving me onward. "Come meet Nona. The old girl's quite a character." When I looked puzzled, she explained, "Nona's my mother. She likes to be called by her name."

"Why?" I asked.

Rusty laughed. "I guess she prefers not to be identified as one of my relatives."

When we walked into the kitchen, Rusty's mother was sitting at

a small chipped enamel-topped table. The first thing I noticed was
that she was as pale and emaciated-looking as most of the patients
in Salvation Nursing Home. I thought, no wonder Rusty works so
well with them.

"Nona," Rusty said, pulling me forward, "this is my friend
Carol, from work."

Rusty's mom nodded a greeting but didn't say anything. So
Rusty added, "Carol's the nurse I was telling you about."

With that, Nona started to wheeze and cough.

Rusty quickly walked over to the sink and got her mom a glass
of water. She stood waiting for her to stop coughing and offered her
a drink. But Nona continued to hack and choke. Finally, when she
could gasp for air, she told Rusty, "There's a cold beer in the refrigerator. Could you get it for me?"

Rusty smiled knowingly and just said, "Sure, Mom. But first
would you let Carol listen to your chest and take your blood pressure?"

Mrs. Russell nodded. "If it's not too much trouble."

"None at all," I reassured her.

"Have a beer, dear," she offered, as I approached her, blood-
pressure cuff in hand.

"No thanks, Mrs. Russell," I said. I couldn't guess how old she
was, maybe sixty-five. But her hair was pinned back on the sides
with two bright little girl's barrettes. She wore a freshly laundered,
starched white shirt. The carefully pressed navy cotton pants hung
on her frail frame. When I placed the cuff around her arm to take her
blood pressure, I had to wrap it several times. She was all bones. Up
close, I could hear her wheeze. "What about going for a checkup?"
I asked. Her blood pressure was high.

"You can afford to suggest that, my dear. You're young and
healthy."

"I'm serious, Mrs. Russell," I said. "Maybe a doctor could give
you something for your emphysema and help get rid of that cough."

"Call me Nona," she directed, and then she added vehemently,
"I'll die here before I'll see a doctor who tells me the reasons for my
sickness are my fault. They all tell you the same thing. Give up
smoking. Don't drink. And you'll get well. Bull!" Nona reached into

her pocket and pulled out a pack of Lucky Strikes. As she lit one, coughing some more, she managed to say, "I know you mean well."

Rusty and I sat at the table talking for a long time, and several times Mrs. Russell got up to get another beer. By the time we decided to go to a diner and get something to eat, Rusty's mother looked pretty tipsy.

"Do you want us to bring you home something to eat, Nona?" Rusty asked before we left.

"No thanks," she answered, without looking at us. "I had a dry piece of cheese between two slices of stale bread this afternoon."

My heart sank. "How awful," I whispered to Rusty.

For a minute she looked puzzled; then she laughed. "Carol, one of Nona's greatest charms is her sense of humor"–Rusty shook her head– "liberally sprinkled with guilt slinging. I went shopping yesterday. She had a cheese sandwich for lunch."

By the time we got back from dinner, Nona was already in bed. Rusty and I went into her room to talk so we wouldn't disturb her mother's sleep. Rusty's room was small, clean and cluttered with religious objects. A statue of the Blessed Mother, a black-and-gold missal, and the Infant of Prague rested on a rose-satin-covered end table. There was a crucifix hanging on the wall and a small woven cross of palm. On top of her dresser lay an ornate dark wooden cross and I walked over to look at it more closely. It was wide and deep, a container of some sort.

"You can open it if you want," Rusty said.

I gingerly pushed the thick wooden cross forward. Inside, there were several small compartments. They held a bottle of Holy Water, two white candles, some balls of cotton and a tiny vial of some kind of oil. I picked it up to smell it. Not a scent. "What in hell's name is this?" I asked her. "And where in hell's name did you get it?" It gave me the creeps, reminded me of some kind of voodoo.

Rusty looked amused again. "It's an Extreme Unction set," she said. "In other words for Last Rites. I got it when I was a kid from the Easter Bunny."

"Oh, God, Rusty. Would you please be serious?" I said, but before she could reply again, we both heard a terrible thump. I jumped, and Rusty leapt up from the bed where she had been sitting. We both got to the door at the same time, but as I started through it, she stopped me. "Stay here," she said firmly. "I'll take care of her."

In the time Rusty was gone, I wondered what was going on. I sat down on the clean worn white chenille bedspread and stared at the cracks in the ceiling, thinking how middle-class and over-indulged my own childhood had been. I had no experience with the kind of poverty that Rusty had grown up with.

Then I started thinking how strange medical institutions were, whether they were hospitals or nursing homes. I'd always known that they robbed the patients of their individuality; that once dressed in a hospital gown, we forgot somehow that patients came from families and were a part of something larger. But before today, it had never occurred to me that those institutions did the same to the staff. Doctors, nurses, aides, once dressed in white, seemed also to exist in a vacuum, to be part of the efficient hospital system, not of the regular world. Once in uniform it was hard to believe that any of us had real and human problems in our personal lives. It was hard to believe that any of us had a history of human suffering.

"She's tucked in again nicely," Rusty announced when she got back. "Not a broken bone in her dear little body. Another bruise or two for sure, but she'll be fine."

"Does this happen often?" I asked.

"Only when Nona overindulges," Rusty answered, "which unfortunately is too often."

I felt terrible for her. Still so young, she had to take care of a mother who drank, she had no father, and she spent her days, every day, working with old people. And I was worried about the quality of my life?

It had grown late while we were talking and I was just about to leave for home when Rusty's mother woke up coughing, sputtering and struggling to breathe. Both of us ran in this time, sat Nona up straight and stayed with her until her breathing eased.

"Maybe I should think about having Aunt Tess from Chicago live with us for a while," Nona told Rusty apologetically. "She's alone now too. . ."

Rusty reassured, "Do whatever you feel is best for you."

I insisted she go to the doctor the following day, and Nona, frightened now, agreed. Once she'd settled down again, I decided to stay over and make sure she didn't run into any more trouble.

At six the next morning, Rusty had to leave for work.

"Why don't you come and live with me?" I asked her over breakfast, and she looked surprised.

There's a function that time serves in intimacy, which I as a nurse had given up long before. It is a luxury of the healthy world–the illusion that we have all the time we need to learn to care for and trust another person, to be sure that he or she is no threat and will offer us no danger. In essence, to *know* someone. But as a nurse I had to learn to reach intimacy quickly to help the patient. I had been forced to drop the tribal dance, the ritual, my protection. There was no room for social distance when within five minutes of entering a patient's room I was looking at and touching the most private parts of someone's body or probing deeply into someone's secret dreams and fears. There just was no time for the many dinners, long conversations and the other niceties which help you know someone. I had to learn shortcuts. So I'd made the adaptation into instant intimacy by developing a seventh sense. My nursing sense: intuition plus observation. It had become a habit. Now it was that seventh sense which let me know that it was perfectly right to ask Rusty to move in though I'd only known her a short while in real time. Besides, her house was dreary even in the early morning. I couldn't shake the feeling it wasn't "healthy" for her to stay.

"You can't live here forever, especially if your mom has company," I continued. "And I could use the help with the rent and the kids if you live with me."

"Can't do that," she said, as she gulped down her orange juice.

"I'm not suggesting that you just abandon your mom," I told her, "but you have to have your own life too."

"I know that, and this isn't the first time my mother's suggested Aunt Tess so she'll have help during the day. That's not it anyway. Nona always says she'd love to live alone. But I can't," she said as she started for the front door. "Come on, I don't want to be late."

Outside, before I got into my car, I asked, "Why then? Is it that you don't think we can live together?"

"Has nothing to do with you . . . or my mother," Rusty said as she jumped into her front seat.

I was standing next to her car. "Okay," I said, "give me a clue?" She started her engine, rolled down the window, and stuck her head out. "Don't have enough time right now. I'll tell you sometime soon," she said, and then she pulled away.

❖❖❖

On the way home, I stopped to see Creede. I pulled in front of the gray Cape Cod house in which she rented an apartment. Her landlady would still be sleeping and I didn't want to wake her so I walked around the side of the house and threw some pebbles up at Creede's window. She stuck her head out. "If there's trouble, I'll pass," Creede said from up above. "I just got home from work and had a harried night."

"No trouble," I told her. "I came for coffee."

Creede opened the front door to let me in. As I slid past her into a large brown-shag-carpeted hallway, she placed her finger over her lips to quiet me. Then we tiptoed up a long flight of stairs to her apartment.

Creede's studio was very dramatic. One enormous room completely decorated in black and white geometrics. Ultramodern oil paintings hanging on the walls, wire and lucite sculptures lining every shelf The loose arrangement of live yellow flowers on her table offered the only color. Books covered the floor, bed and couch.

I plopped down on one of the large black pillows that Creede used as a couch. "To what do I owe the pleasure of your company this morning?" she asked. She placed a cup of coffee for each of us on the low black lacquer table. Then she sat on another of the large pillows, across from me.

"I think I've found someone to live with me," I told her.

"Is this a person I know?" she asked.

I shook my head. Then I picked up the cup and sipped the hot coffee. "She's a person from work," I said. And then for the next hour I explained what I knew of Rusty to Creede.

"So you've decided to snatch someone out of the atmosphere, whom you know practically nothing about, to take up residence in your home," she said thoughtfully.

"That's essentially it," I said, smiling. I knew she thought I was nuts.

"What about your children?" she asked.

"Oh, they can still live there," I teased, "and when you ask a question like that, you have to ask, 'What about your *helpless* children?'" Then more seriously I added, "Creede, a person who works the way Rusty does with old and, helpless people could never be a danger to the kids or me."

"So you trust her already?" Creede asked incredulously.

"What's trust?" I asked. "It's only being able to see someone is enough like yourself to understand what makes them tick. Then because they're a known, they're no longer frightening. Right?" But I didn't wait for Creede to answer before I went on. "Trust me, Creede. I can tell. She's a lot like me."

"For better or for worse," Creede mumbled. Then she shook her head as though I was beyond saving. She lit a long brown cigarette. "Let me ask one question. Does this individual know anything about your plans for her yet? Have you at least given her the courtesy of telling her?"

I nodded. "Yep," I said, "I mentioned it to her this morning and she said she couldn't do it. But she can't keep living where she is, even if she doesn't know it."

"Of course, her opinion that she doesn't want to live with you makes no difference," Creede muttered.

"Just a minute, Creede," I interrupted "I didn't say she didn't *want* to. What she said was she *couldn't*. Want and can't are different things. *Want*, I can fully accept and respect. Can't can always be worked with."

Creede's look softened "So you've really decided," she said.

"I think so," I told her. "My intuition says it's right."

"Well, what's the plan from here?" Creede asked. She got up and took a box of English tea biscuits from the bread box on top of the small white refrigerator in the corner of the room. Then she covered a biscuit with Marmite, a thick salty brown spread. She offered me one but I refused.

"Rusty said she'll tell me why she can't sometime soon," I said. "So how about if I invite her over for barbecue and we can both talk to her? That way you can meet her and tell me what you think."

Creede accepted.

That night my parents dropped Lynn and Jeremy off at home. My parents loved having the kids and the kids enjoyed being there. We had an old-fashioned extended family and the fact that the kids and I lived in a separate house from my parents made little difference. Jeremy, Lynn and I played a few games of Scrabble. Then Rusty called.

"If you're not doing anything special," she said, "I'd like to come over and talk to you. Marta looked okay when I left work, but I think Lenny's in trouble. I brought him a baseball to hold and the pain in his hands made it intolerable. He wouldn't give up, though, and when I left he was still holding it. But I've been thinking and there are some things I want to tell you."

"Great," I told her. "Then you can meet the kids. I've already told them about you and they think it's a terrific idea to have you live with us. In fact the only thing left to do is count the votes."

Rusty seemed to hesitate a moment before she said, "Carol, don't do that until I've had a chance to say what I have to, okay?" The seriousness of her tone worried me.

"Fine," I answered. "Everything will be on hold until you get here."

"One more thing," Rusty said. "What I have to say has to be said to you alone first. Afterwards you can decide what to tell your kids . . ."

We were all sitting on the couch in the living room watching TV by the time Rusty came. Jeremy jumped up to answer the door and

Lynn moved cautiously to the end of the couch.

Jeremy held out his hand. "I'm Jeremy," he said, excited. "You're Mommy's friend, right?"

Rusty bent down. "And you are very smart for a six-year-old person," she told him as she shook his hand.

"Almost six," he corrected. "In December I'll be six. Right, Mom?" he added, turning toward me. I nodded.

"This is Lynn, Rusty," I said, standing.

Rusty walked over toward us. "Hi," she said, and then seeing how shy Lynn looked and how uncomfortable, she made no overtures toward her.

"How about some coffee?" I asked Rusty.

"I'd rather have iced tea if you have any," she said, winking at Jeremy, who was already glued to her side.

"Me too, Mom," Jeremy echoed.

"Lynn," I asked, "what about you?"

Lynn nodded absently, pretending to be engrossed in the program she was watching.

As I went into the kitchen to prepare the iced tea, I could hear Jeremy ask Rusty, "Want to see my room?"

When I came in with the drinks, the living room was empty.

"Hey, guys," I shouted up the stairs, "am I drinking alone?"

I was surprised when it was Lynn who answered, "Be right down, Mom. We're showing Rusty our rooms."

The ice cubes were melted by the time Jeremy jumped off the last step back into the living room. Rusty and Lynn, followed right behind.

"How did it go?" I asked them.

"Well," Lynn answered, "Rusty says she'll teach me how to dance."

Lynn, my serious child, dance? I looked closely at Rusty. I was sure she was the pied piper in disguise. "I thought you didn't like dancing," I said aloud to Lynn.

She shook her head. "Mom, it's you who doesn't like to dance. I don't even know how."

I nodded. "Got it," I said.

"And she'll help me build a tree house," Jeremy chimed in.

"So that means you've decided to take me up on my offer?" I said to Rusty, feeling very self-satisfied.

"Not exactly," Rusty said, serious again. "Not until we get some things discussed, anyway."

Later, while the kids were upstairs watching TV, Rusty and I sat on the couch. Rusty was wearing a light brown blouse and jeans. I could see from the crease in the front that they had been carefully pressed. After only few minutes of small talk, we got down to business. "So lay it on me," I said, smiling, "tell me what's so mysterious that it would keep you from moving in with us."

She didn't look at me when she said, "I have epilepsy."

I laughed with relief. "Is that all?" I asked. "That's what's causing you this grief? I've been a nurse for years–if I haven't learned to hold a tongue blade by now, I'm not much good to anyone." Leave it to me to believe that just because I could hold a tongue blade, I had the problem of Rusty's epilepsy beat. Thank God, she knew better, but of course, I still didn't listen.

At that time, what I knew about epilepsy was just about what my friends who were nurses knew. Everything we, as human beings, do is made possible by the constant discharge of electrical energy between the cells of our brains. In people who have epilepsy the discharge is sometimes too great and it causes loss of consciousness and a grand-mal seizure.

There is also petit-mal, a seizure which alters consciousness but does not cause a person to fall. Instead, a person in a petit-mal seizure will suddenly stop what he is doing, stare, look a little pale, perhaps flutter his eyelids for a brief period of time.

Because in all my years in hospitals I had never taken care of one patient admitted with only that diagnosis, I never thought of epilepsy as causing the people who had it too much trouble. Besides, it wasn't terminal like cancer as far as I was concerned, or even chronic like heart disease and it posed absolutely no threat to me. It wasn't an infection I could catch. I couldn't bring it home to my kids. It wasn't bacteria or a virus or even the kind of unknown that would show up on my X-rays years later. It couldn't harm me at all.

"Are you on any medication?" I asked her then. I knew that most people who had epilepsy could live normal lives if their seizures were controlled by medications. And though medical science had found no cure, epilepsy sometimes went away–no one knew the reasons.

"I take three Dilantin a day," Rusty told me. But she looked concerned that I had taken it so lightly. "What about the kids?" she asked. "Seizures can be pretty frightening to little kids and I can't guarantee I won't have any. With a disease like this–"

"I wish you wouldn't refer to your seizures as a disease. It's really just a disorder, a set of symptoms. 'Disease' sounds contagious. Seizures are just a surge of electrical energy going through your brain, which throws it out of kilter. We don't consider the atmosphere diseased when we see lightning and we don't consider our radios sick when we hear static, do we?"

"Okay," Rusty said, laughing, "I'll try, from now on, to think of myself as a well person who has lightning going through her radio which interrupts the signal and throws her violently on her ass."

"Don't be such a whack!" I said. "It's just that I don't like you to think of yourself as sick.'"

"Hey, Carol," Rusty said before she could stop herself, "I'm not the one who sees me as sick. I'm not the one who keeps locking me up."

I thought she meant in the hospital.

CHAPTER 4

"**W**hat a riot," a girl in green was saying. "Imagine trying to commit suicide by sawing at your wrist with a plastic knife." It was Monday morning and I was passing the nurses' station on my way to Dominic's room. I didn't know the aide who was speaking, but all the nurses and aides looked amused.

"We passed the room a couple of times during the night, saw the covers moving and just figured he was playing with himself. . . so we left him alone," she added. "It was almost morning when we discovered what he'd done."

One of the other aides laughed. "He didn't even need stitches–the nurse just put some butterfly bandages on."

When Mrs. Frick saw me standing there she quieted them.

"Who are they talking about?" I asked Mrs. Frick. I was devastated that anyone should have to resort to such desperate action.

Lenny Kyposky," she said, and then busied herself with reading a chart.

"I'd like to use the phone to call Rusty," I said, as I began to walk toward it. I knew she'd be concerned about Lenny.

"Don't bother," Mrs. Frick said quickly. "Rusty's in there with him now. She's the one who found him."

"I thought today was her day off," I said, puzzled.

"Yes," she said, "but she was on one of her missions again. She came in to give him a smaller ball or something. A handball . . ."

I ran down the hall toward Dominic's room. Penny was standing outside. "Poor thing," she said.

"Lenny, you mean?" I asked.

Penny nodded. Then she said, "But I think he'll be okay. The aide, Rusty, has been with him for over an hour, just holding his hand."

"Good," I said. "How's Dominic?"

"He's been perfect since this whole thing happened," she said. "I think he's frightened." As I opened the door to go in, Penny added, "That little girl is something special. She's more than smart. She's got the kind of sensitivity and compassion that means she's been ground through the mills of the gods, slowly."

"She has epilepsy," I said softly, "and her family was very poor, and her father just died."

Penny smiled and patted me fondly on top of the head. "Those are the facts, ma'am," she said, teasing. "And they're neat and tidy. But I'll bet anything that the experience of those facts is not nearly as neat and tidy. In other words, she's been hammered upon and made malleable by the Master Sculptor."

"Penny," I said, exasperated, "talk English. Are you trying to say that she's suffered?"

Penny nodded. "She's suffered."

Penny left and I walked inside the room. Dominic put his finger to his lips to quiet me and then shook his head sadly. He looked more gentle than I'd ever seen him. The curtains were pulled between the beds but I could see Rusty's shadow right next to Lenny's. I sat down. I could hear them talking.

"They're all laughing at me," Lenny said softly. "They think it's a joke and I'm a fool."

"They don't understand, Lenny," Rusty said. "That makes them foolish, not you."

"What kind of idiot would try to kill himself because he can never again hold a baseball?" he asked, crying now.

"Lenny," Rusty said quietly, "no one thing causes a person to try to take his life. Even though sometimes it looks that way."

Lenny started to sob now, and I could see his small bent shadow shake. Rusty leaned forward and put her arms around him.

"Lenny," Rusty said softly, "it's the feeling of hopelessness that's most destructive. The feeling that nothing ever will change for the better. Now, I'm going to share something with you that I use. There's a place in each an everyone of us that *knows* things will get better. It's a place where the real part of us hides. Whenever we're depressed or scared, we just have to try to keep the outside sounds away so we can hear. And, Lenny, if you listen carefully, the promise for tomorrow will come on the whisper from inside you. That place is the place of hope. . . and I want you to give me your word that you'll try to find it."

Dominic was finally overcome with emotion. He held his shaking hands in front of him and said, "Eh, Lenny, Imma got this good hand but Imma no can throw a ball too. My brainna no work."

When Lenny heard Dominic, he sat back in bed. Rusty pulled the curtains away so we could see then "Thanks, Dom," Lenny said. "I appreciate what you're saying."

Dominic forced a smile. "Whatta room we gotta here," he said, and we all laughed.

❖❖ ❖❖ ❖❖

Rusty stayed until the shift was over and then we left together. "Good job," I said as we walked across the parking lot. "There was no one who could have handled that situation with Lenny better. That thing about the place of hope is nice. Where did you get it?"

Rusty smiled. "It's a long story," she said.

"Well, it's probably one I need to hear," I told her. "I've always had a problem understanding suicide."

Rusty looked thoughtful. "It's hard to explain. I guess you'd just have to be there."

"Are you serious?" I asked. "Do you mean you tried?"

Rusty nodded. "Once," she said quietly, "a long time ago."

I shook my head and laughed involuntarily. "Rusty," I said, "how can it be a long time ago? You can't be more than twenty."

"Nineteen," she corrected. "And time isn't only measured in years."

Sometimes intimate disclosures hang suspended in the air above my head when I find them painful and so it took a little while before I could absorb what Rusty had said about trying suicide. Then I offered what my mother always had, to make a hurt better. "Want to come over to my house and have supper?" I asked. "My mother is picking the kids up from school and taking them to see one of the relatives tonight. So I'm free."

"I'll have to see if Nona's okay," Rusty answered. "I'd like to come over. There's still so much I have to explain–"

I cut her off. "If you mean before you move in, forget it. Nothing that you could tell me would make any difference to me."

Rusty stopped walking and looked at me. "You can't know that, Carol. Not yet."

"Well, come over for a cup of tea at least," I insisted. "You can call your mom from there."

Rusty smiled. "It's not hard for you to get close to people, is it, Carol?" she asked.

"Not to someone like you," I said. "I really think we're a lot alike."

Rusty began to laugh. "I'd watch who you say that to," she said.

❖❖ ❖❖ ❖❖

We both drove down my long gravel driveway to the small brown matchbox house I had rented for the last five years. There were three tiny bedrooms and a center room we used as a den upstairs. One living-room/dining-room combination downstairs with a small kitchen and closet-type bathroom and one huge utility room at the bottom of the stairs which held the washer, dryer, bicycles and anything else we couldn't fit in the other rooms. The one great thing about the house was that it was right on a canal and it had a great big backyard with loads of tall trees. I loved being able to sit on the couch in the living room and watch the boats come and go.

Rusty waited patiently while I struggled to find my key, which lay somewhere in the bottom of my pocket-book. "It's probably underneath my stethoscope, my blood-pressure cuff, my scissors and my wallet," I said.

"Why don't you put it on your key ring?" she asked.

"I'm always afraid I'll lose that," I explained. "And I don't want to lose the car keys and the house key."

Rusty just looked at me but restrained herself from saying anything.

I finally got inside and while I put up water for tea, she called her mom. "Everything's fine," Rusty said. "Nona's having a neighbor over for a drink."

Then we both threw ourselves down on the couch to relax. It had been an emotionally exhausting day.

"Want to tell me?" I asked.

"About what?" she asked.

"Everything," I said.

"Not all at once," she answered.

"All right," I agreed. "How about starting with how you found out you had epilepsy?"

"Sure," Rusty said.

"And don't forget to tell me the stuff that will help me understand suicide, will you?"

"Same story," Rusty said.

I got up to make supper and she began. . .

❖ ❖ ❖

One minute Rusty was cheering for a guy to make a touchdown and the next minute she was hanging by her chin from the bleachers, or anyway that's how it seemed. It was during her freshman year in high school, a Saturday.

A few hours later, when Rusty woke up, she was lying on her back in the emergency room at Community Corners Hospital, strapped on a narrow stretcher. She tried to open her eyes but the overhead fluorescents hammered them shut again. In that moment she could see that the curtains had been drawn around her. She was in a small cubicle. A few minutes passed and she put her hands over her eyes and squinted through the slits between her fingers.

The first person she saw was Dr. Okanowa, the emergency-room house doctor. He was a short man, Oriental, with blackbird hair. He and her mom tried to help Rusty into a sitting position. Then he handed her a small cup with a few pills and said, "Lusty, take these Soon you feel better. Go home."

Nobody told her what was wrong with her but on the small steel table next to the gurney she saw a paper with "Diagnosis: Epilepsy" written on it. When her mom went to pay the cashier, she asked one of the nurses, "What's epilepsy?"

The nurse said simply, "Convulsions."

Rusty didn't know what the nurse was talking about, so when her mother came back, she asked, "What's epilepsy, Mom?" Her mother glanced over her shoulder, her eyes darted around the room. Then she just put her finger up to her lips. Rusty just stopped asking about it.

At home Arlene, Rusty's best friend, called to see how she was. "I have epilepsy," Rusty said.

Like an eagle, her mother came swooping into the room and took the phone away, screeching, "You have no right to tell anyone something like that when you don't know if it's really true." Rusty felt awful. She felt as though she had betrayed a family secret. From then on she was afraid to ask any questions.

Two weeks later, at the school's insistence, Rusty went to see a neurologist. Dr. Angelo, a large white-haired gentle man, examined Rusty. He did an electroencephalogram (EEG) in his office.

When the EEG, or brain-activity tracing, came back normal, Dr.

Angelo shook his head. He was a smart man and so he understood that machines could be in error–that there were areas of the brain too deep or unexplored to register. All Rusty's clinical symptoms pointed to epilepsy, so he put her on phenobarbital.

Several months later when she was still having a few seizures a week and it was obvious that the phenobarbital alone wasn't controlling them, he added Dilantin. He crossed his fingers, hoping that Rusty wasn't in the twenty percent of epilepsy patients whose seizures couldn't be controlled with medication.

The combination of medication seemed to work for while. Now it had been more than six months since Rusty had had a seizure. Good, Dr. Angelo thought, she's in the thirty percent whose seizures can at least be reduced in frequency by medication.

Then, toward the end of her sophomore year, Rusty was in Mr. Drake's biology class when she noticed something was happening again. She heard him talking about the chambers of the heart and saw him point to the diagram before his voice seemed to disappear while his lips still moved. Rusty reached up and pulled on her ear to clear it. It felt as though she had gotten water in it. But by the time she looked up again, Mr. Drake was dismissing the class and Rusty felt as though she had left for a commercial and not gotten back soon enough.

Outside the room, during change of class, the hall was a madhouse and Rusty felt herself pushed along by the crowd in the wrong direction. When she tried to speak or shout, no words would come. She tried to make it down the hall to the nurse's office but never did.

When Rusty fell, she never felt it, she was already out cold. She never heard the kids holler for Mr. Drake and didn't know until later that she had stopped breathing long enough that Mr. Drake had had to do mouth-to-mouth resuscitation to get her back. She didn't see Mrs. Yallow, the nurse, as she stood plastered along the hall lockers just staring at Mr. Drake, and so she didn't understand later when they told her she couldn't come back to school unless her seizures were under control. She didn't know the nurse was afraid. She just felt as though no one liked her.

Several hours afterward, she woke up in Community Corners' emergency room, curtains drawn, and thought: Crap! Here we go again. But this time was different.

Instead of releasing her after her seizures had stopped, Dr. Angelo admitted her to the medical-surgical unit of the main hospital. He knew he had to keep her until he was certain her seizures were under control. First, he would try to increase the dosage of the medications she was already on. Maybe that would do it.

A few nights later, as he stood watching Rusty from the side of her bed, she had another convulsion. Even for fifteen, she was such a little thing. He watched her eyes strain upward, her head pull back, and her muscles stiffen and then relax again and again. She looked so helpless, so vulnerable, and there was so little he could do. Damn things! Seizures. He waited several minutes, until it passed, and then, wiping his forehead in frustration, he left.

"Keep a close eye on her," he told the nurse sitting at the desk. "I'm not happy with the way she looks."

Weeks passed. Rusty didn't know how many days she had been in the hospital, because she never felt fully conscious. And strange things were happening inside her head. There were bright flashing lights that kept shooting like stars in front of her eyes. When people spoke, their voices echoed, and the smallest sound or vibration became an explosion. Several times she heard her name being called, but when she turned around to see who it was, no one was in the room. Everything started going backwards. In order to fall asleep at night, she'd have to force her eyes to stay open, because as soon as she closed them, there was daylight behind her eyelids. But the scariest thing that kept happening was that she would get a cramp in her arm from her head lying on it, or a pain in her side from lying too long in one spot, and when she opened her eyes to turn on her back, she was already there. Her brain often thought her body was in one position when her eyes showed her it was in another. She began to feel crazy. Often, when she tried to move, her body refused and she lay paralyzed, unable to lift her arms or legs. Unable to call for help, she woke up periodically and knew she'd had a grand-mal seizure because her muscles felt sore, a though she'd done too much exercise.

No one told Rusty that all those sensory distortions were another kind of seizure. Sensory, or partial, seizures. The cells in her brain were going haywire, sometimes in the area of feelings, sometimes in the area of sight of hearing or touch, and sometimes when her whole brain was involved she lost consciousness totally and had a grand-mal seizure as well. No one said anything, but Rusty knew something was really wrong.

There were lots of outside clues. They kept the curtains drawn around her bed, and each person who entered her cubbyhole wore a desolate expression. She was allowed phone calls anytime. She was seldom able to talk but still she did notice that the usual limitation on visitors wasn't enforced. Rusty knew this was a privilege reserved only for families of patients who were terminally ill.

Finally, one day when she was awake, after a bad night of seizures, her friend Arlene came to see her. As Arlene, with her long dark curls, stood next to the rails at the side of the bed, Rusty opened her eyes and tried to smile. "Hey," she whispered in a dry hoarse voice, "what's wrong with me?" Arlene's face was getting bigger and littler as Rusty watched.

Arlene just shrugged her shoulders and said, "All I know is the nurse told me not to stay too long because you're on the critical list."

Rusty was confused. She knew nothing about epilepsy, not what caused it, not how long it lasted, whether she could go crazy from it or whether it could kill her. She had tried a few times during that year to find out about it but it hadn't worked. Once, when she and her father went to the library, she had found a book on epilepsy. And she had taken it out while he was still scanning the books on a far shelf. She figured her mother wouldn't like the idea, so she had hidden it under the front seat of the car on the way home and had planned to bring it inside when no one was around. But somehow her mother found it and got so upset Rusty was forced to return it to the library immediately. Another time, she saw an advertisement on TV. An epilepsy association. They offered to send information. When Rusty received the pamphlet, at Arlene's house, all it said that she understood was "disorder of the central nervous system." And she wasn't quite sure what that was. She was upset by the enclosed medal, which had "I am an epileptic" etched deep in red letters. The pamphlet explained that if you didn't wear it you could be taken to jail because people would think you were drunk. Rusty decided she'd rather pretend she wasn't sick than find out any more about this thing she had.

The next time Rusty opened her eyes Arlene was gone and her mother and father were at her bedside. Her mother was pleading with a loud, echoing voice, "Don't give up, Rusty. You have to try."

Rusty couldn't speak but as she lay watching the IV fluid drip from the bottle overhead, she wondered: *Give up what? Try what?* Then she fell asleep again.

Rusty couldn't tell the difference between being asleep and being sedated or being in seizure until after it was over. Then, if it had been a seizure, there were the familiar signs–the bitten end of her tongue, the sore muscles and the concerned looks on the faces of the people around her. She herself had not seen anyone have a seizure in real life, but she figured it must look pretty awful to others because of their reactions.

Especially her parents. One night after a seizure, she heard her mother say to her father, "Well, thank God no children were here to see this."

Rusty kept her eyes closed and suddenly envisioned a horror film she had seen once. The young man, in the daytime, looked like everyone else, but then at night he sometimes fell down on the ground, like her, and had a "fit." Rusty remembered that after about six of these fits, the boy's nose began to grow into a snout and he began to discover long brown hair all over his face and body. Then he'd attack innocent people. No wonder her mother was so afraid.

She promised herself that at the first sign of long hair on her face or body, she'd kill herself. Rusty didn't want to be a werewolf.

When her father realized she was awake, he tried to cheer her up by making jokes and telling stories. This night he told her he had just read a book concerning religious practices in the fifteenth century in England. He added, chuckling, "Honey, you sure are lucky to be alive today instead of then, when they burned people like you at the stake for being witches."

Rusty smiled back at him but in her heart lay a growing terror.

Something strange was happening to her. Something weird, frightening and ugly.

After her parents had gone, and she was alone in her bed, Rusty reached up and unhooked the clasp on the medal she wore around her neck. She held it carefully in her hand, keeping her fingers bent over it. Then she lay on her back and opened her hand carefully. Her Saint Jude medal shone out at her. Rusty had chosen Saint Jude to be her patron saint the year before. Her father had brought her a medal of Saint Dymphna, the patron saint of the incurably ill. But Rusty didn't want her. Nobody had ever heard of her hardly. But Saint Jude–people knew him. He was the patron saint of hopeless cases.

It wasn't really a prayer; all she said was, "Saint Jude, if I can stay alive here and if I'm good, can I just be a regular kid again? I don't want anything special. I just want to have a regular life." She said it in a little voice, she tried not to whine, and she hoped she'd wiped the tear away fast enough that Saint Jude didn't think she was feeling sorry for herself.

The following day, after Rusty spent a restless night because of the bright lights and music in her head, Sally and Ann, two staff nurses on the unit, came in to give her morning care. They were both young and new nurses. They had worked together on Rusty since she had been admitted. This morning they smiled at each other, glad to see her awake.

Rusty really noticed them for the first time. She had gotten glimpses of them before, but nothing really clear. She liked the way they looked in their uniforms. It made her feel safe. And now she decided that she would like to make people feel as good as these nurses made her feel. Safe. A nice feeling. Besides, she figured, if she got a good job like that, she wouldn't ever have to be poor again.

Ann had long red hair and lots of freckles. As she started to walk toward the small sink in the room to fill the stainless-steel basin for Rusty's bath, Sally, a short dark-haired girl, spoke. "Good morning, Rusty," she said, smiling. "Your eyes look bright and you look wide-awake. How do you feel?"

Rusty found it hard to speak because her throat felt sore and dry, so she just said "Fine" and relaxed as the nurses gently washed her and then changed the sheets on her bed. They were chatting to each other and to Rusty, exchanging small pleasantries, their mood light, when Ann asked Rusty, "What are you going to school for? I mean, what subjects are you taking?" Then before Rusty could answer, the young nurse giggled and added, "As in, what do you want to be when you grow up?"

Rusty smiled to herself. That was the first thing anyone had said that indicated that she had a future. It assumed that she would grow up. So at least I'm not dying, she thought.

Rusty answered, "A nurse," and then, having mulled it over, repeated more definitely, "Yes, I want to be a nurse."

Sally was leaning over Rusty brushing her hair and Rusty noticed Sally's hand hesitate for a second. Sally bit her bottom lip. But it was her expression that was the most telling. *But you can't*, it said, clearer and louder than any words. Rusty closed her eyes.

Finally Ann and Sally finished, leaving Rusty alone. For once she was glad that they had drawn the curtains.

She was dozing an hour later when the two nurses came back into the room with the nursing supervisor. Rusty, stunned, realized that it was Mrs. Lobwick, her next-door neighbor. Rusty wanted to pull the covers over her head. Her parents would fall over dead if they found out that Mrs. Lobwick had seen her. It wasn't that she wasn't a nice person, a good woman, as Rusty's father had always called her. But she *talked*, and everything she knew was spread around the neighborhood as quickly as pollution.

Mrs. Lobwick, her curly hair making dark swirls around her starched white cap, came over to Rusty's bed and reached for her hand. "Honey," she said, smiling uncomfortably, "I want to talk to you."

Rusty was in no position to protest so she tried to act happy to see Mrs. Lobwick. She forced a smile and made up her mind to be very careful about what she said.

Mrs. Lobwick lowered her heavy clean white body onto Rusty's bed. She leaned close to Rusty's ear as she pleaded, "Tell me you don't really want to be a nurse."

Rusty didn't see how this could cause any trouble so she said in a determined voice, "I *do* want to be a nurse. And I *will* be."

Mrs. Lobwick's face folded and she sighed, a long low audible sigh. "Rusty, honey, you can't ever be a nurse," she said kindly. "You must know and accept that now, from the beginning. It will be difficult for you to have any kind of a job, with your condition. But because you're smart, maybe you could work in a factory. . . not with the machines of course, but maybe gluing on labels or something. If you take your medicine very carefully, you can have an almost normal life." Mrs. Lobwick's eyes were filled to overflowing.

Now Rusty was really upset. Everyone was telling her what to do and what not to do. And she knew that in spite of the fact that she had some dopey sickness that threw her in the air and flipped her like a pancake, she wasn't going to allow it. "I want to be a nurse and I don't care who knows it," she snapped at Mrs. Lobwick. "I want to."

Then, without any more discussion, Rusty turned over on her stomach, pulled the covers over her head and refused to acknowledge anyone else for the rest of the day.

All that night Rusty lay awake listening to the scary hospital sounds and thinking. She was afraid. She searched her memory for something that she could have done to cause this thing to happen. She couldn't remember falling and hitting her head when she was small, never really hard anyway. That was a question almost everyone had asked since she'd gotten sick. And she couldn't think of anything really bad that she had done. She knew that she had beaten up a couple of the kids in school but she had never hit anyone first; had only hit them back, and then only hard enough to stop them from hitting her again. She realized the way she had fought with her parents, especially her mother, wasn't terrific, but Arlene and her other friends yelled twice as much and nothing like this had ever happened to them.

The night nurse came in, shined the flashlight in Rusty's face and left. The hall light went from fluorescent bright to candlelight dim, and Rusty was lying alone in the pitch dark, when she remembered something that she had almost forgotten. . .

She was very young. And some spooky nun, in a bat suit, was teaching something about *sins*. Big black mortal sins which stained your soul permanently like a scar, and then she talked about little black spots which one could eradicate with confession. Rusty remembered how the nun had taken an eraser to the blackboard to illustrate her point. Those were only venial sins. Of course, the worst of all was ORIGINAL SIN, which you got because someone else had done something wrong and which Rusty thought was too unfair to be in religion. Then, that day the nun's voice got very low and she talked about DEVILS. Devils who got inside people's bodies and possessed them, even small children. And the only way to get them out of you was to have a priest say some exorcising prayers.

Suddenly Rusty knew! And now as the full impact of that knowledge hit her, she sat bolt upright in terror. The nun had been telling this story about a devil and a boy, and Rusty had laughed out loud and said with indignation, "I don't believe you. That sounds like magic and I don't think that happens to real people." At seven years old, that day in Sunday school, Rusty just couldn't believe it. But now she did.

Often, the very things that change our lives irrevocably or finally kill us, originally go unnoticed. The bang that causes the bump on our heads which eventually causes a bleed is gone from our memory. The original pimple which causes the sore that never heals and turns cancerous is forgotten. The small red circle on the ankle of the diabetic which signals impaired circulation and ends in amputation of the whole leg, starts off looking so innocent that we ignore it.

And so it was for Rusty the day that her mother came to visit, bearing gifts, and placed the plastic bag in which her new pajamas came in the top drawer of the bedside table instead of throwing it away in the trashcan.

Rusty had already been in the hospital three weeks. Her seizures had grown much less frequent; she had had only two in the last week. Her head felt clear. Now she was sitting up in bed, wishing she could be outside playing, swimming at the beach with Arlene or riding her bike down the long empty paved road to the local park. Through the large undraped window in her room, she could see that it was a beautiful day. It was getting hot, everything green, summer coming. And Rusty didn't want to be in the hospital one more day, not one more minute in fact.

Her mom had just arrived. She was smiling as she unpacked the brown paper bag and handed Rusty a chocolate shake. As Rusty sipped slowly, her mom carefully took each and every straight pin out of the blue cotton pajamas she had bought, placed the plastic bag in the top drawer, and proceeded to smooth the wrinkles from the gift she had just brought.

"The doctor said that if you don't have any more seizures in the next forty-eight hours, you can come home," Rusty's mother said hopefully as she sat in the chair next to the bed.

"And if I do," Rusty asked between sips, "then how long do I have to stay?"

Nona looked embarrassed when she answered. In fact she stammered, "Baby, honey, if you keep being sick, it's better for you to be here. What can your father and I do with you at home? How will we manage?"

"I can't stay in a hospital forever," Rusty insisted. But before she could say any more, Nona began a fit of coughing.

Rusty offered her mother a sip of water from the paper cup on her overbed table. Her mom refused and lit a cigarette instead.

Sally came in to say, "See you tomorrow," while Mrs. Russell was still visiting.

Rusty, uncomfortable with the IV in her arm and annoyed by the hospital gown which made her look sick, asked Sally, "When can I get rid of this thing?" She pointed overhead to the bottle hanging on the pole.

"Dr. Trevor says as soon as you're seizure-free for forty-eight hours."

"Who's Dr. Trevor?" Rusty asked.

"He's the doctor covering while Dr. Angelo's on vacation," Sally said. Then she waved to them and left the room.

After about an hour, Mrs. Russell started fidgeting and Rusty knew she wanted to leave. Rusty was relieved; she wanted to spend a relaxing night and think about what she would do first when she got out. She thought how peculiar this thing that she had was. This epilepsy. One minute she was so sick and the next she was just fine. Right now, it was hard for her even to believe she had anything wrong with her. Maybe there's some mistake, she thought.

The evening went well and Rusty was hopeful. She had needed no injections of sedatives to control her seizures, and so she felt very alert. She called Arlene and a few other friends to tell them she'd be home in the next few days. The nurse let her get out of bed to go to the bathroom, where for the first time in days she washed herself standing at the sink and finally gave her teeth a good and thorough brushing. Her legs felt a bit wobbly, but other than that it felt great being upright for a change.

At eleven p.m. she fell asleep a happy person. In a few days she was sure she'd be back home playing with her friends, riding her bike, going to the movies and wearing regular clothes again.

Then sometime in the middle of the night she was awakened by a gnawing feeling in the pit of her stomach. She rang for the nurse and asked for a container of milk. She thought maybe it was indigestion. After she drank the milk, she tried to fall back to sleep. But she couldn't. The gnawing feeling in her stomach was almost palpable, like a wiggling, thrashing small animal trying to break out of its shell. In time the feeling started to grow bigger and bigger, moving up into her chest, pushing hard on her heart threatening to burst through her rib cage and out of he body. But now the feeling had changed. It wasn't growing and wiggling any longer. It was biting and clawing and was enraged. She tried to call out, to scream or shout, but the feeling of rage had reached her throat and slammed it shut. Rusty was struggling to swallow, struggling to breathe when suddenly she lost consciousness and felt nothing. She was in seizure again.

Rusty didn't know it then because no one had told her, but there's something called abdominal epilepsy. And sometimes it feels like that. It can be a seizure form in itself or a precursor of a grand-mal convulsion.

But when in the early morning she was conscious again, she knew she had been sick. She knew the signs by now.

Slowly she remembered the feeling in the night, the growing ugly thing inside her, and thought about the devil, the witches and the werewolf. She was certain she'd never be a regular kid again.

Before anyone knew she was awake, Rusty reached over into the top drawer of the bedside table, pulled out the plastic bag and placed it over her head, covering her nose and mouth. Then she quickly wrapped her wrists together with the IV tubing, turned on her side and waited to go to sleep for good.

It was two o'clock in the morning and Rusty had been talking for hours. I got up to make us some coffee, my head in a whirl. She stayed on the couch, silent, until I spoke. "That wasn't a suicide attempt," I shouted in from the kitchen, enraged, "That was a homicide attempt. I think all those lunatics were trying to kill you." When I came back into the living room, I put the coffee cups on the table in front of us and sat on the couch next to Rusty.

"Which lunatics are you referring to?" she asked smiling.

"Well, first, the doctors, who never even told you anything, who never explained anything," I said.

"Dr. Angelo was a nice man, Carol," she said. "I think maybe he thought it was too complicated for me to understand."

"Don't make excuses for him, Rusty," I said, "or for all the nurses, or for your parents, for that matter. It was their default, their errors. You were a smart fifteen-year-old kid, with absolutely no support or understanding from the adults around you. You could have understood about the electrical impulses spreading through your brain. You could have been told what the medicine was supposed to do. Even Jeremy could understand some of it, and Lynn certainly could."

"Nurses weren't allowed to tell anything then," Rusty said. "They assumed the doctor told you. And my parents didn't know any better. In fact, I'm sure they didn't understand any more than I did. Also, they were poor and were probably afraid to cause any trouble because they felt obligated already."

"Rusty," I said, exasperated, "a fifteen-year-old kid needs to be like other kids. By not explaining that this was a physical problem that didn't mean you were crazy, they left you to imagine all kinds of scary things." By now my head was shaking as though it was loose and I was finding it hard to breathe, so I was almost speechless.

Rusty seemed surprised by my reaction. To try to placate me, she teased, "Okay, back to business. Exactly who's guilty," she asked, trying to look serious, "now that we know it wasn't me?"

"Not who," I told her, "What? Ignorance. Insensitivity. Prejudice. Anyone who didn't put himself in your place and try to imagine how it would feel. How were you to know that you weren't going to die from epilepsy, if you didn't even know what it was? How were you supposed to live when they took away all promise of a future for you? A sensitive, gentle kid like you would never have wanted to live and hurt anyone, so if they didn't tell you that you wouldn't hurt anyone else, what were you left with? Only the imagination of a fifteen-year-old kid."

I knew from working with adolescents who had chronic or terminal illnesses that they suffered more than the younger children or adults. Theirs was a world just beginning. They were old enough to dream of possibilities and to understand deprivation. They didn't only miss the "now of not being healthy. . . they also suffered from the future which would never be. Broken dreams are much more devastating than a painful reality.

Rusty looked thoughtful. "I guess they just didn't know," she said, "and I just figured it was me."

"That was the worst thing they did." My fervor was renewed by her acceptance. "They made you doubt yourself."

"I have to admit," Rusty said, "nobody even implied that my future looked rosy. . . . Part of the plastic-bag thing," she said, hesitating, "was that I got the idea whatever was wrong with me was *evil*. I was afraid that something would change me into something else and I wouldn't be me any longer. I felt I couldn't trust myself. I could see the fear in my mother's eyes, and I never wanted to hurt her. So when she left the bag in the bedside stand, I just figured that was the only choice I had. I didn't know whether the seizures would kill me anyway, and I just didn't want to be a bother. I didn't see another choice."

"At fifteen you have no choice but to die?" I said "And nobody's to blame?"

CHAPTER 5

The days were beautiful that week. The grass was a bright vibrant green and the overhanging maple trees, like huge umbrellas, shaded the large backyard of Salvation Nursing Home.

Rusty and I decided to take some of the patients out to have a picnic. Dominic had forgotten most of his problems because of Lenny's "troubles" and had become a whole new person. He talked to Lenny and even talked to me.

"Imma use to work inna garden," he told me one morning as I helped him dress. Rusty was helping Lenny.

"Really, Dominic?" I asked. "You're a landscaper?"

"Imma wonderful inna garden," he answered, his gray eyes shining with excitement. "Imma know everything about 'em."

I laughed. "I'll bet you do," I said. He was standing on two wobbly legs and leaning forward with his arms holding onto my shoulders as I tried to lift his trousers up. The Parkinson's had made it difficult for him to bend his legs. "I don't know one flower from another," I admitted.

"Imma gonna show you." He pointed toward the backyard, which could be seen clearly from his window.

"Eh, Lenny?" Dominic called, and Lenny looked up from the shirt he was struggling to button. "You lika flowers?"

"Sure, Dom," Lenny said, "but I don't know much about them either." Then he looked up at Rusty and forced a smile. "Spent most of my life just working and playing ball, even coached the kids in Little League for awhile. . . didn't seem to have a lot of time to learn about flowers."

"Imma catch you up on 'em now," Dominic said sincerely.

Rusty sat Lenny in his wheelchair and I got Dominic a walker. Though he shuffled, with the support of the walker he could manage on his feet for quite a distance. And I knew by his expression that he felt better walking.

Lenny took a deep breath. "I don't like you to have to push me," he said sadly to Rusty. "I'd feel better if my feet were on the ground."

Rusty immediately bent down and lifted the foot-rests on the wheelchair. Lenny's feet dropped to the floor. "There you go, Lenny," she said. "You can use your feet to help me."

Lenny still didn't look happy. "Thank you, young lady," he said, trying to be gracious. "It's just that a man feels less like a man when somebody has to push him around. Especially a young one like you."

Dominic's ears perked up suddenly and he began lifting his walker and pounding it on the floor. "Dammit! Dammit!" he cursed as usual.

"What's up, Dominic?" I asked, wondering at his change of mood.

"Imma gonna break my neck on thissa thing," he said. "Imma need something stronger." Then he turned to Lenny. "Eh, Lenny? You mind Imma use your wheelchair to rest on?" Rusty and I looked at him puzzled. Then Dominic walked himself over behind Lenny's chair and held onto the handles. "Imma can push while Imma lean, eh, Lenny?"

Marta decided it was time. She told Rusty not to bring her anything more to drink and asked if we could stay with her from Thursday night to Saturday.

That morning Marta had spoken to her lawyer and he told her that the family had consulted a private psychiatrist and insisted he do an evaluation of her mental health right in Salvation the follow-ing week. Marta was terrified. She had to be as alert as possible when he came. That meant withdrawing completely from alcohol as soon as possible.

Both Rusty and I adjusted our schedules. By the time we arrived Thursday night, Marta was a nervous wreck and the symptoms of withdrawal had already begun. She felt weak and nauseated. And as I looked I could see beads of perspiration along her top lip and all across her forehead. Her face was white and strained. Rusty had filled the prescriptions Marta–Dr. Sprite–had written for herself. We had both Librium and Valium in pills and injectable form.

As soon as I saw the way Marta's hands were shaking, I drew up a dose of Librium and gave her an injection.

"Carol," she said, biting her top lip, "don't forget to take my blood pressure and check my heartbeat every half-hour, okay?"

I smiled at her and tried to reassure her. "I will," I said. "I promise."

Rusty had moved close to Marta's bed to stand beside her.

"And do you have Dilantin in case I have a seizure?" she asked.

"I looked quickly at Rusty but she didn't seem upset. I have Valium if we need it," I told Marta.

She misinterpreted my hesitation and asked nervously, "Neither of you is afraid of seizures, are you?"

"No," I said quickly, very aware of Rusty.

Rusty lowered her head. "I'll be fine," she said, and I knew she meant that to reassure both of us.

Rusty and I noticed Marta's long fingernails at the same time. Rusty held Marta's hand up and said, "We'll have to cut these so you don't hurt yourself." She said it as though she was asking permis-sion.

Marta nodded quickly. She constantly was licking her lips now and fidgeting with the sheets, her hospital gown and anything else her hands touched. I could see by her eyes that she was getting frightened.

"Hurt myself or anyone else," she said as she began to laugh hys-terically.

I put my hand on her shoulder to try to reassure and steady her while Rusty ran out to the desk to get the nail clippers and shears.

When she returned and I saw them in her hand, I joked, "They look like my poultry scissors."

"A real chicken," Marta said, and her chest started to heave as though she was about to cry.

"I'll hold–you cut," I said to Rusty. But it was no easy job. It took almost an hour to get through the tough thick nails on Marta's fingers.

"Remember to force fluids on me," Marta reminded us.

"I will," I told her. "And I have an IV set up with glucose and saline if you start to dehydrate."

Marta got very upset. "I thought we said no doctors. I thought we'd do this together. So no IV if we need a doctor to start it."

"I can start an IV," I told her. "I only have it here in case."

She pulled herself together. "I'm sorry, Carol," she said. "It's just that I'm so aware of all the dangers ... and I'm so afraid."

Rusty put her arms around Marta. "You'll be fine," she soothed. "We'll stay with you. We'll help you." And when Rusty spoke, it sounded like a lullaby.

As soon as Rusty moved away, Marta covered her face with both hands and started to sob. "Forgive me," she said, "for anything cruel I say . . . or any harm I do?"

Rusty touched her cheek. "Certainly," she said, smiling. "Without question."

"Wait one minute," I teased. "I never sign a blank contract."

Marta laughed. The Librium seemed to be starting to work and so she leaned her head back on the pillow and closed her eyes.

I walked over to turn off the light but Rusty stopped me. Leave them on," she said. "Dim lights make hallucinations worse because of the shadows."

Rusty and I sat silently in the high-back chairs alongside Marta's bed and waited. We had decided that while Marta was quiet we'd take turns napping because we had to be there for so many hours. As long as we both stayed in the room, one of us would be available if the other needed help. We hadn't made arrangements about food because we figured we could always stick our heads out the door and have one of the aides bring us a sandwich. We had no idea how bad it would be for Marta. Unlike many other acute situations in medicine, alcohol withdrawal plays havoc with the patient's mind as well as his body. I'd be able to monitor her temperature, blood pressure, fluid intake and output but I would have a much more difficult time helping to ward off the terrors and dangers that only she could see. All her subjective fears would now become objective reality. She would see them as though they really existed in the world around her, and for awhile she would have to battle those demons of illusion all by herself. If Rusty and I could pierce her hallucinations, and not become part of them, in her mind, then we would be able to reassure her. The problem was that neither of us knew what lay hidden in her memory, so there was no way to prepare or protect her while she was still alert.

I'd taken care of alcoholics in withdrawal several times before, and their reactions were as different as their faces. Most of the people I'd cared for who went through detoxification had visual and auditory hallucinations, but the variety of them seemed inexhaustible. One young boy at a county hospital where I'd worked took a dive into the concrete floor of his room thinking it was a freshwater pond. He broke his neck and was crippled for life.

Marta's first scream almost knocked me out of my chair. But Rusty reached her before I could stand. "They're making me cut that baby," Marta told Rusty frantically. She was wild-eyed with fear.

"Marta, you're in the hospital with Carol and me," Rusty said very softly. "We're going to see that you're safe. This will pass. . ."

Marta blinked her eyes fast and tried to gain some control of herself "Okay," she said, "I hear you. I'm okay. I'll be fine." She leaned back on the pillow and tried to relax. She was breathing hard and fast. Licking her lips constantly.

Rusty stood next to her, not touching her. Just guarding. With the door closed and the curtains drawn the room took on an eerie quality. The overhead lights were harsh and abrasive instead of comforting. I pulled open the side of the drape and looked outside. It was pitch black. We were one lit bubble in an eternal darkness. Only the three of us existed. I found Marta's fear contagious. It was hard to imagine that just outside in the hall, there were other people and other lives.

I walked over and stood next to Rusty. She seemed calmer than I was. "Are you okay?" I asked.

She nodded and smiled. Marta opened her eyes again and just stared as though she didn't recognize me. "Would you like something to drink?" I asked.

"You miserable fuck!" Marta screamed at the top of her lungs. Then she whispered, "You're going to try to poison me . . . I know you are." In an instant she was up and kneeling on the bed. She reached out to pull my hair but Rusty grabbed both her arms and pushed her down in bed.

I was shaking but Rusty seemed unmoved. "Marta, she was saying soothingly, "Carol and I are here to help you. You're just frightened. No one will hurt you. . . you'll be fine."

"She needs more Librium," I said. "Do you think you can hold her while I give it?"

Rusty nodded. We fought and we struggled and we finally managed to give Marta another injection. I was amazed at how strong Rusty was, and how quick to move.

After several more reassurances by both Rusty an me, Marta drank a glass of juice and seemed to rest. We both sat down again, but this time we moved our chairs closer to the bed. Neither of us closed our eyes.

Marta was quiet for the next few hours, but as we sat we could see her lips move, her eyes dart under her eyelids and her hands wave and struggle in silent argument with the forces within her.

Suddenly she grabbed hold of her head within her arms and began to wail loudly. "That man's belly is black . . . " she sobbed, "and I can't help him. He's too far gone." Then she put her arms down and sat straight up in bed. Her eyes stayed closed. Her face and her voice took on a professional tone. "I'm sorry," she said, "I'm unable to do anything more . . . your husband's cancer has spread too far." She lowered her head and said softly, "I wish it could have been different."

Rusty and I stood alongside waiting to see if she needed our help. There was no need for us to speak. Right now, Marta wouldn't hear us, "Certainly I understand there are dangerous side effects to the medications you're taking," she continued, frowning. "But we have nothing more to offer you."

Over the next hours Marta's face and voice changed several times. We watched fascinated as Marta, like a player in some ancient tragedy, took on different roles. She was the lonely bright child of immigrant parents, then she was the excited bride of a German engineer. She took us with her through medical school. And we watched at her first autopsy. "He's so white," she whispered. "So dead. Like plastic . . ." She never had children, could never. But she'd laughed when she delivered other people's babies, and when she delivered her first stillborn baby, she cried . . . and so did I.

Something happened in the room that night and all through the following day. Rusty felt it, I could see it in her eyes, and I know I did. Marta's whole life was unfolding before us, with all her strengths, weaknesses, joys and sorrows. The pain and the pleasure were so intertwined, and so were the lives and the deaths. All our boundaries blurred .Rusty's, Marta's and mine. We were mixed together as one. Like so many of the other really important things I'd experienced in life, and nursing, there was no way to put it into words. The only thing eloquent enough to express the feeling was the silence, the laughter, and the tears.

By late Friday night Marta had come through the worst of it and she fell into what looked like a deep peaceful sleep. Rusty and I were exhausted too.

"You rest first," I told her. "I'm still too hyped up to sleep. Besides, I want to make sure she's really asleep and doesn't wake up agitated. She might need another shot of Librium."

Rusty nodded and sat in one of the high-back chairs. I pulled over another so she could rest her feet on it and I covered her with a blanket. Then I sat next to Marta and put my head back. I looked at Marta, then I looked at Rusty, and thought about myself. We were all so different and so much the same. The room was full that night, and I felt like crying. Not with sadness but with that bigness of feeling that comes from watching a too beautiful sunset. I thought about how crazy it all was. Here I was almost locked in a room with a doctor turned bag lady turned doctor again and a young girl who acted as wise as an old Zen monk. We hardly knew each other, yet we had just spent twenty-four grueling hours together up to our necks in the human condition . . . and I was feeling as though nothing could ever again be as good.

An hour later Rusty was awake and Marta was still sleeping.

"Your turn, Carol," Rusty said. But I was still wide-awake.

Rusty went out to the kitchen and got us some tea and then we both sat together in the corner of the room.

"How did you learn so much so fast?" I asked her finally. "I mean it can't only have to do with the pain caused by the fear and misunderstanding from the epilepsy, can it? How come you feel such compassion?"

"How come you do?" she asked, smiling. "You don't even have epilepsy."

I laughed. "I'm serious," I said, "and also about nine years older than you."

Rusty sat up straight and tilted her head. "I've spent the last four years in and out of Rambling Woods," she said softly.

My heart almost stopped. Rambling Woods was a state psychiatric hospital. I had done part of my nurse's training there. The experience almost kept me from becoming a nurse. At the time, I thought it was because I was new that the situation seemed so bad. And after working in other psychiatric facilities, I realized that my judgment wasn't good. Looking back, I know Rambling Woods was even worse than I felt it was.

The smell was bad. Not only the urine and feces. People, like animals, smell different when they are frightened, and the one thing I remember most about Rambling Woods is that smell. Heavy perspiration, dry bad breath, and vomit. People throw up when they're frightened, too.

Big old institutional buildings, with plaster peeling and halls echoing, are somehow threatening anyway, and there, while I was learning, raw emotion bounced off the bare gray walls. Battles were being fought in the large dayrooms, private battles with enormous dark demons, vicious buzzards and wire-winged birds. There were struggles, courageous but terrible, with formless monsters set free from the mind's primitive clay. Constant daymares.

I'd seen Purgatory in the sufferings of the physically ill on medical-surgical units. But this was the Inferno. People melted here, their skin spilling like wax onto the floor, when only they could see it. Babies died here, precious babies that only their mad mothers had seen and held. So they screamed, and cried, and shouted "fuck" and "cocksucker."

One patient had asked, "What else can one do, when one is so helpless, but scream? It doesn't matter that no one else sees the danger, it doesn't mean there is none, when you're the one who sees the melting, feels the birds bite, hears the breathing of the demon who waits to swallow you alive." Another patient had said about the doctors and the rest of the staff "It's not their problem, it's not their suffering, that's why it's not their screaming."

My father taught me well. He always said, "Never judge a man until you've walked a mile in his moccasins. And from the time I was a kid, I never found it hard to jump into another's shoes. Then I'd get caught up and forget.

One woman imagined snakes crawling through her head from ear to ear, and out her mouth. They surrounded her, she could never escape them, and when one day she pulled one from under her skirt, with a scream, and threw it, I ducked. For days after, I couldn't believe that snake wasn't hiding down my blouse.

Now I looked at Rusty carefully to see if she was kidding. Although why anyone would kid about being in Rambling Woods, I didn't consider. When I knew she wasn't, I thought about my kids. Then I took a deep breath and asked, "What did you do? I mean, did you hurt anyone?"

Rusty shook her head. "Only myself," she answered quietly.

"The suicide?" I asked, to be sure. I knew that trying to take your own life under the assumption that it was yours to take was one fast way to get put away.

Rusty nodded.

"Do you want to finish telling me about it?" I asked.

"Not really," she said, trying to smile, "but if you still want me to live with you, and your children, I think you have a right to know . . ."

CHAPTER 6

The sparse brown grounds of Rambling Woods covered several acres and the large brick hospital buildings were scattered over the huge expanse like dilapidated old country mansions. Through the many cracked red bricks, tangled ivy pushed its way into the dim sunlight. Heavy hemplike vines hung from under dirty windows like Rapunzel's cast-down hair. But in the fairy tale, there were no bars on the windows.

Rusty's senses were veiled by disbelief as she blindly quietly followed her parents up to the front door of Admissions Building 1. Inside the dark, cell-like room that was the lobby, she sat on the one wooden bench next to her mother while her father went up to the wire-mesh information cage to fill out the admission papers. She heard the faceless woman ask her father from behind the screen, "Why is she here? What happened?"

What had happened was that Sally and Ann had found her when they made rounds. Ann had ripped the plastic bag off Rusty's face so frantically that she had even scratched her, but Rusty hadn't awakened. Both nurses waited until Rusty started to respond before they left her, but then being concerned, of course they had to call Dr. Trevor.

Sally was the one who told him how Rusty was really depressed, even tried to commit suicide with a plastic pajama bag, and after all they should try to do something because she was only a kid.

When Sally hung up the phone, she was angry. "That ass," she said to Ann, who was standing at the desk. "He acted as though what Rusty did, she did to him. He said, 'I'll see her later,' as though it was a reprimand."

Later that afternoon Dr. Trevor visited Rusty. He introduced himself as he stood stiffly at the foot of the bed. He was short, heavy and much too pale. An eggplant plucked before he was ripe. His narrow lips were drawn tight now as he spoke. "I'm going to discharge you from here," he said simply.

Rusty was so surprised she sat up in bed. "Great!" was all she could manage. She had visions of going to the town pool, being with her friends again, eating popcorn at the movies.

Then he added, "However, we have a place. . ."

Rusty frowned and said haltingly, "Yes . . .?"

Dr. Trevor continued, ". . . where they really know how to handle this kind of disease. You'll be with girls your own age. And the staff has experience with this kind of problem."

Something about the way Dr. Trevor had spoken suddenly made her wary. "Where?" she asked quietly.

"Rambling Woods." He turned toward the door.

Rusty jumped out of bed. "You mean Rambling Woods, the nuthouse?" she asked, horrified. The doctor nodded.

After Dr. Trevor left, Rusty walked over to the window and stared out. She was really astonished. Rambling Woods. It was a place for mental patients. Crazy people.

As a child, whenever she and her parents were forced to drive through the town of Evansville and they passed Rambling Woods, her mother would quickly roll up the windows and warn Rusty in a trembling voice, "Don't look! Don't look! They'll see you looking and God knows what will happen. Just don't look."

But Rusty had looked. She had peeked between the fingers of the small hands she held over her eyes. She had seen some poor people wandering around, but nothing had ever happened. Or had it?

Now, years later, Rusty and her parents were sitting in the lobby of Rambling Woods. Her parents looked as nervous as she felt. Nona kept twisting the handkerchief she held, while she repeated again and again to Rusty, "They'll be able to help you here, the doctor said so." Her father kept walking outside for some air.

They had been waiting for more than an hour when an attendant in a faded blue uniform finally came to get Rusty. She wore a large metal ring of keys which hung from a narrow chain around her waist. "Come along," she said curtly. But when Rusty and her parents began to follow, she said tersely, "Only the patient. You can visit her in seven days." Then she unlocked the heavy metal door and gently pushed Rusty through the doorway. As Rusty looked back, she could see her parents' look of surprise. Nona's arms were reaching toward her as the attendant slammed the door.

Without a word, the woman led Rusty into a small room with white concrete walls. This door she locked also. The room was empty, completely bare. Not even a chair to sit on.

After several minutes, when the woman who was lazily leaning against the wall still didn't speak, Rusty lowered herself onto the concrete floor and sat in the corner. More time passed. Then, as though in response to some silent clue, the woman unlocked the door and said, "Take off your clothes. All of them. Someone will be in to examine you."

They searched her. She was made to stand with legs apart and arms stretched above her head. The white-uniformed nurse ran her hands roughly over Rusty's naked body as though she owned it, while the blue uniformed attendant watched rapt. "No scars, no bruises, no tattoos," the nurse said aloud, and the attendant recorded it on the chart she held. Rusty was more embarrassed than she'd ever been. She was made to turn around and keep her palms up and flat against the wall. When the nurse shoved her gloved fingers up Rusty's rectum and reported, "Nothing in here either," Rusty was so humiliated that her cheeks burned and her eyes filled. The shame she felt then seemed a result of her illness and so she transformed it into anger. At herself, and at Epilepsy. What was this thing, she wondered, that had suddenly changed her from a regular kid into something so despicable that others were allowed to take away her freedom and treat her like a criminal? On the inside, she felt the same as always. It reminded her of the story of "The Emperor's New Clothes"; she wanted someone to see the truth and cry out against the illusion.

The nurse, when she had finished, handed Rusty a pair of light blue gingham pajamas and said, "After twenty-four hours you can put on your own clothes again."

"Can't I just have my Saint Jude medal?" Rusty asked her.

"Later," the nurse said sharply. "Ask one of the attendants

upstairs and maybe they'll give it to you then."

Before Rusty went up to the ward she had an interview with the hospital psychiatrist, Dr. Yurek. He asked her name, age and why she had tried to commit suicide. She tried to explain. He seemed nice enough; the only problem was that his accent was so thick they had a hard time understanding each other. That made Rusty nervous. When he explained she was in on a voluntary basis, Rusty asked "Who volunteered?" She managed to decipher that because she was underage, her parents were still responsible for her. And so she now understood why during the drive to the hospital her mother kept repeating, "Don't blame your father." He was the one who had signed the papers to commit her.

After her interview the attendant led her up to Ward 2, an all-female unit where new patients were placed. At the doorway of the immense barren dayroom, Rusty stiffened. About thirty patients, all females, many dressed in the same dirty flowered institutional clothing, sat, stood, paced and ran around in circles as she watched numbly. She remembered what Dr. Trevor had said about "girls like you," and she was appalled. *These people are like me?* The attendant who had brought her up had disappeared, and as Rusty looked around there seemed to be no one in charge.

Suddenly an old woman with long gray hair sticking out in all directions, like a cartoon of a person scared, ran past Rusty and taunted, "Cycloptic whore! Cycloptic whore!"

Rusty jumped backwards and bumped right into a heavy dark-haired young woman. "My name's Jo," the woman said. "Welcome, fairy princess." Jo's voice was warm and as she spoke her eyes wandered over Rusty. "You must be new," she added. The tight black polo shirt she wore accentuated her heavy breasts and looked inappropriate with her khaki pants and combat boots. She held out her hand and asked, "What's your name?"

Rusty almost collapsed with relief. Jo didn't seem as crazy as most of the others. After Rusty introduced herself, Jo grabbed her hand and pulled her toward the hall. "C'mon," she said, "I'll show you around this place."

Then without warning Jo stopped suddenly and looked over her shoulder suspiciously. She shoved Rusty onto one of the splintering wooden benches and asked conspiratorially, "Did they tell you that I was a homosexual, paranoid schiz?"

"No," Rusty said slowly, swallowing hard. In Rusty's mind paranoid was a man in a black raincoat sneaking down cobblestone streets in a fog-blind city, hiding behind buildings, slouching under garbage cans, just awaiting an imagined pursuer, then retaliating by carving the first innocent passerby into soupmeat. And schiz only meant one thing to Rusty. One person who could split at will into two. As for picturing homosexual, well, Rusty couldn't picture that at all.

"Geez," Jo said, nodding sympathetically, "they don't arm you new kids with nothing."

Rusty was confused. Jo, who had been watching a roach scurry across the floor, crushed it into the floor-boards with a loud stomp of her large black boot. Rusty jumped. Jo was complaining about the conditions at Rambling Woods when a middle-aged woman approached them. Her face was covered with white powder, and her matted red hair hung snakelike below her waist. In an agitated singsong voice she ranted at Rusty, "Rumpelfutskin! Hallelujah! Spin me some gold! Spin me some gold!"

Rusty's mouth was so dry that her tongue stuck to her palate and she could feel the perspiration running down her sides. She turned helplessly to Jo, her heart pounding. But Jo just watched as the woman waved her finger angrily under Rusty's nose. Then with a thump at her thigh and a shriek of her voice, the woman demanded excitedly, "What fruit did Cinderella choke on?"

Rusty laughed nervously.

Jo poked her and whispered, "That's Sharelle. Give her an answer or she'll pitch a real bitch and start swinging."

Sharelle was right at her nose so Rusty blurted, "An apple?"

"Dirty lamplicker!" Sharelle shouted as she raised her arm as though to clobber Rusty. But Jo stood up. Suddenly Sharelle put both arms over her head and started to scream as though she'd been hit. From across the room an attendant blew a whistle and Sharelle began to sing softly as she wandered away. The attendant, a pretty young girl with hair as blond as Rusty's, walked over to them and asked, "Is everything okay?"

Jo nodded. Rusty saw by her badge that the attendant's name was Ginger. Ginger walked back toward Sharelle.

"She's the only good one here," Jo told her. Then she added, "By the way, the next time anyone asks 'What fruit' say, 'Banana.'"

Rusty's heart had finally quieted down, so she asked, "Why?"

"It's phallic," Jo answered wisely, "and so a lot of the girls get off on it." When Jo winked, Rusty smiled, though she had no idea what that meant.

The girls walked over to another bench in the far corner of the room. Jo sat down next to the young girl Rusty had noticed rocking before. Now the girl sat stone-still. "This is Dove," Jo said. But the pretty, pale, dull-eyed girl next to her didn't seem to hear.

Rusty asked, "What's wrong with her?"

Jo shrugged her shoulders. "She's just regular crazy", she said simply. "Real harmless. She just talks to her mother when she talks at all."

"So what's wrong with that?" Rusty asked, puzzled.

"Her mother's been dead for years." Jo laughed when she said it.

Rusty looked over at Dove. She wondered if the girl was physically sick. She was so skinny. Jo interrupted her worry by asking, "Want to see some of my drawings?"

When Rusty nodded, Jo left. Ginger had gone also and so Rusty sat as still as Dove. She was scared stiff, surrounded by a roomful of unattended maniacs. Rusty couldn't believe this was true; it looked like some of the bad movies she had seen.

When Jo came back and handed her the sheaf paper, she laughed with relief. Then as Rusty began to flip through the pages, the first picture shocked her, but the others almost knocked her out. The pictures Jo had drawn, all in brilliant color, were grotesque.

Mammoth purple monsters with bright crimson blood dripping from all orifices . . . detailed dismemberment. . . gargoyles with black teeth tearing at each other genitals. And eyes everywhere. On each of the drawings surrounding all the carnage, were eyes, watching. Eyes grew like barnacles on the rough green skin of dinosaurs. Snakes crawled from pink vaginal petals, leaving puddles of red, as the Sun-eye shined and the Cloud-eyes spied overhead.

Rusty was scared to death. She didn't know what to say, so she just smiled.

"What are you laughing at?" Jo asked suspiciously.

Rusty was ready to run when she looked up and saw another attendant walking toward them. This attendant was a pretty, soft-looking black girl whose clothes were so well starched that they seemed to hold her body up.

She smiled at Rusty as she approached. "Hi," he said. "My name's Lenore. I work here evenings." Rusty quickly stood up, ready to follow Lenore anywhere rather than stay in this room. "Have you seen where you sleep yet?" Lenore asked. When Rusty shook her head, Lenore reached for her hand.

Rusty followed her down to the end of the hall, where four large dormitory rooms sprouted like a cluster of grapes.

Lenore led her into the third room. When Rusty saw all sixteen beds placed so closely together, she was horrified. It looked like an army barracks or a prison ward.

Lenore walked over to a bed along the far wall. "How about this one?" she asked Rusty. "It's right next to the window." When Rusty's eyes filled, Lenore added, "Take it. It's a good spot. Dove's got the bed next to you and Simpie the bed behind. Both of them are harmless."

Rusty tried to smile a thank-you. "Where are the dressers?" she asked. "I mean, where will I put my things?" At home, though they were poor, everything was in its place, neatly pressed and stacked.

Lenore shook her head. "There are cardboard boxes under your bed for clothes, but anything else will probably have to be hidden under your mattress. No one around here brings anything valuable if they want to keep it."

Rusty didn't have anything really valuable, but then she remembered. "They took my Saint Jude medal downstairs and said maybe I could have it later. Do you think you could get it for me?"

Lenore smiled. "I'll see what I can do."

The bed itself was a narrow cot with white metal bars on the headboard and footboard. Rusty sat down on the stained green rubber mattress, and as she did, it slid sideways on the springs. "If I sneeze," she said, trying to make light of it, "I'm liable to wind up on the floor." She stood up and straightened the sliding mattress.

"When you get the sheets on, tie them around the mattress onto the spring underneath to anchor it. That seems to work pretty well." Lenore helped Rusty turn the mattress onto the other side, which seemed cleaner.

"Anything else I should know?" Rusty asked. She sat again.

Lenore sat down next to her. "Try to stay away from Jo," the attendant said quietly. "She seems okay until you cross her. Then she can be rough. This is about her fifth admission and I wouldn't tell you she's harmless."

"Sharelle scares me," Rusty admitted, "and so do some of the others."

"Most of them are harmless unless you get to be part of their sickness," Lenore explained, "but Sharelle's a bad one because when she hits out it's usually at people. Another one to watch is Bell." Lenore smiled shyly when she added, amused, "She's a real ding-dong."

Rusty laughed and began to feel a little better knowing that Lenore was there to help her learn the ropes. She was just starting to relax, when she heard a loud rough voice shout threateningly, "Lenore Dartane, where are you now?"

Lenore stood up quickly and her whole face seemed to tense. As she turned to go, Rusty asked, "Which of the patients is that?"

The attendant had just time enough to say, "That's Hester and she's the head attendant on this ward."

Rusty picked up the folded sheets that lay at the bottom the bed and slowly began to put them on the mattress. There was no way she was going out into that dayroom again, where now, besides Jo, Sharelle, Bell and all the other patients, she had to face an obviously tough attendant. It was almost dark as she sat huddled on the mattress trying to figure out what had happened to her in these last days, and more important, what she was going to do about it.

Over the next hour or so, several of the patients walked up to the huge doorway of the dormitory and looked in at Rusty. Many of them wore clothes that were too big, ripped and dirty. No one spoke to her, they just stared curiously, the same way she and the other kids had stared at the scared monkeys at the zoo when they had gone on class trips in grade school.

Finally, just as Rusty was starting to calm down, a large woman with black hair that looked as though it had never been washed, with a dress so torn Rusty could see her underclothes beneath, walked into the room and without hesitating came right over to the bed. She bent over, stuck her face right in Rusty's, and told her in a monotone, "You don't worry, sweets, you're going to be all right."

Rusty was so frightened she didn't want anyone near her, especially this woman. She sat up and moved higher in the bed. "Why are you here, sweets?" the woman asked. She had a hook nose and no teeth. Rusty didn't want to tell anyone anything. She just wanted this woman to go away. Instead, the woman sat down on Rusty's bed. "I'm here because I hurt my sister," the woman volunteered, and then, as though to reassure Rusty, she added, "But she's going to be fine. She always was a pretty strong one. In fact, you just can't get that girl to die."

Rusty had moved so far up on the bed and had pushed so hard against the headboard that she was certain she was going to squeeze like mush through the bars. But the woman finally stood up and began to walk toward the door. "Don't worry, sweets," she repeated, smiling her toothless grin. "Ole Bell here and you are going to make fine music. We're going to be real good friends."

Rusty's heart was beating so fast and so loud that she was sure Bell could hear it. She had been holding her breath for so long, because she had not dared to breathe, that she was dizzy. Suddenly just as Bell left the room, Rusty heard a booming voice that sounded as though it was coming through a megaphone: "Go to the dining room. To the dining room. All patients to the dining room."

Rusty sat up straight and tense. She stared at the doorway.

Like an apparition, a large woman dressed in white appeared and began to walk toward her. She had full, pendulous breasts and gray hair cut as short as a man's. The sound of her white oxford shoes echoed as she walked heavily across the floor. She stood at the foot of Rusty's bed.

Rusty was so upset, she almost cried. But through the lump in her throat she managed to say, "I want to see the doctor."

"For what?" the attendant asked.

"I've changed my mind," Rusty said.

The woman smiled, a slow ugly smile. "So what?" she said.

"I'm here on a voluntary basis," Rusty explained. "Dr. Yurek told me that."

The woman began to laugh. "All that means, honey, is that you get a chance to be evaluated in thirty days instead of sixty or ninety. That's all that means."

Jo ran into the room. "Better come quick, Hester," she said nervously. "Sharelle is acting up again and Lenore can't hold her."

Rusty repeated, "I want to see the doctor."

Hester stopped at the door and turned. "Forget it, honey," she said sharply. "He's gone."

Thirty days in Rambling Woods! It finally hit Rusty–this wasn't the kind of place, like camp, from which her father could pick her up and take her home.

Hester wouldn't let her out of bed that evening. She had to stay in the dorm. And Hester also made her take two of a new kind of pill. Mellaril, she said it was, for psychotic patients, or for behavior problems in children. And then after an hour, another new pill. Elavil, which was supposed to make her less depressed. But she still had to take her regular pills too, her Dilantin and phenobarbital. That was five pills four times a day. Ugh!

"Why do I have to take all these pills?" Rusty asked.

"Because the doctor ordered them," Hester snapped.

And Rusty wondered how Dr. Yurek, whom she could hardly understand, and who had spoken to her for only ten minutes, had made his decision.

Later, Lenore brought her a sandwich, but she was too sick to eat. "Brought you something else," Lenore said, and with that she held out the shiny medal. With Saint Jude hanging round her neck, Rusty felt better.

She managed to keep herself together until just before lights out, when everyone else came swarming into the room to undress. The thought of spending the entire night in a dark room with all these strangers scared her so much she climbed down under the covers and began to cry. Hard, hot tears and sobs.

Rusty heard the shuffling first. The sound of all those feet around her bed. Then she heard the chanting. "Poor baby, poor baby. . ."

At first, it was soft and slow, then faster and louder. Bell, Sharelle and the others surrounded her bed. "Poor baby, poor baby. . ."

Rusty grabbed hold of her medal. Like a bleeding man in shark-infested waters, she placed her hand hard over her mouth to stanch the sobs and dried her eyes fast with the sheet.

❖❖ ❖❖ ❖❖

Rusty was startled awake at six A.M. the next day by the flooding of the dormitory lights and an attendant's rasping voice shouting, "Everybody out of bed!"

She lay there a minute, surprised that she had fallen asleep. It must have been the pills that Hester had insisted she take. Rusty shook her head, trying to clear it, and slowly opened her sticky eyelids. Her eyes and her mouth felt incredibly dry.

Now that she was less panic-stricken than she had been yesterday, she took a better look around. The place was dirty, and one thing Rusty really disliked was dirt. As she sat up and threw her legs over the side of the narrow cot, she kept her bare feet off the floor. She found herself directly across from Dove, who was slouched over on the side of her own cot. When Dove raised her head and saw Rusty watching her, she quickly looked down. But in that moment Rusty caught a glimpse of something in Dove's big brown-yellow eyes that made her wince. She had never seen such pain or such vulnerability. She felt older than Dove, even though Jo had said that Dove was already seventeen. Maybe it's her size, Rusty thought. She can't weigh more than eighty pounds.

Rusty started to dress, with one eye glued on Dove. The rest of the patients in the dormitory were either zombieing around muttering to themselves or had already gone. Dove was sitting as though in a trance and Rusty noticed that she wore a thin torn blouse unbuttoned, and plaid pants so big Rusty was sure they belonged to somebody else. Rusty saw also that Dove wore only one sock.

When Rusty had finished, Dove was still sitting.

A short heavy attendant with kinky black hair and tan skin came into the dorm and walked toward them. When she got close enough Rusty could see that the side of her face was badly scarred. It pulled one of her eyes down and so made her face look crooked. The badge on her blue uniform read "Inez."

"Okay, sweetie," she said to Rusty, "get into the dayroom," and then, turning to Dove, "Get your other sock on and get moving."

The woman picked up a grimy white sock from under Dove's bed and tossed it onto her lap. But Dove still didn't look up or move. "Get it on," the attendant told Dove, "or you'll walk around all day with your foot on this cold dirty floor."

Rusty knew that was no way to make anyone do what you wanted them to, so when Dove didn't react, Rusty bent down and slid the sock onto Dove's foot. She noticed as she did it that Dove's nails had somehow been torn so low that she had thick scabs on all her toes. She was very careful when she put Dove's shoes on, but even so the girl drew back as though in pain.

Inez had gone, and so after Rusty finished dressing Dove, she just took her by the hand and led her into the dayroom. As soon as Rusty dropped Dove's hand, Dove wandered into a corner and sat on the floor with her knees drawn up in front of her.

Rusty didn't find out about Dove till weeks later. Lenore talked to her one night during supper break, and when Rusty heard, she was depressed.

Dove was the daughter of an evangelist minister. Her mother had died giving birth to her. Even as a very small child, her father used to rail, "Thou shalt not kill," and look meaningfully at her during Sunday service.

She was only seven the first time she heard her mother's voice, she told everyone. And when she told the minister, he put her in a closet and fed her bread and water for a week. "Thou shalt not lie, girl," he had admonished. But she had insisted. She had heard her mother's voice. The minister beat her with a whipping stick.

Dove's mother started to talk to her much more when she was ten years old. The day, in fact, that her older brother Harry got mowed down by the wheat thrasher. From the time he died, Dove would eat only bread and water for long stretches.

Her father's beatings and loud prayers couldn't bend her.

Finally, when she was thirteen, she told the minister that her mother had called for her. When he sent her to the barn to punish her, she shot herself.

She had been in intensive care on the critical list for a long time, but when it was time for her to be released, her father refused to take her, so she'd been sent to Rambling Woods.

She had never been transferred out of the Admissions building because she had never been able to ask for an evaluation, so she had never seen a doctor. And because she was never any trouble, everyone forgot about her.

Once Rusty knew about Dove, she wanted to take care of her. Nobody so young should have had such an awful life, she thought.

There were at least twenty patients hanging out in the bathroom waiting until breakfast call. Rusty hated to use the bathroom. The low sinks and white toilets were all out in the open with no stalls to separate them. And you had to ask an attendant for toilet paper, if you wanted to use any. That was one of the worst things about being in Rambling Woods–the lack of privacy.

At home, no one walked around without a robe on, and the bathroom door was always locked when someone was bathing or using the toilet. She had never been allowed to stay over at anyone's house; she had never gotten used to dressing in front of other people.

Now Rusty was mortified. She tried to wait until the bathroom was empty. Finally she gave in and went. And to her relief, most of the patients were so spaced out they didn't even notice her.

When she got back out to the dayroom Ginger began to herd all the patients together and march them into the dining room for breakfast. When she saw Rusty, she waved and smiled. "How did you sleep?" she asked, as Rusty walked past her to sit at one of the long tables.

"Okay," Rusty told her. "I think they must have drugged me."

"You ain't seen nothing yet," Jo said, as she sat in the chair next to Rusty. "Wait till you get your morning meds."

When Rusty noticed that Dove wasn't there, she told Ginger.

"I'll get her," Ginger said pleasantly. But Rusty was concerned.

How often was Dove just not noticed?

When Ginger brought Dove, she sat her next to Rusty.

"Hey, princess," Jo teased Rusty, "you waiting for somebody to deliver your food?" Then she got up and walked to the end of the long line in front of the cafeterialike counter.

Rusty sat for a few minutes trying to coax Dove up, but when she saw it was hopeless, she decided to just get twice as much food and let Dove eat from her tray. The line was almost gone when Rusty reached it.

The room behind her was buzzing with the sounds of chattering, moaning, crying out and shouting. All separate. As though each instrument in a huge orchestra had decided to play a different tune. Rusty wanted to cover her ears but she needed her hands to carry the tray.

The black woman behind the counter asked, "What'll it be this morning, child?"

Rusty looked at the watery oatmeal, the weak coffee and the powdered eggs and almost said, "Forget it." But then she remembered her mother wasn't allowed in for at least a week, and she didn't want to wind up dying of starvation before she got out. Besides, there was Dove.

"I'll have some of everything," she said, and the woman behind the counter smiled, pleased.

It was more awful than Rusty had imagined. She found a black bug in her oatmeal, the coffee had been mixed with tea from the night before and the eggs had rubbery lumps in them that could not be chewed. She ate the toast. And Dove ate almost nothing. Rusty managed to get one spoonful of oatmeal into Dove's mouth but she just kept it there.

"Let's get out of here and have a butt," Jo said, as she roughly pulled Rusty out of her chair. Rusty reached for Dove's hand and pulled her along.

In the dayroom, Jo explained, "After breakfast, we're allowed our morning cigarette. One cigarette in the morning, one just before lunch. One after supper. There are set times for smoking–these people are sports. You can't just smoke when you want to."

Rusty didn't smoke that much. She had tried it once or twice in the ladies' room at school when some of her friends had dared her to, but she didn't really like it. She was afraid she'd start to cough like her mom. Still, she'd seen how tough some of the women looked with cigarettes dangling from their lips, and she thought she might just need to use them as a prop. To scare people off.

❧❧❧

Two days later, Ginger told Rusty, "This morning you can go to the shower with the girls."

Jo took Rusty's hand and led her down the hall. There were four open gray concrete shower stalls, no curtains for privacy. Nothing to separate one girl from another or the attendants from the patients. As she stood watching, Inez shoved Dove's too thin, shaking body into the shower. The girl's lips turned blue almost instantly from the cold water.

"Wash that pussy, honey," the attendant cooed at Dove, "or I'll wash it for you . . . *good.*" Dove's eyes widened and she began to scrub frantically.

Jo tugged at Rusty's hand. "C'mon, let's get a towel," she said; and then, noticing how stricken Rusty looked, "She'll be okay. That attendant has a big mouth but she ain't going to hurt her." Jo gave her a sneaky grin and added, "Inez *likes* little girls too much."

Sunday. Rusty's parents were coming. She paced most of the morning trying to decide how she felt. Was she angry with them? Would she tell them it was unfair of them to have put her in this place? She imagined herself pointing to the door, telling them to go, she didn't even want to see them. Then, she imagined herself running toward them as they walked through the door.

The other patients seemed restless too. Ginger said, "That's how it is on visiting day."

Rusty wondered how she would cram in all she had to say, all she wanted to ask. By one o'clock in the afternoon she was pacing up and down in front of the heavy metal door. As the attendant unlocked it, she tried to peer through the crack to see if they were there.

Her father walked in first, but Rusty almost pushed him out of the way to reach Nona. She wrapped her arms around her mother and buried her head in her chest. She cried. Nona cleared her throat and patted Rusty's shoulder. "Come on, Rusty," she said, "come on. Let's sit somewhere."

The three of them sat on a wooden bench in the hall. Rusty kept rubbing her mother's arm, kept clinging to whatever part of Nona was free. Her father hummed a little tune now and then but didn't talk. Several times Nona urged, "You have to try harder, Rusty. Will you honey?" And Rusty nodded.

"I will," she promised. Her voice was soft, her throat almost closed with inchoate longing. "I will."

❖ ❖ ❖

Firsts are always the hardest. So after the first week, after the first visit, the time seemed to pass and Rusty managed. One afternoon, Rusty, Dove and Jo were sitting at one of the long tables in the dining room having lunch and Rusty was fooling around. She picked up the small blunt knife that she had been using to cut her hot dog and dropped it down her shirt into her bra.

Simpie was sitting at a table far across the room. She was a short fat woman of fifty with Raggedy Ann red cheeks and two gold front teeth. Simpie was slow and childlike. A slow mover and a slow thinker, but she loved Rusty with all of her confused little heart.

Simpie saw Rusty drop the knife down and quick looked around to make sure no one else was watching. In fact, she was looking behind her when Rusty took the knife back out and placed it on her plate. So she never saw that.

As soon as lunch was over and everyone was being herded into the dayroom, Simpie approached Etta, a Student nurse, and whispered, "Rusty has a knife and she's going to hurt herself. Help get it back so Rusty can't hurt herself."

Etta never approached Rusty. Instead, not knowing what to expect, she told Hester and Hester called the doctor. He didn't know Rusty. No one came up to Rusty and asked her about it. No one even just grabbed her and frisked her. Instead a huge conspiracy began.

For most of the afternoon Etta, Hester and the doctor tried to decide what to do. When the other student nurse arrived, they were warned and so Rusty finally noticed that something funny was going on. It was usual for her be followed by a few of the students–she was bright and funny so they enjoyed her. But she could see that during exercise period in the yard, more than being followed, she was being surrounded by them.

One of the student nurses jumped each time Rusty moved. What the hell is going on here? she wondered.

Finally, back inside the building, back on the ward, Hester approached Rusty. "Dr. Li wants to see you," she said, and Rusty was surprised. She had never heard of him.

Hester seated Rusty on one of the heavy oak benches in the hall outside the doctor's office and asked her to wait.

Suddenly another patient, a white-haired old lady called Janie, approached her and whispered, "Hey, why don't you just give the knife back? They're starting to hassle all the rest of us."

"What are you talking about?" Rusty asked.

"The knife you took at lunch," Janie answered.

"I didn't take any knife," she told the woman.

"Somebody said you did," Janie said, and then she disappeared.

Once inside, Rusty was seated across from another strange doctor. With a different accent. Different but still difficult. He began to ask Rusty all the questions she had been asked before. "Do you know where you are?"

Rusty frowned. They wanted crazy, she'd give him crazy.

"Do you know what day it is?"

Rusty smiled.

"Can you tell me the president of the United States?" he asked.

Rusty frowned.

Finally, she couldn't stand it another minute. "Why don't you just ask me if I took the knife?" she asked, annoyed.

He looked confused. As though she had given him information that he wasn't prepared for. He ignored her and asked, "Why are you so angry?"

"Because," she answered, furious now, "you keep insisting on playing Sherlock Holmes instead of asking simple questions which will clear this whole thing up in no time." Dr. Li didn't understand.

Throughout the rest of the day, there were conferences held in the nursing office while the staff hypothesized about Rusty, using the theories they had learned.

"It's just a bid for attention," the nursing supervisor said.

"She's symbolically being aggressive," Hester said.

"I think I read that knives are phallic," Etta said. "So maybe she's having an identity crisis. You know about penis envy, don't you?"

Rusty had been pacing outside the room and finally she got frustrated. "Damn all your theories," she screamed at them. "I was just fooling around. My big mistake was that I forgot, for just a minute, that I was not supposed to be a regular kid. I forgot just how sick everybody in this damn place is."

They said, then, that she was agitated, and so they asked the doctor what to do.

"For agitation, give tranquilizer," he said.

And so they did.

Simpie was sitting outside under a large maple tree, deep in thought. She was wondering why they had punished Rusty by giving her an injection the night before. She was really happy though that Rusty hadn't taken the knife and that she wasn't going to hurt herself. In fact when she looked up and saw Rusty walking toward her she was so tickled, she started to giggle and wave frantically. So she was totally unprepared for Rusty's anger, and devastated when Rusty grabbed her by the arm and shouted, "First of all, around here you never tell what you see, and second, why the hell did you do it to me?"

Simpie collapsed onto the grass and sobbed into the dry brown earth. Then she groped around blindly, until she latched onto Rusty's leg. She tried to explain why she did it. Rusty was brokenhearted and angry with herself when she understood. What's happening to me? she wondered. Then she bent down and put her arms around Simpie.

Rusty had been in Rambling Woods for almost a month. It had become more familiar, and so sometimes she was able to relax. She was just hanging out in the dayroom when Jo walked up behind her and said, "Come on, let's get some food."

Rusty followed Jo to the dining room and they stood in line. She was looking for Dove and so she didn't notice Sharelle behind her. "I hate your fuckin' guts, sweetie," Sharelle hollered. And then she slammed her tray right into Rusty's face. Rusty was so stunned she never had a chance to regain her balance before Sharelle picked her up by the collar and flung her across the room into a pile of folding chairs. She heard the attendant's whistle blow just before she fainted.

When she woke up, Dove was sitting on the floor next to her bed, rocking. "What happened?" Rusty asked, but of course Dove didn't answer. Then Jo stopped in.

"Boy, they fixed Sharelle good," Jo told Rusty. "They trans- ferred her to the third floor."

"What's that?" Rusty asked, rubbing her head. She had a bump where she'd hit the floor.

"That's where they send all the real sickies," Jo said, and she whistled. "It's almost as bad as Graylock Pavilion."

During this time Rusty had some seizures. She never could tell when one was coming on. It always was a real surprise. During one of them, as she hit the hard tile on the bathroom floor, a tooth went completely through her top lip. But no doctor was called, and none of the staff or the patients seemed to take any particular notice. When she looked in the aluminum mirror, she felt like a member of some primitive tribe who had just gone through a strange initiation rite.

Another time, she fell against an old-fashioned iron-coil radiator and burned her cheek. And when she was conscious again, she was furious. She didn't understand why the TV was kept up and out of reach of the patients, why no glass mirrors were allowed, and yet in the main rooms like the dining room and the dayroom, red-hot radiators were left exposed and the patients left unprotected. Her anger seemed to improve her vision and make her thinking clearer. She began to question why they had put her in this place for her own good, to protect her, when if she fell at home, she would only hit the wooden floors or the soft front lawn. She began to wonder whether they really were trying to keep her from hurting herself.

When her thirty days were up, Lenore took Rusty aside. It was the night before her staff evaluation, Lenore warned, "Just don't tell them the truth. Whenever they ask something, just agree with them and thank them. But remember . . . anything but the truth about how you feel."

Dr. Li sat up front on the steel folding chair. Rusty could see Ginger and some others she didn't know, she was so nervous that she felt the fake cotton of fear in her ears and was almost blind anyway.

"Are you sorry?" Dr. Li asked.

"Yes, sir," Rusty answered.

"Will you do it again?" Dr. Li asked.

"No, sir," Rusty answered. And the rest of the questions went about the same. Half the time Rusty didn't understand Dr. Li's accent, the other half, she didn't understand the questions. But it didn't matter.

Rusty passed staff. She had done what Lenore suggested and so she was going to be released. She thought she should feel happier, but the idea that she had lied to them somehow made her feel she had betrayed herself.

The day she left, she had mixed feelings, but only because of Dove. She was certain Dove could get well, if only someone cared enough about her. She wasn't as crazy as some of the others. It was just that she hadn't had much love in her whole life and Rusty knew that could make people sick.

Rusty's mom and dad came to get her, smiling. Simpie and Jo walked her to the elevator. Ginger waved good-bye. Dove was not around. Rusty had tried to explain it to her but Dove didn't seem to hear.

"I almost feel bad about leaving," she said to the others as the elevator door opened.

"Don't," Jo said dryly. "You'll be back. Once they get you, once they say you're crazy, you never really get away.

It was dawn when I stopped Rusty from finishing her story. Through the window, the world outside Salvation was in a rosy gray haze. I was crying.

"I'm so sorry," I mumbled between sniffles. Mindlessly I got up from the chair and walked over to check on Marta. I had to do something while I got myself together. I automatically put the cuff on her arm and checked her blood pressure. It was normal and so I went back to sit.

"For what?" Rusty asked.

As a nurse, one of the oaths I had sworn, one of the things I had promised, was to do no harm. Medicine and Nursing might not always be able to help . . . but it was that "do-no-harm" business that was upsetting me now. I was a true believer in Medicine. God knows by then I'd seen miracles: we could bring dead men back to life by pumping on their chests; we could relieve pain with a shot or a pill; we could make the blind see again, with cataract surgery and corneal transplants. And now as I listened to Rusty, I felt like some medieval nun who had joined the Church because of her belief in Good and God and had just heard about the Inquisition. Rusty in a state hospital was my clear look at the Inquisition. My idea of Justice was threatened; my faith had been challenged.

"I couldn't have survived," I said "and I feel bad as a grown-up, and as a nurse, that a kid had to go through that, because of our ignorance."

Rusty smiled and protested, "Fate had something to do with it. And so did I."

"What was that?" I asked caustically. "Are you responsible for having the epilepsy? Or for people being afraid of it? Or for the incompetence of the doctors and nurses, the psychiatrists and the institutions that were supposed to help?"

Rusty watched, amused by my outrage. Then as I got up to listen to Marta's heartbeat again, she said softly, "It's my life, Carol. That's why it's my responsibility. And the way I look at it, all of life is an obstacle course. I just have to keep practicing my jumps."

"Oh no," I swore. "What happened to you before can never happen to you again."

Rusty could see how I felt. "Don't look so upset," she said. "It was bad but I survived."

"Funny you should say that," I told her, trying smile. "Until now, I've also judged everything by it's 'terminality. If it didn't kill you, it wasn't important. But now I'm beginning to revise my philosophy, to include some subtleties. Now I want to know *how* you survived."

Rusty leaned her head back against the chair, obviously remembering. "The hospital itself was bad," she said quietly, "but if you knew where to look, you could get a great education. It might not be Yale and they might not have meant to, but they did help to prepare me to live normal . . ."

"Wait a minute," I hissed, looking over at Marta to make sure I hadn't awakened her. "Let me try to get handle on this. Let me tell you what I heard . . . and then you can tell me if that's what you said." Rusty nodded. And I began. "A miserable man, who happened to be a covering doctor, made a decision knowing almost nothing about you to put you in a filthy state institution at the tender age of fifteen. Why? Because medicine failed you. But let's not nit-pick. Then the uneducated staff there humiliated you by examining you as if you were a prisoner. They endangered your life by putting you in a dorm with really disturbed patients. They gave you medication which could have destroyed a mind not as strong as yours, prescribed by a doctor who couldn't speak English well enough for you to understand him—and it seems to me that communication is an essential part of psychotherapy. Not to mention the fact that Elavil shouldn't be given to patients with seizures, to treat a depression that isn't pathological. But all that is absolutely understandable? All that helped prepare you to live a normal life?"

Rusty laughed at me. "That's *part* of what I said. This is the rest. Of course, when I first got to the nuthouse I was scared to death. And though most of the time I wasn't helped by the staff, the patients did me a lot of good. From Sharelle I learned that often when other people hit out at you, it's not your fault, it's not even personal. It has something to do with what's going on in their minds.

"I wasn't a kid whose parents had money, and much as that shouldn't matter to everyone, it does. In Rambling Woods, the clothes most of the patients wore were so awful, most of them thought I was spoiled. I'd never had people feel like that about me. But one of the best things was, because I was so young and had led a sort of sheltered life, I didn't know that patients in nuthouses weren't credible, so when they told me I was pretty or smart, I believed them. It felt good to me. I felt really special. I began to get a sense of myself as having value. As soon as I saw Dove, I knew I was less frightened than she was, and she had stayed alive. So I figured out that fear didn't kill.

"When I saw the way the attendants treated the patients, I knew I could do better. So I found out something about myself that I had no way of knowing before. I was good at taking care of people, and more than that, it felt good inside of me. From the day I put on Dove's sock, I was even more certain about what I would do with my life. If, of course, I ever got out.

"So I made it into a game. I tried to figure out how I could learn the things that would help me live a better life. And whenever I found one of them, I didn't look at it as being bad or good. The experiences that helped me survive, I tried to learn well; the ones that impaired to my survival, I tried to avoid. It was almost like hopscotch."

"Talk about a glass being half full rather than half empty," I said, admiring. "Where did you learn to 'see' like that?"

Rusty was embarrassed by my reaction. So she smiled and said flippantly, "I must have inherited it, I guess. I was born this way."

"Neither of your parents sound like they have it," I said.

With only her eyes to show her amusement, Rusty explained. "I didn't mean genetically. I meant it came with my soul." I raised my eyebrows to show my confusion and she lifted her hands and added in her storytelling voice, "I've always had this vision of a soul being unripe or ripe. Something like a butterfly in its cocoon. The shell that protects it when it's changing or growing is like pessimism. But after the shell of pessimism falls away, you have optimism, and a full-grown soul."

❖❖ ❖❖ ❖❖

Marta woke up and began to blink her eyes. I walked over next to her and reached for her hand. Rusty was right next to me. "Welcome, sleeping beauty," I said to Marta and she smiled.

"How was I?" she asked.

"Good," Rusty said.

"Not too terrible," I teased.

Rusty and I washed Marta and changed her sheets. She even managed to get out of bed to go to the bathroom with our help. And after she sipped some tea for breakfast she seemed to want to go back to sleep. "You can go," she said to both of us. "I'm sure I'll be all right now."

I looked at her. She did seem fine and I knew rest would do her good. "What about it, Rusty?" I asked "Ready to leave Dr. Sprite to her own resources?"

"I think that's wise," Rusty said, laughing. And we left.

In the parking lot, I looked at her. "Come live with me? It will work for both of us, I'm sure."

Rusty dropped her smile. "Don't say that, Carol," she said. "You haven't even heard the whole story. Other things happened that made me understand there are never any guarantees."

"Oh yes there are," I told her. "According to the ancient established Buddy Doctrine, as long as I'm around what happened before can never happen again, because I won't allow it."

"But what if I fall again?" she asked cautiously.

"Jeez," I wailed, "don't make it sound like a fall from grace. . . And if you 'fall,' I can catch you."

"How can you be so sure?" she asked.

"Because that's one of the basic Buddy Laws, which are always the natural outcome of following the basic Buddy Rules."

"Sounds like simple loyalty to me," Rusty said, smiling again. Her brown eyes glittered with fun.

"Oh no," I said, laughing, "you don't understand. It's about four inches longer, seven inches wider and infinitely higher than simple loyalty. The Buddy Doctrine is a much more complex theory."

The theory, though I could never have put it into words then, was written on every cell of my being. It had something to do with primitive man's climb out of the slime of the earth; it had something to do with no longer whacking another on the side of the head with a club because you were afraid of him or wanted something he had. It had everything to do with man standing upright on two legs and being able to raise his face to the sun, in gratitude and victory, after so many centuries of struggle.

Rusty turned and looked over her shoulder at me. Still smiling, but her voice strained and serious, she asked, "Just so I can really understand, and I don't mean to sound rude, but what's in it for you?"

"If I fall, you can catch me," I said quietly.

She smiled. Then she nodded. And we laughed. All seemed perfectly right with the world.

CHAPTER 7

The shining sun flickered on the rippling canal as Rusty and I sat on the grass in my backyard talking. It was Sunday afternoon and Creede had called early that morning and offered to pick the kids up and take them to the beach. Rusty and I had stayed home, still recovering from taking care of Marta.

"When the kids and I get back we can have that barbecue you mentioned," Creede had reminded me.

"Sounds terrific," I had said.

Now, with the kids and Creede gone, I watched as Rusty snapped off one long blade of grass and held it out. A large black ant carrying a huge bread crumb climbed on. She waited until he'd gotten solid footing and then she very slowly and carefully lifted the blade to the anthill, which was several feet away.

"You just saved that ant a couple of days' hard labor," I told her. She looked at me, tilting her head slightly, and said, "That's assuming, of course, that I've delivered him to the right place. For all we know, even with the best of intentions, I've just sealed his fate by placing him in an enemy camp with a large enough food supply to give their soldiers days of extra strength."

Rusty had a funny way of speaking. The things she said were often hilarious but her delivery was deadpan. At the beginning I could never be sure whether she was serious or kidding. The only giveaway was the look of amusement in her eyes. Even when what she said was serious in content, she had a certain objective ability to recognize her own absurdity as well as that of the situation. It made her fun to listen to.

Now we both watched in silence for agonizing minutes as the struggling ant slowly and laboriously descended into the black hole of his destiny.

Finally, when he had disappeared and there were no shots from below, I asked, "There were no clues about your epilepsy until the football game?"

"Nope. Up until that time I was just a regular kid, you know, with horns, antennas, hooves and a tail. Cut up a little in school, had a few friends who were fun-loving and kind enough to hang out with me even though I could only see the ones who stood on my right side."

"Okay," I said, playing the straight man, "I don't get it."

"I'm legally blind in my left eye, which does cut down peripheral vision," she explained.

"Look," I wailed, holding my head, "this is what's called loading the dice. Are you sure you're not kidding me? I never heard of anyone with so many handicaps."

"Don't feel bad," she said, grinning. "I was one of the few people turned down by 'Hire the Handicapped' for just that reason."

Sometimes when things seem so bad it almost destroys me, I react with hysteria. So this time I laughed and said, "Well, you've got beautiful long dark eyelashes."

But I wasn't fast enough to beat her. "Yes, I know," she said, pretending to be serious. "The Lord is good at token gestures."

Finally, when I stopped laughing, I asked, "What happened to your eye?"

Rusty looked thoughtful. "My mother told me that I was born with a lazy eye," she said, "Eventually, I guess it got so lazy it retired from active duty."

"Rusty," I said, "would you try to be serious? A lazy eye can usually improve if the good eye is patched. Why wouldn't your parents have done that?"

"I told you my parents were poor," she said, as she shrugged. "Maybe they couldn't afford a patch."

"And you're not angry about that now?" I asked. That was a question I was to repeat so many times over the next few years that I should have made a flash card for it. And each time I asked it, Rusty gave me a rational answer.

"They did patch it for a short time," Rusty admitted, "but I was a tomboy and I kept riding my bike and running into trees. My parents were kind of nervous. I guess they were afraid I'd wind up killing myself."

I understood the reasons now, but I'd still be furious if it were my eye.

Rusty had turned over and was lying on her stomach, searching for a four-leaf clover. She told me she was always on the lookout for them. No wonder, I thought. I got up and started toward the house. "Want anything to drink?" I asked. "I'm thirsty."

I brought some lemonade back and scanned the lawn. Rusty was gone. Nowhere to be seen. I stood holding the glasses, when I heard a laugh from the willow tree up above.

"Real funny," I said as she climbed down.

"I had a tree house when I was little," she said. "I spent hours in it pretending I was stranded on a desert island. I was always perfecting survival techniques."

"I can tell you didn't have a mother like mine," I told her, "or you'd never find yourself stranded, even for a minute. The woman stuck like glue."

"You're wrong," Rusty said as she took the glass of lemonade from my hand. "I *did* have a mother like yours. And hiding from her was half the fun."

"So go on," I said, sitting on the grass again. "Tell me the rest." "You don't have time for the rest right now," Rusty said, "but I'll finish this part anyway . . ."

After Rusty's discharge from Rambling Woods, she expected to go back home, go out with her friends and live essentially the same kind of life she had before. But she found that everything had changed.

Though her father was happy to have her home again, her mother was so nervous she picked on Rusty constantly. She was terribly overprotective. When Rusty had seizures–and they occurred far less frequently now–Nona Russell would immediately call in a neighbor and phone for an ambulance. Daniel Russell would try to convince her to let him try to handle it, but Nona just ignored him. And so they would fight. Often, after Rusty went to bed at night, she could hear them and it made her feel guilty.

Nona Russell wasn't a young woman but her life had aged her even more. She was pathetically thin with scant gray hair and suspicious-looking brown eyes. She'd had great hopes when she married Daniel Russell all those years before. She had believed in his dreams even more than he did. But while he never could see what had become of them, Nona could, and it had made her bitter. Until the time Rusty got sick, she had planned to live her dreams of the good life through her daughter, but now even that was gone.

"Mom," Rusty said, sitting at the small kitchen table across from her mother, "Arlene and I are going to the beach. Do you want anything from the store on my way back?"

Rusty's mother's face contorted in horror. Then she said cautiously, "Rusty, you know you can't do that anymore. Swimming is dangerous, you could drown."

"Mom," Rusty said patiently, "I said Arlene was coming with me. I'm not going alone," and she reached out to touch her mother's arm. "Anyway, nothing will happen."

"Rusty," her mother said sweetly, "wait until later on, then your father and I can take you."

"What's the difference?" Rusty asked, confused.

Her mother looked down when she answered. "Well, later, when it gets dark, most of the other people will have gone home."

Then Rusty understood that her mother was not so much worried about her drowning as she was about what other people would say if Rusty had a seizure at the beach and they saw her.

Rusty was angry. "I'm not staying home, Mom," she insisted. "I'm going out."

With that her mother began to choke and cough and wheeze so badly that she almost turned blue. Her father walked in and asked, "What's going on here?"

Rusty shook her head and said, "Nothing."

Rusty's father was helping her mother up the stairs to bed with his arm around her waist when he looked over his shoulder and said to Rusty, "Why don't you go outside and start mowing the lawn? I'll be out right away."

Nona Russell was breathing easier now. Rusty went outside, knowing her father wouldn't be out until she had finished the lawn, same as usual. She wondered why it would be all right for her to get sick in the front yard while she was doing something her parents needed, rather than at the beach where she would be enjoying herself.

When Arlene rode up on her bike, Rusty was already half finished with the lawn. "Can't go to the beach now," she told her friend. "Want to come with me later, after dark?"

In order to get back into school, Rusty had to be under the care of a psychiatrist. She figured that the teachers were nervous about having her around, especially after they found out she had been in Rambling Woods.

Dr. Gunner was the psychiatrist. He was kind and understanding but he kept encouraging Rusty to leave home and find a place of her own. He offered a number of other suggestions, all of them appropriate for an older person but absolutely impossible for a fifteen-year-old to accomplish.

Dr. Gunner told Rusty that her father was senile and her mother was neurotic. He obviously didn't like Rusty's parents, which didn't help her deal with them. Rusty felt, in every session, she had to make excuses for them to try to calm the doctor.But it did feel good to have him so firmly on her side; that helped her think better of herself. Yet, after a few sessions he moved to another city and Rusty was sent to Dr. Bettina Weintraub for a consultation.

Rusty disliked Dr. Weintraub. She was a woman in her late sixties with close-cropped wiry brown hair and a matronly figure. The day Rusty's father took her to the office, the doctor was wearing a black-and-white-striped dress with black oxford shoes.

When she opened the door to let Rusty in, Dr. Weintraub snapped at Mr. Russell, "You sit in the waiting room," and promptly pulled Rusty in and slammed the door in her father's face. Rusty knew how bad he must have felt. He had spent the entire morning searching for the appropriate clothes to wear and finally chose a pair of his best dress pants, which, though clean, were so old they had been pressed to a high sheen.

Dr. Weintraub pointed to the single chair across from her wooden desk and indicated that Rusty should sit.

Rusty nervously perched on the edge of the chair and watched as Dr. Weintraub read through the single chart on her desk, frowning often and shaking her head.

"It doesn't look good," Dr. Weintraub said aloud, and Rusty's throat closed with fear. What could the chart say? She knew she'd never put a plastic bag over her head again, and that was the only thing she had done that seemed even a little bit strange to her. So they couldn't really send her back to the nuthouse and yet she had the feeling that Dr. Weintraub was threatening her.

"Okay," Dr. Weintraub said, sitting up very straight, "tell me your side." Rusty didn't know who was on the other side. Her mom and dad, Dr. Gunner, the principal from school, the staff at Rambling Woods? So she didn't know what to say.

"What do you mean?" Rusty asked quietly.

"Don't play dumb, dear," Dr. Weintraub said firmly. "Just tell me everything that happened."

Rusty couldn't do that. She was shy, not used to talking to other people about her private life, and right now she was very uncomfortable. Besides, she didn't know what the doctor expected.

"You want me to tell you everything that's happened since I was born?" Rusty asked nervously.

Dr. Weintraub pushed her chair back from the desk and stood up. "Don't be smart, young lady," she said, annoyed. "I want to know how you feel." It sounded like an order. Rusty thought about her father sitting in the waiting room. He'd be nervous too by now, afraid Rusty was telling this stranger all about him. Things that would certainly embarrass him.

"I feel like I don't want to talk to you," Rusty said, thinking she was giving Dr. Weintraub what she wanted. The truth. "I feel too uncomfortable."

"Then why are you coming?" Dr. Weintraub asked sharply. She was already closing Rusty's chart.

Rusty stood up too. She hated anyone standing above her. "I really don't want to," she answered honestly again, "but the school wants me to." Rusty knew she wasn't crazy and she didn't need a shrink. Especially this one.

"Then leave," Dr. Weintraub said, feigning indifference. But Rusty heard the doctor slam her desk drawer as she left the office.

That night Dr. Weintraub called and talked to Rusty's father. She insisted if she were ever to see Rusty again, she wanted a full letter of apology. Rusty refused to write it.

She had to go on home teaching, as long as she wasn't seeing a psychiatrist and as long as her seizures weren't under complete control. Rusty was still taking lots of pills. Three Dilantin and three Phenobarbital a day to help control her seizures, and Elavil as an antidepressant.

The school gave her a little black box to keep on her bedroom dresser at home. They put one in each of her classes. Like a ham radio. When she wanted to ask a question, she had to push the red button, and the teacher would acknowledge her. But it was hard to understand her lessons from her bedroom; she couldn't see the blackboard.

One day, she had worked especially hard on her social-studies lesson. She had Nona ask her all the questions so that when Mr. Lyman asked, she would be able to buzz him and tell him the answer. She got up early that morning, dressed and ate, then sat in front of the machine just waiting till classtime. At nine o'clock she turned on her machine. But she heard no sound. She pushed the red button. She pushed it again. "Hey, Mr. Lyman," she shouted at the little black box, "it's Rusty ..." But there was no response.

Nona called the office at school and they said they'd send somebody down to class to tell them. They had simply forgotten to turn her on. At ten-forty, just in time to hear Mr. Lyman say, "See you tomorrow," the intercom went on. Rusty picked it up and threw it on the floor.

The school sent tutors. That was better. But Rusty missed terribly being able to hang out with the kids at school. Only one time did she try to visit. They threw her off the grounds. They told her she had no business there, and when she went to the office to complain, the principal told her, "I'm really sorry. But we can't be responsible."

Rusty thought in time her mother would adjust and get less fearful, but even after a year, there was little change. Her mother watched her constantly. At night after Rusty was in bed, she would sometimes hear the door creak and see Nona's shadow. Several times when Rusty was showering, her mother would peek into the bathroom. She forbade Rusty to lock the door. Rusty found that her mother had even opened and read letters of hers written by one of the boys at school whom she'd dated for a while. Rusty was angry. She and her mom fought. Daniel Russell went outside for a walk. And Nona said several terrible things to Rusty.

Finally Rusty ran inside to her room and threw herself down on her bed. Nona followed her. She could feel her mother standing there waiting for her to say something. "Mom," she said, still crying, "please stop being mad at me. I can't stand not being allowed to do anything. I can't go to school, I can't be a nurse, I can't play with my friends, I can't even drink Coke because it has caffeine in it. Is that living?"

Nona's shoulders sagged. "The doctors say there are people with worse handicaps. Some people have no arms or legs. And we shouldn't feel so sorry for ourselves," Nona said weakly.

Rusty sat up on her bed, tears still running down her cheeks. "Mom," she said, her voice coming in choking sounds instead of full words, "you know that's not true. Those other handicaps aren't always worse. If a kid has no legs, when he looks down he understands why he can't walk. And no one else expects him to walk. And if he tries to get up and stand on fake legs, everybody claps and sends up balloons. No one claps when I spend a day on my feet, and when, God forbid, I fall on my face, everybody acts as though I've done something disgusting, like throwing up in the middle of a room. Mom, I don't look any different to me. Do I look different to you?"

Nona walked over and put her arms around Rusty. "I'm sorry, baby . . . but it wasn't my fault."

"Help me, Mom," Rusty cried, burying her face in Nona's chest. "I don't want to be like this anymore."

Rusty didn't know quite when it started, but her parents began to tiptoe around, afraid of her, afraid to aggravate her or trigger her seizures and start the cycle of the crazy house again. She, sensing their fear, angry at them for the restrictions that they were helping to impose, acted crazy. It was like dominoes. Several times when she was bored at night–and she was bored often because they wouldn't let her do anything except work in the yard and play with the cat–she'd walk into the kitchen and sit on the yellow countertop in the dark. When her mom came in to get a beer, she'd turn on the light, see Rusty and panic. And Rusty did nothing to allay her fear.

Once, out of sheer frustration, while her parents were sitting quietly in the living room, Rusty slid down the banister, flapping her arms like wings and crowing like a rooster. "Cock-a-doodle-doo–cookoo," she screeched as she landed on the floor right next to the couch. Her father and mother were visibly shaken.

"Honey," her father asked, "why did you do that?"

"Cause I'm mad, Pop," Rusty said as she crossed her eyes, "because I'm crazy mad."

She was mad. Angrier than she had any right to be, she told herself as she went outside to sit on the front stoop in the dark. That was as far as she was allowed to go, except for Thursday nights, when she went food shopping with her parents so she could help them with the heavy packages.

Rusty watched as several kids across the street talked and laughed loudly. When she recognized them, she was going to holler hello and run over. But she didn't. She just sat in the dark on the stoop because everyone had told her that for now this was how it had to be.

Rusty tried. During her second year at home, her seizures were fairly well controlled and she worked hard on her studies so that she could graduate with her class. She tried to respect the school administration's wishes and not visit her friends and loiter on the school grounds. At home she cleaned and helped Nona in every way she could around the house. In her spare time she read or played with the cat, Fred.

So when the principal requested that she not attend commencement exercises and her parents refused to allow her to go to the ceremony to pick up her diploma, Rusty was furious.

Graduation day, while the other kids in her class, dressed in blue-and-gold caps and gowns, listened to the many speakers congratulating them, Rusty, dressed in jeans, stormed into the principals office and demanded her diploma. But the only woman there didn't know what she was talking about, so Rusty had to leave without it.

She ran, her heart beating fast, across the huge front lawn of the school. She had to get away. The last thing she heard was the school band playing "My country, 'tis of thee, sweet land of liberty, of thee I sing . . ."

❖ ❖ ❖

"I can't believe this," I mumbled, again destroyed. "I really can't."

Just then Lynn and Jeremy came running into the yard with Creede walking behind. Jeremy threw his arms around my neck and said, "Mommy, we went to the ocean to see the sharks! Wanna come next time?"

Creede had tied her red hair back with a yellow scarf and wore her usual faded cut-off jeans. That morning when she had picked up the kids, Rusty was already asleep, exhausted from our night with Marta, so they hadn't met. I had only a few minutes to give her a summary of what had been said, and her only response was raised eyebrows. Still, I knew she was enough my friend to support me in whatever I chose to do. "Sharks?" I asked, looking up at Creede.

"Never can tell what you'll find when you get out of the house," she said. Creede was always teasing me about being housebound, ignoring nature and the gifts of beauty in the universe. But as much as she loved the outdoors, I loved the indoors. "You must be Rusty," Creede said, bending down to shake Rusty's hand. "I'm Creede."

Lynn moved closer to Creede, grabbed for her hand and explained, "Creede *thought* she saw a shark but I think it was just a piece of driftwood floating in the water." Lynn's cheeks were rosy from the sun and her dark brown hair glistened with red highlights. I smiled at her.

"For an eight-year-old child," Creede told her, pulling her down on the grass, "you have no imagination."

Jeremy was lying next to Rusty on the grass and now he too was looking for a four-leaf clover.

"How about both you kids running inside for a quick shower," Creede said. "Then we'll start the barbecue."

Lynn got up right away, but Jeremy was deep in concentration. "Jeremy?" I said, slapping him lightly on the butt. "Get going. Get clean, and later you can look with Rusty again."

"Oh, Mommy," he cried, "just one more minute."

"Now," I ordered.

The kids ran toward the house and Creede moved closer to Rusty and me. She took my glass and sipped some lemonade. Then she turned to Rusty and said, "I hear you're thinking of moving in with Carol and the kids."

Rusty looked at me quizzically and I knew she wanted to know if I had told Creede about her. When I smiled and nodded, she seemed relieved. "I just have to see if my mom can manage," Rusty said, "and I'd really like that. I love kids and would be willing to do any kind of work to help around."

"Great!" I said. "Can you start a fire? If you can get the grill set up, then Creede and I will get the kids and the food ready."

Rusty jumped right up while Creede in a very droll voice said to her, "By the way, she" –pointing to me, "is a great friend, a terrific general and a good person. But in truth, she can't work for shit. All she does is read."

"Not fair," I said, frowning. "That's not at all true. As a nurse, I practically kill myself every day."

"I concede," Creede said, laughing. "As a nurse. She saves all her energy to fight the important battles. So around here"–and she put her arm around Rusty's shoulders– "it'll be just you and sometimes me, kid."

Rusty moved in the next week, and everything went well. When I offered her Jeremy's room, she said, "I'll sleep on the couch in the den upstairs. I don't want to take either of their rooms." She didn't have much. Only a few green uniforms, a couple of pairs of jeans and half a dozen blouses.

"I just worry about your not being comfortable," I said. The sofa in the den opened into a bed but it was pretty uncomfortable.

"I'll be fine," she reassured me. And then, really smiling, "Compared to some of the places I've stayed, these accommodations are so good I can hardly believe it."

She said everything with such good humor and acceptance that I wondered where the anger or bitterness she must have felt at times had gone. How she had developed the philosophy she seemed to live by now? I'd heard it said that adversity builds character, but I'd always thought that in some way, it was a con. I'd seen too much adversity destroy people as well as their character. Adversity, I thought, was almost like salt in cake: too little, it tastes bland; too much, you choke.

Together, that night, we made a great dinner, and the kids and I got her a cake. She looked embarrassed but pleased. She spent the evening playing with them while I relaxed on the couch and read. God, it was great having another adult in the house again. I felt good.

CHAPTER 8

"Get up, Carol," Rusty called from the foot of the stairs. "Your clothes are ironed, the hot chocolate's on the table and the kids have gone to school. If you don't hurry you'll be late for work."

I pulled the covers down from around my head and tried to focus on the hands of the clock radio. Eight-thirty A.M. Rusty was right. I dragged my body to the edge of the bed and stood up slowly. The floor was cold. Thank God Rusty had ironed my uniform and gotten the kids off to school or I'd never make it, I thought. I stumbled downstairs to hear Rusty whistling happily in the utility room. By the sound of the washer and dryer, I knew she was doing the laundry again.

"Anything you need from the store today?" she called from inside when she heard me land in the living room. "I'm going grocery shopping after you go to work."

"Umm," I said as I sipped the hot chocolate she had made. It was still too early for me to think clearly. "I guess you'd better get some hot dogs and some pancake batter so I can cook tonight. The kids put in a special request, remember?"

Rusty came out of the utility room balancing a pile of folded towels. After she put them away in the linen closet upstairs, she came over and sat across the table from me. "Jeremy wants to go to the circus this weekend," she reminded me. "If you don't mind, I thought maybe Arlene and I could take them both on Saturday. You're welcome to come along if you like, or if you'd rather just relax and hang out, that's okay too. What do you think?"

"Sounds great," I said as I jumped up and raced into the bathroom to shower. "I could use a break. And I hate the circus."

During the two months that Rusty had been living with us I thought I had died and gone to heaven. She was like one of those little elves who seem to work at night while the rest of us sleep. The house was always neat and clean and I began to believe the salt and pepper shakers automatically refilled themselves. I dipped my spoon into the sugar bowl with confidence now. I knew it would come up full. When Rusty and I worked the same days, we took one car and rode together. But today I was driving alone.

Dominic's new medication had agitated him so much the day before that he had been almost impossible to deal with. Even Rusty couldn't calm him down.

His physician, Dr. Roberts, had to order tranquilizers. But, Dominic had gotten worse. Now, as I walked down the front corridor, I saw Dr. Roberts. He had come in to examine Dominic.

He stood alongside Dominic's bed, leaning on the rails, and asked, "What's the trouble, pop?"

Dominic held out one shaking hand and began to sob.

He wouldn't talk. Finally, when he just kept sobbing, the doctor left.

"I don't know what to do with him," Dr. Roberts muttered as we walked together to the desk.

"When kids have minimal brain damage," I offered, we give them Dexedrine or Ritalin to calm them down. Why can't we try that with Dominic? Maybe it will help his depression and calm him down."

Dr. Roberts looked surprised and then he laughed. "Okay," he said, "we'll try it. And if it works, I'll send you to medical school."

"Thanks," I told him, "but I don't want to be a doctor."

He looked puzzled. "Why not?"

"It's sort of too limited," I said, smiling my don't-be-offended smile.

"Are you serious?"

"Sure," I said. "You don't really have such a great deal, you know. As a doctor you only get to take care of the sickness. You don't have the time to get to know the patient. And some of my most priceless moments come from really getting close to them, having time to spend with them. I like nursing."

Dr. Roberts pointed toward the door. We could both hear Dominic banging on the side rails. "You like patients like Mr. Gragone?" he asked.

When I nodded and said, "I really do," he laughed.

"You're a funny girl," he said.

He left and I went back and tried to talk peace to Dominic.

The day passed fairly quickly. After one dose of the Ritalin, Dominic calmed down. I was thrilled and so was he. He jabbered like a magpie all afternoon. Lenny had gone for X-rays at the nearby hospital complex and so Dominic had the room to himself. Because there was no one to make him feel self-conscious, he spent the after noon practicing walking with his walker. He was getting pretty good at it. "If Imma catch you, Imma kiss you," he teased.

"If you can catch me," I teased back, "you can kiss me." But I managed to keep one step away until the end of the shift, when, just for good luck, I kissed him anyway.

"I expect better tomorrow," I told him.

"No reason to worka hard," he said, gray eyes glittering. "Imma get a kiss anyhow."

He seemed happy when I left.

I had promised Rusty I would stop by Marta's room to help her wash up and fix her bed. She was still keeping to herself, and after the interview with the lawyer she had agreed to stay in Salvation long enough that the family could be sure she was "dry." Because Marta was so angry, she still refused to allow anyone but Rusty, and sometimes me, into her room.

Marta was sitting, as usual, in the high-back chair which was planted in front of the window.

"Hi," I said as I walked over to her. "How is today going?"

She didn't answer. "Marta," I said, "you've got to start getting out of your room. You can't stay cooped up in here forever." When she still didn't say anything, I walked over and began to change her sheets. Several times when I looked at her, I had the feeling that though she was staring out the window, she was looking inside herself. Then I saw a small tear run down her cheek. She quickly brushed it away.

"Anything you want to talk about?" I asked, but she shook her head. I continued to fix the bed.

Suddenly she turned to me and said, "That night you and Rusty stayed with me, I had a dream . . . something about Rusty and Rambling Woods."

I hesitated. I couldn't believe she had been able to hear us. She had seemed so out of it, so locked inside her own world. Of course I should have known better. I'd taken care of people in comas who had been able to hear the insensitive things that were said by doctors and nurses, and as soon as they woke up, they called us on them. That's how I had learned that hearing was the last sense to go. But that night with Marta and Rusty, I'd forgotten. "What was the dream about?" I asked softly.

Marta quietly repeated Rusty's story.

I wasn't sure what to say. I didn't want Marta to doubt her own perceptions. At the same time, I didn't want to betray Rusty by admitting it was true. Finally my choice was made the only way I knew how-I sacrificed Rusty because she wasn't the patient now. She and I had been the caretakers, so we were obligated to do everything possible to help Marta get well. Lying to her wouldn't help. I hoped Rusty would understand.

"It wasn't a dream, Marta," I said, coming over to stand in front of her again. "It's true."

"Those bastards," she said vehemently. "They had no right to do that to her!"

"You sound like me," I told her, trying to smile. "But we can't undo what's been done."

"Idiots! Assholes!" she hissed and hollered in a way reminiscent of her bag-lady days. "That's why I'm staying in this room. The world is full of assholes."

"I don't think staying in your room is the solution to the ignorance in the world," I said, trying to be gentle. "As a patient you're twice as vulnerable in an institution."

"And as a doctor in an institution," she snapped, "you think I'm not vulnerable?"

"Hold on a minute, Marta," I told her. "I'm not the enemy. You don't have to shout at me.

"I'm not shouting," she shouted, "I'm trying to tell you that being a doctor is no picnic either."

I answered before I could think. "If I had my druthers," I said, "I'd still rather be a doctor than a patient."

"Hmph!" she snorted. "That's because you have no idea what it's like. You're just a child."

I looked at her seriously. "Marta," I said, "I'll listen if you'd like to talk to me. And maybe I'll even be able to help. Pain and suffering don't discriminate by age. Life's taken a few shots at me too."

She looked at me just for a moment, then silently turned to stare out the window again. "You wouldn't understand," she said after a few minutes, and she made it clear that the issue was closed.

I finished her bed and I straightened her room. Then I helped her over to the sink to wash herself and brush her teeth. She didn't say a word to me until I was ready to leave. Then, "Is Rusty working tomorrow?" was all she asked. When I nodded, she said, "Good."

Marta was still staring out the window when I left.

Jeremy ran up to the car as I parked in the driveway. It was a beautiful sunny day and the big trees in the backyard were lush and green. "Rusty and me made the tree house," he shouted excitedly right into my ear. He was hanging from the open window as I pushed the car door open.

As soon as my feet hit the gravel driveway, he pointed to a far corner of the yard. "C'mon, Mom," he said, already running.

By the time I reached the bottom of the tree, Jeremy was already climbing up. He had pulled himself onto one of the lower branches and was now, like a small monkey, swinging up to another, higher one. I closed my eyes, afraid he was going to fall like a rock onto the ground at my feet. I kept my mouth shut, though, because I didn't want to call a halt to his life just to keep myself comfortable.

"Mom," he hollered down, "grab that branch and follow me."

"Can't, honey," I shouted back up, as the big smile on his face fell. "Really. I'll break my neck. I'm too old."

"Rusty climbed," he said, sulking. "We even ate peanut-butter sandwiches in the hideout."

"Sounds great, Jeremy," I said, "but Rusty's braver than Mommy, honey . . . and younger."

The tree house was built of a varied assortment of planks that Rusty and Jeremy had collected from the woods in back. They had capped the roof with plywood and then covered it with an old tattered floral rug they had unearthed from some junk in the utility room.

It looked as though the whole thing had washed up on a beach somewhere. I was happy that the tree's green leaves camouflaged it so my neighbors wouldn't try to run me out of town.

When Jeremy saw me turn to walk back to the house, he frantically jumped down from the tree. In one minute he was on a new track.

"Mommy, Mommy," he said breathlessly, "come and see Mr. Bibble and Pokey." As I bent to give Jeremy a kiss, I could see Rusty walking up the path toward us. I smiled and waved.

"Who's Pokey?" I asked, looking down at him.

I'd met Mr. Bibble the year before. Jeremy had been telling me about this friend he had who always seemed to pop up when he felt lonely or afraid. He was bigger than Jeremy, so Jeremy said, and could frighten away anything or anyone who frightened Jeremy. But for almost a year Mr. Bibble never seemed to be around when I wanted to meet him. Then one morning, as the sun was blasting through the window across Jeremy, who was sleeping in his bed, I bent to kiss him good-bye before I went to work. Half-asleep, he reached up and put his small arms around my neck to hug me. And as he did, his face was turned toward the wall opposite the window. "Mom," he whispered quietly, "it's Mr. Bibble. Look slow . . ." As I stood to look, Jeremy carefully sat up. "There he is," he said, smiling, and added, "Mr. Bibble, this is Mom."

"Where, Jer?" I asked. All I could see was the wall and Jeremy's shadow.

Jeremy slowly got out of bed, and just as slowly walked toward the wall. "Watch him grow, Mom," he whispered. And as I watched, the shadow on the wall got bigger.

"Jeremy," I said, laughing, "that's your shadow. Everyone has a shadow."

"Then where's yours?" he asked as he looked around the room.

I was standing away from the window and so there was no other shadow but Jeremy's on the wall. Jeremy looked thoughtful. "A shadow appears when you block the sun. Then it can't hit the wall, and so where your body blocks the light, there's darkness. See?" I said as I moved in front of the window. A large dark shadow stood next to Jeremy's on the wall.

Jeremy's face lit up. "Oh, Mom, how great. Now you have a friend too. What's his name?"

"Jeremy," I said as I sat on the bed and laughed again, "you haven't been listening. That's not a friend of mine. It's my shadow. It's only a dark spot on the wall where my body blocked the sun."

Jeremy looked sad. "Oh, Mommy, I'm sorry," he said, and he crawled up on the bed next to me.

"About what, honey?" I asked him.

"About you only have a shadow and I have Mr. Bibble," he said, shaking his blond head. His hair from sleep was sticking up straight on one side.

"What do you mean, Jeremy?" I asked, still not sure he understood.

Jeremy looked very serious as he tried to explain. "Mom, maybe one time I only made a shadow of empty dark, but then Mr. Bibble came to be my friend and he walked into the space and stayed there. And now he's always there."

"Okay, honey," I said, because I was sure if I stayed any longer I would be late for work. "I have to go. See you later." When I bent down to kiss him, he said, "Mom, look harder. Are you sure there's nobody in your shadow? Are you sure it's empty?"

"I really don't see anybody, Jeremy," I told him as I left. And he had looked so sad for me that even I felt bad.

Now Rusty was standing beside Jeremy, the afternoon sun making her blond hair shimmer. "How was work?" she asked. "Is Dominic any better? And did Lenny go to X-ray? And did Marta leave the room?"

I laughed. "Hold on," I said. "You've only been off two days. How much could have happened?"

Jeremy was getting impatient. "Mom, please hurry, you can talk later," he said. "The sun will go down and then you can't see Pokey. He'll disappear."

"Sounds like an unreliable little fellow," I told him, grabbing his hand, "so you'd better lead me to him."

"Rusty, c'mon," Jeremy prodded, "let's show Mom." He blinked both eyes in an attempted wink.

They took me down to the boathouse in back. It was a dark brown shack which hung over the dock into the canal. Then they positioned themselves so the falling sun was behind them.

"See Mr. Bibble, Mom?" Jeremy asked. When I nodded, he added, "Now look behind him."

And sure enough, on the side of the shed, in back of Mr. Bibble, was another shadow, a little elf much smaller than Mr. Bibble. I looked quickly behind Jeremy at Rusty. She was doing something with her hands. And as her fingers moved, so did the little man's legs and arms. He seemed to dance.

Jeremy was standing in front of Rusty, his back to her, his head turned so he could watch what happened on the shed.

"Is that Pokey?" I asked them both.

Jeremy laughed but he never turned around. "No, silly," he said, "that's Sebastian. He belongs to Rusty."

When I looked puzzled, Jeremy pleaded, "Rusty, make him talk to Mom. Just one time?"

Rusty looked embarrassed; then she said, "Jeremy, he told you he doesn't like to talk to grown-ups. He only trusts kids."

"But Mom's not really grown-up," he protested. "She understands about Mr. Bibble." Then Jeremy turned toward Rusty. And she just as quickly lowered her hands. "Oh, look what happened now," Jeremy said, raising his arms in a gesture of despair. He ran over to Rusty and explained to me, "See, Sebastian is so shy, he can't have anybody look at him. That's why Mr. Bibble and I didn't turn around. Whenever we do, he disappears."

He put his arms around Rusty's neck. "Can't you ask him to come back for just one minute? To say just one word to Mom?" Jeremy begged.

"I don't know, Jer," she told him. "Sebastian is pretty stubborn."

"Just try, please?" he asked.

"Okay," Rusty said. "You guys turn around."

"You too, Mom," Jeremy ordered, and so I turned away from Rusty and stood in back of him.

Soon the elf appeared again and danced over to tap Mr. Bibble on the shoulder. Jeremy giggled. "Say hi to him," he whispered.

And though I felt terribly silly, I said, "Hi, Sebastian."

Then, like the whistle of a high wind, "Pleathed to meet you," came back. It seemed to come not from where Rusty stood but from the side of the shed.

"How did you do that?" I asked as I turned quickly around, but Jeremy's screams interfered with Rusty's answer.

"Now look what you did, Mom," he wailed. "You disappeared him again. And now maybe we'll never see him again, because he hardly ever comes out."

"Out of where?" I asked, feeling very much like a grown-up.

"Out of inside of Rusty," Jeremy explained. "He lives some-where in her middle and he has a locked box he takes care of that has all her bad feelings and big dreams in it. He has to guard it, that's why he can't come out a lot."

Rusty lowered her head. "Jer . . ." she said.

Jeremy's eyes widened and his hand flew up to cover mouth. "I'm sorry, Rusty," he said, almost in tears. "I forgot it was a secret."

Rusty said, "Don't worry. It's all right." But she wouldn't look at me.

"Don't worry. It is all right," I repeated, for both of them. Then, "Where's this fellow Pokey I'm supposed to meet?"

"Rusty," Jeremy asked, "is it still okay?"

She smiled at him. "Sure," she said. "Get set!"

"I'll watch from over there on the grass, out of your way," I told them.

I saw Rusty pull a magnifying glass out of her back pocket, and I wondered about it. Jeremy turned around so both he and Mr. Bibble were crouched down again with their backs toward Rusty. Suddenly, from around the top corner of the shed I saw a small round yellow light, which looked just like a ball, fall toward Mr. Bibble. "There it is, Mom," Jeremy shouted. "It just poked around the shed, and here it is!"

The way Rusty held the magnifying glass toward the sun made the little yellow ball bounce or fly. It shone over Mr. Bibble's shoulder. They played hide-and-seek, with Pokey disappearing each time Mr. Bibble got close enough to grab him. And like a well-choreographed dance, Rusty moved Pokey so Jeremy could have Mr. Bibble bounce the circle of light.

"Okay, Jer," Rusty hollered, "have Mr. Bibble catch this one." And as Jeremy reached up with empty arms toward the sky, Mr. Bibble caught the small bright yellow piece of the sun.

CHAPTER 9

It was another of those long weekends. Rusty and I'd both had the weekend off and the kids had gone to visit their father for a few days so we had plenty of time. "Tell me about your next admission to Rambling Woods?" I asked.

"Let's go walk through the park while we talk," Rusty suggested.

It was one of those sunny bright three-dimensional days when the rich yellow and orange autumn leaves seem carved against the clear blue of the sky. The grass was a vibrant green and when Rusty and I reached the park, I felt like one of those animated characters who walk themselves into a picture and become part of it. We were standing along the bank of the small lake in the center of the park when Rusty explained . . .

"It all started again the summer after graduation when I'd been admitted to the hospital to have the muscle in my left eye corrected. There was some trouble with the anesthesia and I went into a long period of seizures in the recovery room. That began another cycle where everything went out of control again.

"When I woke up back in my room, my right wrist and forearm was bandaged, and I was puzzled. I asked what had happened and the nurse said, 'You'll have to ask your doctor.' So I kept trying to peek underneath the dressing to see what they'd done to me." Rusty was kicking pebbles and dirt as she walked with her head down. "They said I broke a glass and cut myself with it. But I couldn't remember anything, so I couldn't defend myself."

I wondered if it could possibly have had anything to do with a disruption of the electrical discharge in some special cells in the brain. Certainly I had no question that she could have had legitimate rage enough to turn on herself and be self-destructive, but I was certain something else was happening here.

"What did the doctors say when you told them you didn't remember doing it?" I asked. That seemed like an important diagnostic clue.

"Nobody ever asked me that," she said as she bent down and picked up a small rock from the path. She threw it hard and we watched as it spun and jumped across the surface of the lake.

"You didn't volunteer the information?" I asked.

Rusty shook her head. "For one thing," she said, "no one seemed very interested in my version of what happened. For another, they didn't seem to believe anything else I had to say. Third, as long as they never asked, I figured it wasn't important. All I kept repeating was, I wasn't trying to kill myself. But no one ever believed me."

"I believe you," I said immediately. I couldn't put my finger on why, but I knew she was telling the truth. Now all I had to do was discover the reasons in some medical text, and I knew I could validate my intuition.

Over the last six years that I'd been a nurse, I had begun to play a game with myself about being able to make a correct diagnosis before the doctors could. I'd bend down and smell someone's skin and take a guess on the electrolyte that was imbalanced. And when the lab slip showed I was right, both Penny and I would be stunned. I'd make a guess about a diagnosis of a new admission, before the doctor saw him, and tell Penny. When I was right again, we'd be shocked. I knew I used a lot of information that was scientifically based, complaints and symptoms and other clues, but when they all fell together into a pattern I could easily recognize, it felt like magic to me. I could never figure out quite how I did it. But by whatever gift or talent it happened, I was grateful for it and tickled by it.

Rusty and I sat on the trunk of a fallen tree. "I even tried to picture myself doing it," she explained, "and I couldn't. If I had done it, I wouldn't have lied. It was a point of honor with me even then."

"It must have been terrible to have everyone doubt you like that," I said.

"When they accused me of cutting my own arm, I felt as though I'd been tricked. I was sure the glass had broken accidentally and I had just fallen across it when I got sick."

I could identify with Rusty's feeling of being tricked when she didn't remember. When I had given birth to Lynn, I had been medicated with Scopolomine, a drug which causes amnesia. And when they handed me my baby, I tried to throw her off my chest: I didn't believe she was mine. I thought they had switched her with another baby because I had no memory of having her. At that time, I was told that I had bitten the nurse who took care of me, and I myself had a fresh bite on my left arm. When I first saw it, I thought someone else had done it to me. Except there was no mistaking the teeth marks. The skin on my arm wore the same pattern as the skins of the apples I had bitten as a kid. Besides, if that wasn't proof enough, I had deep scratches on both my legs–and blood under my fingernails. I was stunned at first. Then I was alternately shocked, horrified and hurt. I stared at myself in the mirror. I think I expected fangs. But the eyes were the same, and the teeth were still short, even and white (of course I expected bloodstains) and my hair was still long and tied back in a ponytail. Didn't look like the kind of girl who would hurt herself or anyone else. I was terribly ashamed. I apologized to everyone at least a hundred times, trying to assure them that I wasn't the kind of person who would do a thing like that knowingly.

They reassured me. All the doctors, nurses and the staff of the hospital. They understood. It wasn't my fault. It was the medication they had given me. But nothing helped me get over the spooks. Nothing helped stop my crying or the creepiness I felt. I had done something absolutely against my nature and I had no memory of any of it. I could never make it up to the person I had injured or defend why I had done it.

How much worse it must have been for Rusty, I thought, with no more control than I had had, and no one else to share the blame. Now, hearing Rusty's story, I wondered about the mechanics involved. If amnesia could be caused by medication, was it possible the brain could produce a similar substance which would cause the same effect? I knew our brains produced endorphins, a compound similar to morphine, for pain relief. Was it possible that the brain could mimic the medications that we produced or was it the other way around?

And that feeling of being tricked–is it possible that the brain itself reacts to being robbed of a memory? That it feels cheated, and can only transmit that by way of a feeling? Were alcohol blackouts caused by the same accidents of the brain and chemical reactions? Was all amnesia chemical and not psychological? And if we could invent or discover a medication that could cause amnesia, could we also develop one which could retrieve memories? I was driving myself crazy with questions. Damn, I thought, I have to read and research and study to find the answers. The only thing I knew for sure was that I did believe Rusty. Without a doubt.

"Weren't you afraid it would happen again?" I asked.

Rusty smiled and shook her head. "No," she said, "I never worried about that. I just thought I'd have to concentrate harder and pay more attention to my life. Then maybe I wouldn't forget so easily." I made a face and laughed. "Remember," she added, "I was always accused of daydreaming in school and out. So I thought maybe this was the same thing."

"But now you know that your daydreaming might have been seizure, right? Lots of kids are blamed for not paying attention when in truth they suffer from petit-mal seizures."

"Really?" she said, surprised.

"Didn't anyone ever explain that to you?" I asked.

Rusty shook her head. Again I understood how little she knew about her own epilepsy.

While I was trying to explain to Rusty and absorb what she had already told me, we walked silently around the lake. Then we went to the snack bar to get a Coke and hot dog. We sat on top of the large black cannon, a symbol of somebody else's war efforts, while Rusty continued to explain about hers. . .

The morning Rusty's arm had been cut, Dr. Weintraub stood at the door of the hospital room looking at Rusty while she slept. Dr. Angelo had called in Dr.Weintraub because she was now the psychiatrist in charge of Community Corners.

For weeks, Rusty had been waiting to be transferred to Hillsdale Hospital, which had a good neurology department, or Calvary Neurological Center, which had one of the best. Dr. Angelo had wanted to have some tests done to rule out brain tumors or blood-vessel damage, and those hospitals had the sophisticated equipment and the staff to do the most complete workup. So on that morning they came to get her, that's where she thought she was going. But when the white-uniformed attendants put her on the stretcher, in addition to pulling a strap across her chest and thighs, they tied her hands onto the metal sides. That frightened and upset her.

They were pushing the stretcher down the hall when Rusty saw her parents. "Mom," she asked, "where am I going?" But her mother just turned her head and looked away.

Rusty asked again as they all got into the elevator. But her mother still didn't answer. "Mom," Rusty called softly, trying to raise her head, "Mom, are you there?"

The nurse who rode in the ambulance with Rusty was a mean-faced woman with a corrugated face and a muscular body. Her language was as rough as her voice.

"Where are we going?" Rusty asked anxiously. But the nurse was kneeling in back of the ambulance driver, chatting and laughing with him and the technician.

From what Rusty could gather, the woman's name was Toni, and Rusty kept listening for clues to where they were going.

She asked a few more times, and when no one would answer, she tried looking out the crack between the curtains on the windows to see if she could recognize the landscape.

Toni lit a cigarette. "Want a drag?" she asked Rusty.

And when Rusty nodded, she held the cigarette right in front of Rusty's lips. Rusty lifted her head to reach for it, and Toni pulled it away.

At first Rusty thought it was because Toni was laughing and talking to the guys up front. But when Rusty lifted her head again and Toni again pulled the cigarette away, she looked up at the woman's face, her smirk, and understood the game the woman was playing. Rusty put her head back down and turned her face toward the wall.

Her heart was pounding and her eyes filled. She knew, then, where they were headed.

This time when Rusty's father had been asked to sign the commitment papers to Rambling Woods, he had refused. So Dr. Weintraub and another psychiatrist, 2 pc'd her. A 2 pc is a two-psychiatrist consent for commitment. It's an *involuntary* commitment. It seemed not to matter to anyone that Rusty had never even met the second psychiatrist.

Rusty was put in a private room on the second floor of the Admission building. Toni was in charge.

Rusty was lying on the bed, still trying to figure out what had happened, when an attendant brought in dinner.

"I'm not hungry," Rusty snapped. "I'm sick to my stomach."

The attendant shrugged and left with the tray.

Five minutes later, Toni came in, carrying the same tray. "You'll eat this or we'll tube-feed you," she threatened. "You're not going to kill yourself in here."

Rusty was angry. "What the hell are you talking about."

"Slicing your arm up, sweetie," Toni said, "and it's a damn shame. A kid as young as you."

Rusty was sure Toni was crazy. That they were all crazy. Why would she want to hurt herself that way? She had been taking

Dilantin and phenobarbital at home. Why wouldn't she just have swallowed some pills if she was sick of living? They're crazy, she told herself again and again, or they're trying to drive me crazy.

Toni slammed the tray down on the table in front of Rusty. "Now, let's see you eat that all up," she ordered.

Rusty wasn't going to argue with her. Obviously she was stuck here again for some wacky reason. She sat up on her bed, looked straight at Toni, stood up and left the room to go to the hall linen closet. The mattress was too dirty without clean sheets.

"Get back here," Toni shouted.

Rusty refused.

Suddenly, like white water, the staff was upon her.

The restraint was like a long canvas sack, only it had a hole for her neck and sleeves for her arms. Once they got Rusty into it, they tied the top and bottom to the head and foot of the bed.

"Now, you'll eat, you brat," Toni said as she took the hot tea and put it to Rusty's lips. It burned. When Rusty pulled away, Toni deliberately spilled it onto Rusty's chest. Toni began to shovel the mashed potatoes in fast. Several times, Rusty choked. Finally Rusty couldn't stand it another minute. She pulled her head, like a turtle, down into the restraint.

"Come out," Toni warned.

But Rusty wouldn't.

Rusty woke up on the third floor. She knew from her last time in Rambling Woods that there was no place worse except Graylock. Bell was on three, and of course, Sharelle. But Dove and Simpie were there too. Rusty was surprised and wondered why they had been transferred.

Dove, it seemed, had inadvertently pulled the fire alarm; she thought it was a telephone. She had been trying to call her mother. The staff had gotten a big kick out of that, picturing a phone booth on a cloud.

Sandra Lee told Rusty about that. Sandra Lee was an older woman, had been an attendant for years, and somehow had still remained kind. Rusty guessed it helped that she had a limp. She understood something about pain. Sandra Lee also told Rusty that Simpie hadn't spoken since she got there, just cried constantly. When Rusty asked, "What did she do to get sent here?" Sandra Lee told her: "They say she gouged Hester's eye out ... but it could be they're exaggerating."

Rusty heard many tales of violence about the patients. And sometime during her stay, she decided that was another tool the staff used to intimidate the patients. They tried to make the patients afraid of one another so they couldn't band together. It didn't work that way, though. Usually what happened was that the staff believed their own rumors, which made them more afraid of the patients than they already were. Rusty learned that if you really wanted to know who was dangerous, you had to check with the patients. For the staff, propaganda was more effective than truth. On only one patient did all of them agree. Sharelle.

Sharelle was now kept in full restraints in one of the back rooms of the ward for over twenty-two hours a day. She was allowed up only to get some exercise. At first, that reassured Rusty, but one incident made it clear that Sharelle was a regular escape artist and was staying in those restraints for her own unfathomable reasons.

One night Sharelle called out from her room to say she was wet and wanted her bed changed.

Megan Magenta, the night attendant, was a dirty mean woman who took out her anger on the patients and even stole from them. She was not too bright, and very rough. She drank and so she was often lazy. This job was a cinch as far as she was concerned, and she didn't take kindly to anyone who made it more difficult than she thought it should be.

Magenta was napping at the desk in the nurses' station when Sharelle called, and so she hollered back, "Cut the crap. I'll he there when I get there." A few minutes went by and Sharelle called again.

"Okay," Magenta called back groggily, "I'm coming, you pain in the ass. I'll be with you in a minute."

The next thing Magenta knew, she was being tapped on the shoulder.

She turned around.

It was Sharelle. "I said I was wet," she told the attendant in strong measured tones, "and I want to be changed, now!"

But Magenta didn't move fast enough. It took her too long to get her feet off the desk. Sharelle grabbed her by the arm and rearranged her. Magenta came to work the following week with her arm in a cast which only made her meaner.

❖ ❖ ❖

Third floor's routine was much like that of admissions, though the patients were more disturbed. The day Rusty arrived, Bell was transferred to Graylock for "breaking the head" of another patient, who unfortunately reminded her of her sister. Rusty never got to see her or the patient whose head Bell was supposed to have broken.

Because of her seizures, Rusty was allowed to have a private room. The two large dormitories were down at the end of the hall and the staff wanted Rusty closer to the nurses' station, which was a card table and a few chairs in the hall outside the dayroom. The food on three was worse. And because there were fewer visitors and more restrictions, it was harder than admissions. Rusty just hoped she'd be able to adjust. She tried to stay pretty much to herself.

When Sharelle found out she was there, she began a continual night chant for Rusty. Every night, as soon as the night shift began. For hours each evening; for evenings on end. "Rusty baby . . . Rusty honey." Finally, after several tormenting evenings and just as many sleepless nights, Rusty couldn't stand it any longer. It was just too creepy to listen to another minute. She was afraid that ignoring Sharelle would enrage her more, and then she would just get up and come after Rusty as she had Magenta.

Rusty stood in Sharelle's doorway. It was a small dingy room, and the windows were so encrusted with dirt that it seemed dark as night. Sharelle was lying on her back, in restraints. God, she's big, Rusty thought, as her whole body involuntarily trembled.

"Don't be nervous by me," Sharelle crooned in a low monotone "How could I hurt you?"

Rusty stared at Sharelle. Her arms were tightly crossed and pulled against her chest by a straitjacket, which was tied to the sides of her bed. Rusty felt a little safer. She moved cautiously into the room. "Read to me, Rusty," Sharelle crooned, and Rusty looked down into Sharelle's white powdered face. Her red snaky hair was spooky, but nothing like her demon green eyes. Clear as green marbles, empty enough to see through. Not made of flesh and blood, but something cold, clear and hard.

Suddenly, without warning, Sharelle's eyes changed. Darting, frightened animal eyes, but now real eyes. Flesh-and-blood eyes. "Read me the Bible, Rusty?" she asked softly, and at that moment she seemed completely sane.

Rusty smiled at her. She smiled back. So Rusty sat beside Sharelle's bed in a small metal chair and read. After a while, when Rusty could see how dry and parched Sharelle's lips were, she lifted Sharelle's head and offered her some sips of water. Sharelle seemed calmer. Rusty felt sorry for her now.

After a few more nights, it became a ritual, and the attendants even began to bring Rusty's meds into Sharelle's room in the evenings.

❖ ❖ ❖

After the first two weeks, Rusty was allowed an honor pass for the grounds. Vast open areas surrounded the several buildings in Rambling Woods. She was unsupervised except for a grounds patrol, a kind of security police, who never even looked to find you if you happened to get lost. She was one of the few patients on third floor who had a pass and so she could go to the commissary or the recreation rooms, which were in other buildings. Rusty didn't understand how people who couldn't be trusted outside an institution were allowed an honor pass to spend so much time unsupervised, but she had just about given up expecting intelligent reasons for anything. Besides, she enjoyed being out for the day.

The weather was usually clear and crisp, and the sun was shining. She liked the feel of it on her face. And the colors were great. It smelled good outside, clean and fresh and healthy. She could run and jump until she was exhausted. She could climb the big pine trees. It was less restrictive in some ways because here they seemed not to believe her seizures were real. Most of the time, if she fell inside, the attendants just walked around her. No one ever called a doctor, and if anyone helped her up, it was one of the other patients.

Beebie, a funny old woman with white hair and a large sturdy body, never talked at all except to say, "Abba, dabba, digga, digga, digga." All the staff had tried to get her to speak. They threatened her, they cajoled her, they ignored her. They placed bets on who could get her to break down and talk. She refused. It had been years since she'd spoken, and everyone finally figured she had some kind of damage which prevented her from speaking. Rusty doubted that. The staff twisted anything you had to say anyway, so Beebie was probably just standing her ground. It drove the staff crazy if they couldn't play with you. Rusty figured if, one day, something was important enough, Beebie would speak.

For Rusty, all that didn't matter. Beebie, without words, obviously cared more and was smarter than any of them. Rusty was grateful. Because it was Beebie who was there when Rusty came to after a seizure. She'd just look Rusty right in the eye, nod vigorously once, help her up and go back to the corner of the dayroom to sit on the bench in the same place she always sat. She looked like one of those war memorials made of concrete.

After a month, Rusty's dad and mom came to visit, and while her mom stayed to talk to her, her dad went downstairs to request Rusty's day pass from the doctor. They were going to have a picnic under one of the big trees on the lawn. When he came back, he was almost skipping.

Rusty asked, "Did you get my pass to go out?"

Daniel Russell smiled and said, "I did better than that. I got you a pass to come home."

Rusty smiled. "I can come home for the day?" she asked.

Her dad blinked his eyes comically and said, "I did better than that. I got us a pass for the weekend. I can keep you till Sunday."

"Wait a minute. What's going on here?" her mother asked in a panicky voice.

Rusty was really worried. Dove kept getting even thinner and paler. Her black hair had grown much longer so Rusty started braiding it after she washed it. And Rusty had to wash it because Dove acted as though she didn't even know it was hers. In the showers one morning, Dove had put shampoo in her hair, imitating Rusty, but when she walked out of the shower, her head was still full of suds. So Rusty put her back in and rinsed her off.

Then Dove started coming down to Rusty's room at night. Rusty often had to let her almost fall asleep before she walked her back to the dorm to sleep in her own bed.

It made Rusty nervous that Dove, who never spoke to anyone real, had been having long conversations with her mother and her dead brother Harry lately. About being with them. But even more important, Dove still wasn't eating. Rusty had talked to everyone about it. She had even suggested that Nona bring in jelly sandwiches, which she hand fed Dove. Mostly, Dove ate nothing.

That was another frustration for Rusty at Rambling Woods. There never seemed to be anyone who had authority with whom Rusty could share her concerns. Hester was impossible and most of the others were so young they had hardly any experience; the doctors couldn't talk English, and they were never around. The only one left was Denise. And that wasn't a real choice either.

Denise was the other attendant on the ward during the day, she and Sandra Lee and maybe forty patients. Thank God, Rusty thought, most of us *aren't* crazy.

Denise was nice enough, but she was usually in as much of a fog as Dove, so she had enough to do just to see that the patients got their pills. And there was a ton of them. After watching Denise pour them into the small paper cups a few times, Rusty was sure the girl went by the colors rather than by dosage or purpose.

Rusty was thankful that Denise wasn't brighter, because otherwise she would have had to take all the pills she was given. She was still on the pills for epilepsy: three Dilantin and three phenobarbital a day. The new doctor who was doing his internship, Dr. Phillipe, just read her chart and decided that she was depressed so he added Elavil again to raise her spirits and then Mellaril again to calm her down. With all those pills he added Cogentin, in case she started to shake from the others. And, of course, Taractan liquid in case she got agitated.

Rusty asked both Denise and Sandra Lee if she could talk to Dr. Phillipe because all those drugs were making her feel terrible. She couldn't think straight, she was almost always nauseated, had awful headaches and was getting moody. "And I'm not a moody person," she told Denise. But they forgot and so Rusty simply stopped taking most of the pills. She just dumped them down the toilet and she was amazed that often there were several other pills in the bowl by the time she had added hers. She kept taking the Dilantin, though. This was no place to be unconscious.

One day after Rusty had been on third floor for several months, she had to have some lab work done. It seemed every time a new doctor walked onto the ward, he would arbitrarily order a blood test. Rusty never could figure out what they were for and no one she asked seemed to know. "Probably for some kind of research," Denise told her as they walked into the back hall, "to find out if there's some physical reason for schizophrenia."

"But I don't have that," Rusty said. "I have epilepsy."

For a moment Denise looked surprised, but then she just shrugged and led Rusty into one of the small halls by the chemistry labs and sat her on the bench. There she waited.

Rusty was thinking about Dove, wondering how to get her to eat, wash and take care of herself. She felt like Dove's mother. She started wondering what it would be like to grow up without a mother, as Dove had. Then she thought about her own mother. . . and about herself. Did she want children?

She remembered one doctor at Community Corners telling her, "You can have children but if there's the possibility what you have is hereditary, would you want your children to have the kind of life you've had?"

"I can't answer that," Rusty had said. I'm only fifteen years old. I haven't had a life yet."

Now, two years later, in her heart she knew that she would never want a child of hers to feel as awful as she did sitting on a bench in a crazy house waiting for her blood to be drawn.

Preoccupied, she didn't notice Sharelle until the woman was standing in front of her.

"You're just too cute, honey," Sharelle said, so close that her knees were against Rusty's. "And that's why I don't like your face." Sharelle's green eyes were spinning wildly.

Rusty at first tried to talk her down. She spoke slowly and softly. Then she tried to slide along the wall, but Sharelle was blocking her path. Rusty frantically looked around for another patient or an attendant, or the lab tech who was supposed to draw her blood. But it looked to Rusty as though Sharelle was going to beat him to it.

Just then, there was a noise from behind them. "Abba, dabba, digga, digga, digga." And there stood Beebie.

When Sharelle turned to see who it was, Rusty crept past her and sneaked into the bathroom. Sharelle followed hot on her trail.

Rusty hid in one of the toilet stalls and locked it. It was the lab technicians' bathroom and so it had doors.

"Rusty . . . Rusty baby . . ." Sharelle chanted, a deep, drawn-out, ominous sound. Rusty didn't answer.

Then: "Abba, dabba, digga, digga, digga."

"Beebie, get help!" Rusty hollered. Sharelle was banging on the stall door, kicking and hitting it. "Beebie?" Rusty hollered again, but no one answered.

Sharelle laughed. "A smart and pretty little thing. . a pretty little smart devil." And Sharelle bent down and began to crawl under the stall.

"Beebie!" Rusty screamed this time. But there was no response. Rusty was standing on the toilet ledge, and Sharelle was crawling under the metal door like a snake. She swiped at Rusty as though she was a fly. She was almost into the stall, only her legs outside. Rusty was frantic. "Beebie, help!" she screamed one more time.

Suddenly Sharelle collapsed flat on her face and her body hit the tile floor. "Abba, dabba, digga, digga, digga," Rusty heard.

Beebie was sitting on Sharelle when the lab tech found her.

A voluntary commitment was thirty days. An involuntary commitment was sixty days before evaluation and decision. In Rusty's case, it was decided, she had to stay another ninety days.

When Denise handed Rusty the paper and she read it, she asked, "Why? Why do I have to stay? What's wrong with me? Who said I have to stay?"

"Everything you need to know is on there," Denise told her.

Rusty read it carefully. "The only thing it says is 'Ninety days,'" Rusty repeated.

She was confused. She wanted someone to tell her what was going on. They could keep her forever.

She ran from one nurse to another, asking, "Why?" Then from one attendant to another.

"She's getting agitated," Denise said.

And so they medicated her.

Rusty learned to stifle her emotions. She was smart; she learned quickly not to let her feelings show.

❖❖ ❖❖ ❖❖

Dove was really getting worse. Especially late at night. And that's when Magenta did some of her finest mean work. Several times when she found Dove in Rusty's room, she grabbed her by the hair and dragged her out.

Then one night when Magenta was on and obviously drunk, Dove awakened with a terrible nightmare. She screamed. Rusty heard her and sneaked down to the dormitory to see if she was all right. On her way, Rusty looked for Magenta, but couldn't see her anywhere. So she felt safe enough to sneak Dove back into her own room for a while

Dove's big eyes were wide with fear as she sat on Rusty's bed, her nightgown soaking wet from sweat. In the dim light from the hall, Rusty could see that Dove's lips were almost blue, so she pulled the rough wool blanket off the bed and wrapped it around Dove to try to keep her warm. When that didn't work, Rusty put Dove in her bed and lay down next to her. Dove put her arms around Rusty's waist and hugged her; it was the first time Rusty remembered ever

seeing Dove reach out for anyone. Maybe there's hope, Rusty
thought as she held Dove close to warm her.

When Dove calmed down, when she stopped shaking, when her
hair, wet from sweat, had dried, Rusty took her back to the dormitory and tucked her in.

It was very late at night or very early in the morning when Rusty
awakened to see–or rather feel–Dove standing by her bed.

"Rusty," she whispered, "I feel funny."

Dove's voice was so soft, and she was so pale standing there in
the long white hospital gown, Rusty thought she was dreaming.

"Dove," Rusty asked, "are you talking to me? I mean, do you
know what you're saying?"

"Yes, Dove said, "I have to go . . ."

But before she had finished, Magenta was standing behind her
and grabbed her by the hair again. "I told you not to come in here,"
the attendant shouted. "You little slut . . ." Rusty watched as Dove's
arms flapped like the wings on a pinned butterfly.

Rusty couldn't fall asleep again. And that's why she was up so
early. When she walked into the dayroom, she was surprised to see
Beebie already sitting on a bench in the corner of the room. Rusty
stopped in her tracks. She could hear Beebie keening, making piti-
ful whimpering sounds.

Rusty started to walk toward her, but Beebie turned her face. It
was then that Rusty noticed Dove, lying on another bench. Her back
was toward Rusty, and through her worn nightgown, the bones in her
thin back looked like wings.

Rusty walked over to her. "Dove?" she whispered, bending
down and touching the girl's shoulder. She didn't want to startle her.
"Dove .." But before she turned Dove over, she already knew.

Tenderly Rusty touched Dove's white cheek. She ran her hand
lightly over the girl's smooth black hair. Then she gently closed the
lids on Dove's sightless eyes. Finally Rusty unhooked the clasp on
her silver chain and took off her shiny silver medal. She pulled open
the fingers of Dove's left hand and placed the medal inside her palm.
Then she carefully closed Dove's cold fingers over it. Saint Jude, the
saint of hopeless cases. Saint Jude for Dove.

Rusty stood up straight. She looked at Beebie, who looked back at her. And Rusty could see her helplessness. No cry could sound so deep a hurt. In Beebie's gray eyes was the pain of a mortal wound. Rusty walked toward her. Without a word, in a slow and fluid ballet, Beebie stood up and Rusty lifted her oak bench. It seemed light as air.

Then, with a fury she had never felt before, Rusty broke every window, turned over every table, smashed the TV. She destroyed the dayroom. By the time all the others heard the racket and came running, it was already done.

Magenta appeared. "Who did this?" she demanded.

"Abba, dabba, digga, digga, digga, Rusty did it!" Beebie shouted. "Rusty did it!" There was victory for all of them in her voice.

When Rusty had finished her story, the shine had gone out of the day. I couldn't react. I didn't know what I felt. When a body is beaten, it bleeds, and if it bleeds enough, a person goes into shock. And maybe that's what happened to my mind, my heart and my emotions that day. Feeling shock. I was dizzy with fear, anger, guilt and compassion all mixed together. I wanted to throw up and get rid of it all. Instead, I just tried to look normal, while I wondered how she survived that second admission to Rambling Woods.

When I asked her, she smiled her wise smile. "Most of all I learned that there were times I could deal with situations and there were times that situations were dealing with me," she said. "During those times, reality is understanding a set of rules, a way of thinking that isn't necessarily your own. I had to work my way into and through that maze. In order to get what I wanted, I couldn't just ask. First the people in power had to have satisfaction, then I had a chance."

"I don't get it," I said, still muddy-minded.

I watched her blond hair blow in the wind and her brown eyes twinkle, and I could see again that her sense of humor was a special kind of shield. Even when she spoke of serious things, she told them in a way that sounded funny. As though she weren't involved. As though she didn't take what life had done to her personally.

"Once I went to staff evaluation over a weekend pass," she explained, "and when the shrink asked me whether I got along well with my parents, I told him the truth. Well, I did such a terrific job that they made me a ward of the court until my parents could shape up. You see, they felt helpless unless they could do something," Rusty explained. "When I admitted I didn't have the situation in hand, they were forced to keep trying. That was what brought satisfaction to them. They could only help by keeping me away from the situation they saw as a problem. After three months, I went before staff again, and I told them everything at home was fine. I thanked them and gave them credit for the change in me, and so they were happy and I was allowed home again."

I was outraged. I never knew when Rusty's story was going to throw me into a fury again. This time, I slid off the cannon and started to pace around it as she sat looking down at me. "You're in a psych hospital because they say you have problems, and when you tell them those problems, you're punished for them? That doesn't make sense," I shouted.

"Out here, it doesn't make sense," Rusty said simply. "In there, it's reality. Most of the staff there was uneducated. The state doesn't pay top dollar for talent. They did what they could; they weren't smart enough to do anything else. And in truth, there were some good people there, but no one big enough to fight that kind of system. It just shouldn't be called a hospital . . . it should be called something else."

I threw myself on the ground and pounded on the earth with my fist. "If you don't stop being reasonable," I screamed, "I'm going to go crazy. How come you're not furious? How come I'm so much angrier than you? How come no matter how many times you explain, I think the whole thing shits! And how come you can handle the injustice in your life and I can't?" I sat and looked up at Rusty. "Really, Rusty," I said, "every time you tell me more, I can barely keep myself from wanting to kill everyone you ever dealt with. I walk around like a seething volcano for days."

Rusty slid down from the cannon and fell on the ground opposite me. Then she grabbed my hand. "Carol," she said softly, "thank you for being angry about what happened to me. I can understand it-but it's a luxury I can't afford. Being angry is a privilege reserved for the sane. If you have been diagnosed as crazy, any display of anger is interpreted as loss of control. If people get frightened, I get locked up. Also, and more important, I know that it can help bring on my seizures. I understand that anger at others acts like a boomerang and can hurt me more than it ever could hurt them."

"But what do you do with it?" I asked. "Where does it go? Not being allowed to feel it doesn't mean you don't feel."

Rusty got up and began walking across the lawn. "On a day like today," she said, "it's too hard to remember I was ever unhappy. The trees are solid and green. The grass smells like grass and the sky is clear blue."

"It's often like that," I said. "What has that got to do with anything?"

"It's not often like this," she insisted. "Not for me anyway. Sometimes the flowers and trees wave and wiggle and the wind smells like bananas."

I thought she was kidding me again. But something in her expression as she sat down next to me told me different. "What's wrong with the wind smelling like bananas?" I teased.

"Nothing," she said, taking a deep breath, "if it smells like that to everyone else. But when it doesn't, when you're the only one who smells it, it makes you feel crazy and you get lonely." Then, as though trying to forget, she shook her head back and forth and fell back onto the grass with her arms behind her head. "Yep," she said, "that not-getting-angry business was a hard one to figure. But I've been lucky. My brain is smart even if it shorts out, causing me a lot of grief. It allows me to see situations from other points of view. And understanding things helps me not get angry."

"So," I said, "it's the site of your illness but it's also the tool of your healing." She nodded and I teased, "The line between a nut and a guru is silk-string-thin. You're a regular philosopher."

"It helped me understand my parents better," Rusty volunteered. "It helped me see them more clearly."

"I wonder if Lynn and Jeremy will ever see me clearly," I said, thinking that maybe I should treat them a little less well: maybe it would help their vision later.

Rusty laughed. "I think they see you as you are. Competent, intelligent, funny and good. They know they can depend on you, that you can take care of them."

"Does that mean I'll have to take care of myself in my old age?" I asked, laughing.

Rusty nodded. "Only the weak get taken care of." But as she said it, I could see her face change and she looked upset.

"What are you thinking about?" I asked.

"Dove." The way she said it, I could hear gentle bird sounds and fragile wings flapping overhead.

"That was hard for you," I said, because I could see her pain. "Do you want to talk about it?"

Rusty was as close to anger as I had ever seen her. "There was something so very, very wrong," she said, tight-lipped, "that someone could die like that. Dove might not have had the will to live, but she might not have had the will to die either. Her body gave out while her will was suspended. And because no one took the time to try to bend her will toward life, her body deteriorated. She really died of apathy and neglect. She was forgotten in that mayhem, because all the others ran or rocked or chanted or shrieked. They shouted and hit walls and banged feet on the floor. Patty, a little girl who was blind, deaf and dumb, tore around that dayroom like a jet, never bumping into anyone. She attracted attention. Though they said she was retarded, she had sense enough not to allow them to ignore her. The staff always said Dove was good. It was certainly not 'good' for her. She had a total lack of aggression."

Now I understood even better Rusty's fury when Dove died. Her rage in destroying the dayroom that day was her challenge to life. If too much goodness impaired survival, she would state her claim so there would be no misunderstanding

CHAPTER 10

Rusty was raking the one thousand leaves that had fallen all over the backyard, and piling them into huge heaps that she would later deposit into large plastic bags for the garbage men to pick up.

"I don't get it," I told her. "It seems like a lot of extra work when they'll eventually dissolve by themselves."

"But it's fun," she said, "and besides, all the neighbors lawns have been done."

I was sitting on the couch reading through a medical book on diabetes and neurology, and a psychology text on depression. I was trying to figure out how to better help Mr. Gragone.

"Why are you doing that?" Rusty asked as she came in to get a drink of water.

"Because it's fun," I told her.

"I don't get it," she said, laughing. "It's a beautiful day. How about sitting outside to read?" she asked. "I'll rake, you'll read. And that way you can at least smell the wind."

"Jeez, Rusty," I said, "you're getting as pesty as Creede about me experiencing my environment." But in truth, I was glad she wanted my company. And even I could manage to move my body from the couch to the porch steps. So I slipped on my shoes and followed her outside.

She raked. And she raked. And she raked some more. And each time I looked up from my book, another area of brownish lawn showed and another large pile of leaves appeared. She waved. And she smiled. And she sang.

It was a beautiful day. And I was in the middle of a chapter on electrode implantation of the brain, when I looked up to see Rusty spinning with arms outstretched, in front of me. Her head was back and she had a glorious look of pleasure on her upturned face as the sun shone on her freckled nose. Soon she flopped down in front of me.

"Whew!" she said. "Is that a terrific feeling!"

"I'll bet," I said, laughing at her twinkling eyes and rosy cheeks.

"Try it?" she asked. "Just try it once?"

I looked at her and made a face. "No way," I said.

"Come on," she said, standing. "Just see if it's fun for you. Just try it once to find out for yourself."

"You sound like Jeremy," I told her.

"Well, why not?" she asked.

"Cause I'm supposed to be a grown-up." I said.

"Who says grown-ups can't have fun?" she asked. "And that's not the kind of grown-up you want to be, is it? Grown-ups who let the kid in them go, get dull . . . and boring. Is that the kind of grown-up you want to be?"

"Of course not," I said, "but if anyone sees me, they'll think I'm crazy, and I don't want that either."

Rusty looked thoughtful for a minute. Then excitedly she said, "I think I've got it. I've got a great idea. Stand up."

"What now?" I asked, laughing. Sometimes she was so responsible she put me and anyone else I knew to shame, and at other times she did remind me of Jeremy. I stood up.

She stood up straight and stretched her arms out. "Now. get behind me and do the same thing," she said. When I hesitated, she pressed, "Come on, just stand right behind me, as close as you can, and put your arms out like this."

I stood directly behind her and did as she said.

"Okay," she ordered, "now put the palm of your hands against the back of mine, and put your fingers through mine.

"You're crazy," I said, but I did as she asked.

"That's what everyone else will think too," she said as she started to spin. "Because from the front, they'll only see me, so you're safe." She laughed as she shouted, "Hang on!" And I did.

At first we were clumsy and I tried to stop, but she clutched my fingers hard and sang, "Spin, Spin," as around and around we went. With my head tossed back, the blue sky flew by and the green of the trees melted too, the wind blew through my hair and the feeling I had was of flying and freedom. I was dizzy and falling and yet far from the ground, as faster and faster we spun. As everything spun around me, I felt my borders blurring as though my body had no edges. I was surprised when Rusty stopped. I had forgotten that we were attached. We fell in a heap. I laughed as I hadn't since I was really small.

"See?" she said, winded. "I knew it would be fun for you. Let's try jumping in leaves." She grabbed my hand and pulled me forward.

"Hang on," I said. "Enough is enough. I've had enough fun."

She looked crushed. "Just once?"

"Hey, give it up," I said. "I jumped into a pile of leaves once when I was a kid and almost fractured my skull on a rock underneath. I can't afford a broken head now."

This time she stood behind me. This time, with arms outstretched, her fingers twined through mine. "Okay," she shouted, "fall back!" But I got scared and pulled us both down sideways.

"I'm right behind you," she told me, as we stood again. "When you fall, you'll fall on me. You won't get hurt." It reminded me of when my father taught me how to roller-skate, by having me stand on his feet while he wore the skates and skated for both of us.

We fell back. Again, and again and again, until I had leaves in my hair, leaves in my mouth, leaves up my nose. But I had to admit, it was fun.

Afterward, when we came inside to wash and change our clothes, Rusty said, "Why do you think it's so hard for you to act silly? To have fun?"

"I don't know," I said. "I guess I'm too self-conscious. Or maybe it's because I can only manage one role at a time. Now I'm supposed to be a responsible adult, a mother, a nurse. . . so I have to act grown-up. And acting grown-up gives me confidence. I don't want to confuse myself by acting like a kid."

Rusty laughed. "You make it sound like a costume party," she said, "and I'm glad it's just your outfit. Because I was afraid you'd forgotten how to be a kid."

"Aside from the dull-and-boring business, why would that be

such a disaster?" I asked her.

Rusty sat at the foot of my bed while I looked through my drawers for something to wear. "Because," she said seriously, "I think the part of us that stays a kid is the part of us that keeps us alive. It's the part that can hope for a better tomorrow because it can forget the hurt that's been done to it today. It's the part of us that stays innocent enough to trust and forgive the people who hurt us, because that's how kids are, you know. It's the part that believes just because we don't have the answers doesn't mean there are no answers, it just means we haven't found them yet. And it's the part of us that can love without reason, without logic, and completely, just because it's a child's nature to love. Even more, it's a child's need to love–and be loved back."

Rusty stood up and walked in front of my wall mirror. "Carol," she said, "stand behind me again." And I did. "Now, wrap your arms around the front of me, like you're hugging." And I did. Rusty did the same. But the mirror showed only Rusty, with four arms hugging her. "That's how it should really be, in each of us," she said. "The grown-up behind, and the kid up in front, hugging each other making a whole person."

That night after supper when my parents dropped the kids home, we all went shopping. Rusty had an idea that she figured would help Lenny out. The X-rays had shown that he'd never get more movement back into his fingers and so he had gotten really depressed again. "We have to find something," Rusty said. That's what we were looking for now. Something.

"Can I have one thing, Mom?" Jeremy begged as we walked across the parking lot of the enormous toy store.

"We'll see," I told him. "Let's see what we find." Then I turned to Lynn. "Do you want anything special, honey?" I asked her.

She reached over and held my hand. "Maybe just a record, Mom, if we have enough money," she said.

"I have money," Rusty told her. And then when Jeremy ran over to her and looked up at her with big blinking brown eyes, she poked him in the chin and added, "Even enough for something for you, Jer."

Jeremy gave her a prize winning smile. What a con man, I thought.

Up and down the long aisles we walked, each of us studying the large stacks of toys.

While I looked over some books in the paperback rack, and Jeremy jumped up and down next to me as though he was on a pogo stick, Lynn and Rusty walked up and down the far aisles.

"Mom," Jeremy said, his voice vibrating with the movement of his body, "can I have a fishing pole?"

"Maybe," I said. And he kept jumping. I wanted to hold off as long as possible before I bought him anything, because as soon as I did, he'd start nagging to go home to try it.

Rusty and Lynn came over holding a card game. I could see it was a baseball game. A guess-the-player type. "This will make Lenny feel better," Rusty said. "I'm sure there's not a baseball fact he doesn't know. If he takes it into the lounge, he can show off in front of everyone."

"Sounds right," I said. Jeremy kept hanging onto the end of the box to try to see what it was. Lynn was standing quietly next to Rusty. She had a record clutched in her hand.

"Got what you wanted, babe?" I asked, smiling at Lynn.

"Really, I did," she said, brown eyes alight.

"Rusty," Jeremy begged, "what about fishing? What about a fishing pole?"

"Sounds good," Rusty said, and the two of them went to find the fishing equipment.

Rusty had an armful of stuff when she came back, and Jeremy had an ear-to-ear grin.

"Live with us another two months," I told Rusty, "and you'll be on welfare."

She laughed. "Won't be the first time."

On our way to the cash register, Rusty spotted it. The very thing she really wanted. "Can you believe this?" she said excitedly. It was a pinball machine. A very large colorful one. The green neon base-ball diamond blinked on and off, demanding our attention.

I looked at the price tag. Expensive. I showed Rusty.

She nodded. "How much have you got?" she asked me, smiling.

"Enough to split with you if we're all willing to eat cereal and hot dogs for the next few weeks." I said.

Rusty told the kids about Lenny, about how his fingers wouldn't open up enough that he could hold a baseball anymore, but how if he could have this pinball machine, because his fingers worked like lobster claws, he could manage enough to play. Then he could put it in the lounge and all the other patients would think he was a hero. "How do you feel about eating cereal?" she asked them.

Jeremy looked at his fishing pole. "Fine," he said. "I'll just catch a fish."

"Lynn?" I asked.

"Fine, Mom," she said, smiling. Then she held up her record. "I'll just dance."

So Rusty bought Lenny the machine. She would have to assemble it for him and get clearance to put it in the lounge, but I had no doubt she could do that. And the timing was perfect. Two days later was his birthday.

When we got home, Rusty asked, "Are you sure you didn't mind about the money?"

"Don't be silly," I teased. "I can take it off my income tax."

Maybe Lenny hadn't expected a party. Maybe that's why he cried. But it was great seeing all the old people, dressed in their finest clothes, all wearing pink and purple party hats, and all waiting anxiously for Rusty to wheel Lenny in.

That morning Dominic had insisted we help decorate the dining room. He spent hours blowing up red, yellow and green balloons and tying them with multicolored ribbons. Louisa and Howie made streamers for the aides to hang from the ceiling and Mrs. Frick surprised us all by bringing in a gold banner on which she herself had written "Most Valuable Patient." Lenny had somehow penetrated her rock-hard heart.

But, of course, it was the pinball machine that got Lenny. As soon as Rusty wheeled him close enough, he stroked the side of the big machine as though it was his favorite pet.

"I can't believe it's for me, young lady," Lenny said, tears falling faster than he could brush them away. "I didn't know I still had so many friends."

I couldn't decide whose eyes shone more, Rusty's or Lenny's. After lunch, the cook carried out a three-tiered cake that he had specially designed with a brilliant blue baseball cap in buttercream frosting. When all the candles were lit and all the patients began to sing, I could feel a large lump in my own throat.

The afternoon sped by with each of the patients taking turns playing baseball. Lenny began to organize them by numbers so they didn't have to fight for a turn, and Dominic finally suggested, "Eh, Lenny? You thinka maybe we shoulda put a few money here and maybe save for a football machine?"

Lenny wasted no time. Sherry got him an empty coffee can and placed it on his lap. "Ten cents a game," he hawked, smiling wide. "Ten cents a game." By the end of the day, Lenny had become a combination carnival caller and proud entrepreneur.

Several times during the afternoon when I had looked around, I couldn't find Rusty. I knew she had gone to try to convince Marta to join Lenny's party. But Marta never came.

Now it was time for us to go home and Rusty was nowhere to be found. I marched down to Marta's room.

I opened the door and quietly walked in. Rusty was sitting face to face with Marta, both of them in geri-chairs in front of the window, and Rusty was holding her hand. On her bedside stand was an untouched piece of Lenny's birthday cake. The whole scene looked very private. "I'm sorry to disturb you," I said, turning to go, but Marta stopped me.

"Stay, Carol," she said softly. "It's time we all talked."

I sat on the bed across from them and waited for Marta to speak. She turned to Rusty. "I know about Rambling Woods," she said cautiously, and Rusty immediately looked at me.

"She thought she'd been dreaming," I explained, "and when she asked, I couldn't lie."

Rusty nodded and then she smiled at Marta. "It's okay, Carol," she said gently, turning toward me. "I don't mind. I trust Marta. It would be different if she were dressed in mink coming from a cocktail party."

And with that Marta put her head in her hands and began to sob. "Rusty," she cried, obviously touched by Rusty's understanding, "I have to ask something. And it's very personal. If you can help."

"What is it?" Rusty asked, concerned. "How can I help?"

I felt like an intruder, but Marta wanted me to stay, so I just tried to quiet my breathing and not move a muscle to disturb them.

"Rusty?" Marta repeated, and I could see that she was clutching Rusty's hand hard. "Were you ever in Graylock Pavilion?"

Rusty's body stiffened and she turned her face toward the window for a moment. Then she looked back at Marta and nodded.

"Did you know a woman, Flora Eldrich?" Marta asked anxiously. It seemed very important to her.

Rusty nodded again.

Marta's eyes were pleading when she asked, "Could you tell me about her, Rusty? Could you tell me everything you remember?"

"Can I ask you why?" Rusty asked.

Marta's hand involuntarily covered her mouth. "I killed her," she whispered. "I killed her."

Rusty sat up straight.

"Rusty," Marta begged again, "just tell me what you know."

So Rusty did.

Flora was about seventy, with wiry white hair and a pleasant face. She dressed in dresses she had worn when she had been committed to Graylock eight years before and so they were patched and sewn in a hundred places. One side of her skirt was always shorter than the other, giving her a lopsided look. She spent her days knitting clothes for her microscopic children, using rubber knitting needles made for her by a kindly occupational therapist. She always had a neat little pile of woolen clothes on the bench next to her.

Flora always wore a colored scarf around her neck. She had worn it for years, telling everyone that something was eating at her neck, and the kerchief was there to keep her head from falling off. One day she began to complain that the thing had finally shown itself-the thing that was eating her away.

Everyone had laughed at her. Except Rusty and a girl named Mickey Pet. Finally one day Rusty had removed Flora's scarf. There was a lump the size of a grapefruit on the side of her neck. When the attendant called the doctor and made him come up to the ward, he was annoyed. When he saw the lump, he was amazed. "Can't believe I missed it," he had said, chuckling. And then, "Well, you can't win 'em all." Rusty had been furious but there was nothing she could do. That was the last time she had seen Flora.

"I was one of the surgeons who operated on her," Marta said gloomily.

"Wait a minute, Marta," Rusty began, but Marta put up her hand to stop her.

"Let me finish," Marta insisted. "It's time I got it off my chest. I've held it in a long time." She looked at both of us and then she explained. "I'd been a surgeon for many years and at first I loved it. I looked forward to a nice clean operation which would remove a diseased part and make my patient whole again. But then as medicine progressed and there were new advances in surgery, I had to do more and more radical surgery. I had to remove more and more of my patients to try to help them. I had to do pelvic exenterations on old and young women, and later . . ."

Marta began to cry and I could understand why. In a pelvic exenteration all a woman's reproductive organs are removed, her large intestine goes and her bladder is removed. In the ones I'd seen, everything on the inside of a woman s body from the waist down was gone and what was left was a gaping hole. The woman can't urinate normally, she has a colostomy and she can never have intercourse again because her vagina has been removed.

"I began to take sedatives," Marta continued, as though wanting to rid herself of it all. "Not enough to endanger my patients, just enough to keep my hands from shaking." She took a deep breath and continued. "After a while, when the pain got too bad, I took Demerol, and then Dilaudid. Still, I couldn't bear the feel of the knife cutting into so many of my patients. I began to doubt the wisdom of what we were doing . . . and I began to feel fear all the time."

"Why didn't you stop operating if you stopped believing in it?" I asked.

"I couldn't," she explained, looking deep into my eyes to see if I could understand. "There were always patients waiting in my office; always people insisting I do something for them. People who would die if something wasn't done. . ."

"And Flora?" Rusty asked, reaching out to hold Marta's hand again.

Marta started breathing hard. Then she began to cry, but through her tears she continued to explain. Faster now, looking down, pulling her hands back from Rusty, wringing them together in her own lap. "The night Flora came in through the emergency room, I had already been up for thirty hours. I had just finished an emergency appendectomy and was ready to go home. But Flora was in trouble, her tumor started bleeding and it had to be removed. I didn't do head and neck surgery but the surgeon on duty asked me to assist and because there was no one else around, I agreed. In the bathroom, just before I gowned for the operating room, I gave myself an injection, but even that didn't help."

Rusty got up to get Marta a glass of water and I handed her a box of tissues. Because I didn't know what else to do, I just stood for a few minutes with my hand on her shoulder.

"A lot of this is unclear in my mind," Marta explained. "The doctor began to cut away the tumor. I watched as he put the scalpel under her nose, deep in her throat and cut away most of her face. Suddenly there was a bleeder, a big one, and the surgeon got a cramp in his fingers. He told me what to do; he tried to explain it carefully. But I froze. I couldn't move. I couldn't clamp. I couldn't sew. The nurses tried to stop the bleeding but it was too late. I just stood and watched as Flora bled to death." Marta's whole body was heaving with her anguish now. But she was too fragile to touch, so both Rusty and I stayed away.

Finally Rusty said gently, "There are worse things than death. Flora's dying was kind. And it was better she died there than in Graylock."

Marta tried to force a smile. "Thank you," she said. "Thank

you. . ." Then she looked straight at Rusty. "Will you tell me about it? Maybe if I knew more about it, I could find some way to live with this."

"What was Graylock like?" Rusty asked in a faraway voice. It was bad . . ."

CHAPTER 11

Graylock Pavilion was a place for the criminally insane. And the day Dove died, Rusty was on her way there. Rambling Woods was so large that in order to get from one building to another, you had to take a bus. Rusty shook throughout the ride. She had never been so frightened. She was sure she wouldn't make it this time. She was sure she couldn't cope. She'd heard so many awful things about the place. But the hardest thing to deal with was the disbelief that she had somehow done it again. Not that she didn't remember what had happened this time, she did. But tearing up a dayroom didn't make her criminally insane, did it?

Magenta had jumped her with another attendant Rusty didn't know, and had given her an injection of something which had made her pretty groggy. So now, instead of seeing details, she only got impressions.

Graylock was dirty, dark and dingy, a very old concrete building. Into a small creaky elevator and out into a narrow dirty hall. Even smaller, narrower corridors shooting off the main like spider legs. The walls so drab it was hard to call it a color. It smelled, an incredibly strong smell of urine, and there were thick bars on heavy metal doors leading into God knows where. "There are four wards on the top floor," the attendant told Rusty. "You'll be on Ward Four." Rusty knew the top floor was the worst. The attendant unlocked a heavy dark metal door that led into another hallway. Rows of these heavy metal doors lined the hall. From some of them, grabbing, grasping hands were extended through the bars. Rusty didn't know if there were patients in all those rooms. She saw expectant faces peering through the mesh-covered windows down the hall. She didn't know whether one of these locked rooms would be hers from now on.

Then, as they reached the end of the dismal hallway, through blurred vision she saw several white-haired wrinkled-looking patients standing in what must have been the dayroom. She had seen Snake Pit and thought of it now. She began to shake, her whole body vibrating with terror. In the corner she thought she saw a woman eating like a dog off a metal plate. And then she saw Sharelle. Sitting on the bench in the main dayroom? With all the other patients? Rusty tried to clear her mind. She looked closer. The long red hair was knotted and tangled as always, but when Sharelle looked up, Rusty was petrified. Sharelle's green eyes were no longer spinning, no longer angry . . . they were absolutely vacant. And she drooled.

After a few minutes Rusty was taken into the dorm, a crowded stinking room with more than thirty filthy cots, and given an injection by the main attendant, Gloria Goodall.

"This will calm you down," Gloria told her. "And you won't need another dose for fifteen days. It's a new medicine, Prolixin, just out, and it seems pretty good."

"Is this what Sharelle is on?" Rusty asked apprehensively.

"Sharelle's not on anything," Gloria said.

"She was violent on Three ..." Rusty explained.

"Oh, that must have been before her operation," Gloria said, smiling.

By that afternoon, Rusty couldn't sit still. She began to pace. Whenever she sat, she rocked. Her hands shook so badly that she couldn't hold a fork to eat, but that was just as well. The food was garbage. Besides, she could never sit long enough to eat. She couldn't even sit long enough to go to the bathroom. She was agitated and she thought it was her fear, her reaction to being in Graylock.

That night she couldn't wait to go to bed. But then she had to rock . . . on the mattress covered with stiff plastic that reeked of urine. The sheets refused to stay on, no matter what she did. And her head kept rolling off the hard pillow. It was like a rubber ball. Each time she moved too quickly, the mattress slid off the springs. Rusty spent most of that first night awake. Several times she heard what she thought was water dripping onto the gray linoleum tile. It was almost morning when she realized it was urine: some of the more disturbed patients were peeing in bed.

For the first week and a half, whenever she rocked-and she always did now–she'd find herself on the floor. Then, something seemed to happen. As quickly as it had started, Rusty's body stopped racing her around.

Graylock was filthy; she always had to watch where she sat or where she walked, because the older patients would urinate and defecate wherever they happened to be at that moment. There were mice, many of them, and the food was often inedible because of the bugs. The staff took home much of the best in fruits, meat and canned goods.

Because Graylock was for long-termers, there were few visitors to impress or complain to. The furniture, what there was of it, was old and broken, having been there for so many years it had practically begun to grow roots into the walls and floors. Most of the patients were old people and kids. Not average kids from average families, but kids from the streets, from broken homes, from single mothers who had ten kids and wanted none of them.

Bennie, a beautiful black girl of twenty-four, was one of them. She had an awful reputation, and one of the attendants told Rusty that she had killed someone, but Rusty didn't believe it.

Bennie was big and tough-looking, until she smiled. Of course she never smiled at the attendants. She was the one who explained to Rusty how it was for her.

"I was brought up on the street," Bennie told her as they sat on the floor in the corner of the dayroom. "There ain't nothing else out there. Here there's food and a bed; it ain't a good bed, it's a dirty bed–but it's a bed. Out there you have to fight off your ass to get that. It ain't gonna rain on me in here. And here's people who tell you what to do. They tough, but they care about you."

One of the other girls, Mickey Pet, was twenty-one and had been there for seven years. Like Rusty, she had seizures. She was a sweet-looking small brown-haired girl who reminded Rusty of a squirrel. When Mickey fell on the floor in seizure, the attendants deliberately ignored her. They said she just did it for attention. It was Bennie who usually helped her, saying, "If she's doing this for tention, let's give it to her. She must need it pretty bad."

Rusty didn't know whether Mickey was faking or not, because she had never seen a real seizure. But it gave her time to think one day when she watched Mickey. The girl had stiffened and fallen to the floor. Her eyes had rolled so far up in her head, you couldn't even see the black parts, and her eyelids didn't close. But it wasn't spooky or scary. She didn't hurt anyone and there was no foam coming from her mouth. They couldn't treat a person badly because of this, Rusty thought. It's no big deal. Maybe mine are different, she said to herself. But the next day when it happened again and Mickey's tooth went through her lip, just as Rusty's had, Rusty knew better.

Mickey, Rusty and Bennie were sitting in the dayroom that night and Rusty was furious. She had been angry all day, had ranted and paced around; now, as she thought about it again, she stormed at the other girls. "Do you think these institutions are good for anybody at all?"

Mickey, fully alert now, smiled good-naturedly and put her hand on Rusty's shoulder. "For a few people who need someplace to stay. But mostly, I guess, it's for the doctors, nurses and attendants. It gives them something to do. It keeps them off the streets."

❖❖ ❖❖ ❖❖

The day Rusty came back from her first weekend pass, she went directly to the nurses' office. She had had a good weekend and was looking forward to her next pass, so she wanted to be sure she did everything that was expected of her.

Jeannie Raven was at the desk when Rusty walked in. The Raven twins were the head attendants on Graylock. They were both thin and dark-haired. Both pretty and smart. But Jeannie was much softer than Joannie. They wore glasses, of course the same kind, and only if you looked close could you see that Joannie had a small dark birthmark near her hairline on the right side. Jeannie worked days and Joannie worked evenings. Rusty was sure that was another plot to make the patients feel crazy. Anytime you told one of them something, they'd swear you'd mixed them up and told the other. As a result, nobody talked much to either of them. "Hi," Rusty said, smiling at Jeannie. "I was put on the honor system and told to remind the attendant when the fifteen days was up, so that I could have another dose of medication."

"Thanks," Jeannie said, looking through the charts on the desk. "You're right. It's due."

Rusty followed Jeannie into the treatment room and willingly submitted to the injection. "By the way," Rusty asked, "do you know a patient called Bell?" Jeannie just shook her head. And Rusty realized, horrified, that in an institution like this, patients could disappear without a trace. When she'd gotten her shot, Rusty walked out into the dayroom where the other girls were.

Bennie and Mickey were happy to see her. "Did you bring anything special?" Bennie asked. Rusty reached into her bag and pulled out some cookies and a jelly sandwich that she had brought from home. Bennie quickly stashed it inside her sweater. "I found out something about you," she told Rusty. They were all sitting around the big wooden table, Bennie alongside Rusty. "I sneaked a look at your chart when Joannie was in the dining room last night. You're a paranoid schizophrenic just like me and Mickey here." She said it as though she was glad to have Rusty aboard.

Rusty figured anybody in their right mind would feel the way she did when so many people watched everything she did, and talked about her, and made decisions for her, including when and what she should eat, when she could smoke, when she could get up and go to bed. They treated her as though she was crazy, not trusting her with anything. She couldn't have matches, knives, forks or a spoon that was too big. She had no rights. She told Mickey and Bennie all of this, adding, "The combination of all this stuff is enough to make anybody look behind his shoulder. I don't own my own body. I don't own my own mind."

"Hey, man, don't take it so seriously," Bennie said. "It's all about money, not for real. Only the staff thinks it's real. They can't put you up in a crazy house and make the government pay for it unless they give you a 'crazy' diagnosis. It's just how life is in this world; but, man, you don't want to believe it."

Suddenly Rusty was aware that she was rocking again. She couldn't sit still. First she thought maybe the conversation had made her more nervous than she knew. Her hands began to shake and she had to stand up. She thought: This is how it must feel to be crazy. But suddenly it hit her. The medicine! The injection! How stupid!

She ran to tell Jeannie. Because of the time span, and the symptoms, the attendant was convinced Rusty was having an adverse reaction. The attendant quickly called the doctor. But there was not much they could do. They tried to give her a sedative to counteract it, but the only thing it did was knock her out. For the next several days, all Rusty did was sleep.

During the next months, Rusty tried to set up a routine. She washed and scrubbed the floors in the dayroom and bathrooms and then she started on the dorms. She washed windows and even convinced Mickey and Bennie to help. She began to help some of the sicker patients dress and eat, and so the months were passing. She even managed to survive spending Christmas and New Year's there, but it wasn't easy. Finally she had persuaded some of the patients to come along with her and act as a cleaning squad. But that almost did her in. The staff thought she was gaining too much power; they were afraid of mutiny, and so one day for no reason she could know, they jumped her and medicated her. They did it the next day too. She was getting scared.

That night as she lay in bed struggling to unscramble her groggy medicated brain, something inside her decided it was time to turn her life around. The last months in Graylock had made her aware that it was different here from the other buildings. Here, so many of the patients were lifers. And the staff was intent on doing their jobs. They had to justify those jobs by believing most of their patients were crazy, and so the patients had to have serious diagnoses and be treated with strong limits, heavy medications and restraints. Rusty was one of the few patients who had been there less than a year, and she knew if she didn't watch herself, she'd wind up a lifer without ever knowing what hit her. She couldn't have that. She had a normal life to get on with. She had used Rambling Woods up. There was no more to learn here, and only the danger of getting stuck in its revolving door. She had to find a way out.

The next afternoon, Rusty, Bennie and Mickey were sitting on the dark pine table in the dayroom, singing, to the tune of "Frére Jacques": "We are crazy. We are crazy. We are nuts. We are nuts. Happy little morons, happy little morons, da, da, da . . ."

After a little while, Rusty said, "Fellas, I think we have to get ourselves together."

"What do you mean?" Mickey asked.

"What about signing up for the work program?" Rusty suggested.

"Not me," Mickey said right away. "I'm not working in that dungeon."

"It's too dangerous for me," Bennie added.

"Why?" Rusty asked.

"Once they find out I can work, they'll put me right back out," Bennie said.

"So what's wrong with that?" Rusty asked. That was all she hoped for.

Bennie shook her head. "You sure don't know nothing about out there," she said. "They'll get me an apartment someplace in lower New York . . . the Bowery or something . . and I'll be with the hookers and the winos. Shit, I got too much class for that."

So Rusty alone started working the following week, in a factory on the grounds of Rambling Woods. A bus picked her up at eight AM. and dropped her off in front of another building. There, in the basement, she sewed two pieces of material together to make slips. She worked nine hours a day, five days a week, and earned four dollars total. But it was the beginning for Rusty. She was eighteen years old.

As Rusty had been talking, there was a noticeable change in Marta. Her expression went from guilt and depression to pure, unadulterated anger.

"Those idiots!" she fumed. "How could they even suspect hysterical seizures when real injury resulted? That's one of the diagnostic criteria for organic seizures. And for what purpose were they giving you a powerful psychotropic drug? Where were the doctors?"

"The problem was," Rusty said, "that there weren't too many doctors who cared enough to look past the obvious. I had been diagnosed before, and so they just continued routine treatment."

When I saw how upset Marta was, I said, "You have to go back to medicine, Marta. There are too many defenseless patients who really need you." When she bowed her head, I added fervently, "You don't have to do surgery again. You could be a medical doctor. Think about it, Marta," I pleaded, walking over to hold her hand. "Think about going back. Think about all those patients all those years who didn't die. Think about all those patients you really did help."

Marta squeezed my hand and then she smiled at Rusty. "I'll think about it," she agreed softly. "I will."

In my heart I knew that being a doctor was so deeply rooted in Marta's soul that she'd have to return in order to live. I also knew that her trial by fire, her testing at the hands of the gods, and her success in grappling with her own real and human personal problems would make her a far better doctor than most.

CHAPTER 12

"Fire, Mommy, fire!" Lynn screamed as she came running into my room.

I jumped out of bed, trying to untangle myself from my red nightgown. "What happened?" I asked as I ran after her into Jeremy's room. I was sleeping late because I had worked for Penny the night before. Her father had gone into uremic crisis.

"My mattress is on fire," Jeremy said as he stood alongside his smoking bed. The room was thick with smoke and my eyes burned. I tried to open the window as I screamed, "Jeremy, get out of here. Lynn, bring me my boots!" Jeremy stood frozen until I flung his small body toward the door. When Lynn handed me my boots, I held one by the top and let it fly into the window. The glass shattered all over the roof outside and the floor inside. I tried to shove the smoldering mattress through the window. It wouldn't fit. Jeremy was now standing in the doorway staring at me. He looked confused as I struggled into my high black boots. Suddenly, he started to laugh.

"You look like a crazy fireman, Mom," he said, giggling. In my panic, I was ready to throttle him for his enjoyment.

"Run downstairs and open the door," I hollered. "And, Lynn, help me drag this mattress down the steps." She grabbed the bottom and I grabbed the top and we struggled and stumbled with the heavy smoking mattress down the narrow staircase. We coughed and our eyes teared but soon we had it on the porch and finally we had it in the backyard on the snow-capped concrete cesspool cover. "Get some water, Jeremy!" I screeched. "And get your coat on." Lynn's lips were blue and my whole body was shaking. It was freezing out, especially with nothing but a red nylon nightgown on.

Lynn and I ran inside and threw on our jackets. Then all three of us grabbed some pots and brought water outside to splash on the still-smoldering mattress.

Afterward I asked, "How did that happen?"

Jeremy didn't answer and he wouldn't look at me. Lynn moved close to him as he stood at the bottom of the stairs in the living room. She held his hand.

"I'm going to ask one more time, before I punish you both. Now, how did it happen?" I said.

"I don't know," Lynn said, but I could see she wasn't telling the truth. I sat on the edge of the couch and just stared at both of them. My heart was still beating like a bongo and I was both angry and terror-stricken. I had just finished doing a year of burn nursing and the incredible damage that fire can do to a human being had been a constant nightmare. It was my biggest fear. That, and something happening to my kids. The combination now made me completely unreasonable.

"You have three minutes or you'll both get it," I warned.

Jeremy came forward and stood in front of me. "I didn't burn the mattress," he said solemnly.

"Stick out your tongue, Jeremy," I said firmly. When he did, he did it so hesitantly, I knew he was lying. "It's purple," I said firmly, as though it was true. "Jeremy, you're lying." He backed away from me shaking his head.

"Honest, Mommy, I didn't burn the mattress. I burned my book," he said with tears in his eyes. "I only wanted to burn that book."

I jumped off the couch to grab him by the hair, but Lynn was immediately at his side pleading, "Mom, don't spank him. He didn't mean it. He didn't know what he was doing."

I grabbed them both and sat them on the couch. "Do you both know what fire can do to you?" I asked, more frightened now that I didn't think they understood the danger of it; knowing that Jeremy had actually set fire to the mattress by playing with matches while I slept. "Haven't I told you a hundred times that you can get dead? Or worse yet, that you could have more pain than you could stand and it would drive you crazy? Or that you'd be so scarred that you'd have no friends ever?"

They swallowed hard, both of them, and looked as frightened, as I hoped they would. I figured that fear could be handled in therapy later, death couldn't.

"All of that for a book you didn't like?" I continued my tirade. "Do you know how senseless that is, Jeremy? And where were you, Lynn?"

"I was in the bathroom," Lynn said. She looked crushed.

But suddenly Jeremy looked angry at me. "I was right, Mom."

I shook my head. I wanted to throw him over my lap and spank him hard but I just read several books on the psychology of child rearing and all of them warned of the dire consequences to the child's psyche of hitting. Nothing, not a word, about a parent's psyche.

"Okay," I said, trying to think of something that would punish enough but not too much and still discourage so they couldn't wind up destroyed. "Take your shirt off and go into the bathroom. If you like lighting matches so much, you can do it until you're sick of it." I'd read about aversion therapy in one of the books. "But you'll do it under supervision in a place that's safe." I figured that with no shirt on, his clothes wouldn't catch fire, and in a tile bathroom the walls would be safe. "Lynn," I said, "collect all the matches you can find in the house and bring them to me."

Then, Lynn went upstairs to finish her homework, and I sat in the bathroom with Jeremy and insisted he light all the matches we had found. There was almost a shopping bag full and I was sure before he was finished he'd holler uncle. But I was wrong. After almost three hours, when I was certain we would both die of sulfur asphyxiation, I asked, "Do you understand that what you did was wrong?"

Jeremy looked at me with tight lips and narrowed eyes when he said, "No, Mom, 'cause you don't understand the reason."

I was so upset by then that I just grabbed him by the arm, stood him up, smacked him hard a few times on the butt and yelled, "There isn't any reason good enough. Now, you get upstairs and stay there until you're really sorry. Until you can promise you'll never do it again." Jeremy ran upstairs. Tears were streaming down his face, but he did not make one sound.

When Rusty came home from work, she knew by the way I looked that I was upset. When I told her what had happened she asked, "Can I do anything?" and when I shook my head, she added, "Would you mind if I went up to speak to Jeremy?"

"It won't do any good," I told her. "I tried to talk to him several times and now he's not saying a word."

"I'd still like to give it a try," she said, "if you don't object."

"No, I don't object," I said. "In fact any parent who won't accept the assistance of four psychologists, three educators, a guerrilla army and anyone else who's willing to help raise her kids doesn't understand her responsibility to her children, or her own limitations. Just try to impress on him how much damage fire can do, will you?"

Rusty nodded and went upstairs. It was more than an hour before she came back down, and when she did, she was smiling. "You've got some terrific little boy there," she said, sitting on the couch next to me. "He's got a lot of what you'd call principles."

"Great," I said, "and I hope he'll keep them if he ever survives childhood and grows up. Which is possible if I can just get him to understand about fire."

Rusty interrupted. "He understands perfectly how destructive fire is. He knows exactly how much damage fire can do. He says you told him it could destroy big buildings and even melt steel. He said you told him that nothing has a chance if it gets caught in a bad fire. That's why he used it."

"I think I've got to kill him," I said, exhausted. "He's so stubborn."

"I think you've got to kiss him," she said, "and anyway, you owe it to him to hear his side."

"Listen, Rusty," I said, "maybe you'd better give me a practice run. I'm not exactly reasonable about things I'm terrified of, so I'm liable to blow it. Run through it with me once, as long as it makes sense to you."

"Sure," she said, smiling, "but then you have to hear it yourself. It'll lose something in translation."

And it did. But not enough to make me totally forgive myself.

Upstairs, I sat on the bed with Jeremy, his big brown eyes sincere and trusting as he explained, "Mom, Mom, I wasn't bad. It was the Grinch, the Grinch who stole Christmas, who I was burning. Mom, you told me about how fire can destroy everything. And, Mom, that Grinch was a bad Grinch, and all the poor children wouldn't have any presents for Christmas if he got away. What about the children, Mom?"

I hugged him, still worrying that the next bad guy who showed up would get us all burned to death.

"But you do know you can't do it again, don't you, Jer?"

"Sure," he said, his small head shaking so fast that his blond hair flew from one side to the other. "Rusty said how with especially bad creatures, with magic creatures who do bad things, even real fire doesn't work. So only use magic fire."

"Jeremy," I asked, my heart in my throat, "what's magic fire?"

"Well, Mom, it's like this," he said, holding my hand and speaking very slowly. "You have to make it in your mind. You can make it really big. But you have to only destroy bad things with it. And you have to light it with a good wish, a wish for better, not for bad. Got it?"

"I think so, Jer," I said. "But what about matches?"

"Oh, you're a silly," he said, laughing. "Real matches only burn real people, so Rusty said I can't touch those. But I don't need 'em. Only my good wish. Like for the children. Got it?"

"Got it," I told him. And then we both told Lynn and went downstairs to thank Rusty.

That night after the kids had been tucked in, I was sitting on the couch reading and feeling good that my life seemed all right. My kids were fine, work was okay and I liked having Rusty share my responsibilities. The world was spinning at just the right speed for me right at that moment. "I'm happy," I told her. "What about you?"

Rusty was ironing our uniforms for the following week. She looked over at me and smiled. "I'm happy too," she admitted.

"That sure is a beautiful sight," I said, indicating the row of freshly pressed uniforms that hung on the doorjamb. "I don't know how you do it all ... and look as though you enjoy it besides." The living room smelled like a Chinese laundry. It was great.

Rusty laughed. "Stop making such a big fuss over such little things," she said. For the first time, I saw what looked like pride in her eyes.

I went back to reading but found my mind wandering. Since Rusty had moved in, I had decided her troubled home life and the incompetent medical treatment she had all those years were the biggest factors in her seizures going out of control and her consequent commitment. So with some dense blanket defense, both Rusty and I managed to avoid ever talking about what we'd do if her seizures ever went totally out of control again. I had, in theory, no question of what I would do. Neither of us ever discussed the practical aspects of the problem.

She was so happy now, so functional, so healthy, that whenever we spoke of her past, I had a difficult time accepting that we were talking about the same Rusty. It played with my perceptions. I was always looking for the connecting threads. I had an insatiable desire to know everything that had happened.

Now, as she whistled and ironed, I said, "I want to hear how you got out of Graylock. We might as well get it out of the way while we're both feeling strong. Then, because it will never happen again, we can both try to file it away somewhere like a bad dream."

Rusty was frowning.

"What did I say?" I asked, puzzled.

She walked over and sat on the floor next to the couch. "You said, 'It will never happen again.'" And then, in the same tone I had used to tell my kids there was no Santa Claus while hoping to preserve their faith in people, she explained, "I have a sickness where my brain plays tricks. Sometimes it looks like my mind is crazy. You yourself told me there is no cure, and so there's always the possibility the same thing can happen again. I can't stop it from happening and the doctors can't either. If there's no control, there can't be promises."

I reached over and grabbed Rusty's chin in my hand, as I did with my kids when I wanted them to pay special attention. "Rusty," I said, my voice firm, "you are not crazy by any criteria. Therefore, you will not be locked up in a nuthouse ever again, no matter what happens. You no longer live with your mother. I am neither as old, as poor or as tired as she was, and I will fight along with you for your rights as a sane person, whatever they may be. Nothing will shake my belief in you, in your mental health, and therefore even if something happens, we will deal with it together. Nothing will change."

Rusty's eyes were wide as a child's when she looked at me and said, "Carol, even the seasons change. Everything changes."

"Except me, I said with the pomposity of ignorance and youth. "I'm constant. Relentless, some people say. Through wind and sleet and storm, et cetera."

Rusty put her head down on the cushions of the couch. "I hope so," she said in a soft voice, "I really hope so." When she lifted her face, I could see fear in her eyes, and tears.

CHAPTER 13

Rusty began . . .

The following month during a weekend pass at home from Graylock, Rusty was sitting at the kitchen table eating breakfast with her parents when an idea popped into her head.

"Maybe if I got a real job and became a working member of society, they'd release me," she told her father.

He was absently chewing a piece of toast and his eyes lit up. "Now, there's a thought, girl," he said cheerfully, "that just might work."

Nona looked up from her coffee.

Rusty spent that afternoon poring through the papers and setting up interviews at nursing homes for the following week. They seemed to need the most help and she was good with older people. Her father would drive her.

"And you might think of learning to drive yourself," he suggested that night. "I could use the help."

Rusty could finally see what sad little figures her parents were. They both looked so pathetic, especially Nona, and so poor. Her father wouldn't even wear his teeth. He liked them so much that he had kept them on his dresser next to his wallet. Suddenly the two of them seemed weak and naive, unable to defend themselves against life, against the system. She saw how frightened and exhausted they were, how they disliked each other even though they needed each other so desperately. They once had such pretty smiles, she wanted them to smile again.

Rusty began to feel responsible for them. She felt bad about having added pain to their life, about having helped make life harder for them. They had done their best, though it had hurt her. But she knew she was stronger and would survive better than they. That day, she could see so clearly, that she was the only one who could help any of them.

Rusty hadn't had any seizures for almost six months, driving seemed a good idea. Her mother had never learned, and as Rusty looked at her dad's thinning white hair and wrinkled skin, she saw just how tired he had grown. He was almost seventy now, time to rest.

During that week, while Rusty was trying to stay out of trouble in Graylock, her dad was standing on long lines in the motor vehicle office applying for her permit and road test.

The next weekend he gave her driving lessons. "You're a natural driver," he complimented her.

"And you're a natural criminal," she laughed and teased. He had forged her signature. Rusty thought it was to save time and expedite the application. But Daniel Russell did it so he could falsify the information. He knew what Rusty was up against and he wasn't sure that she would be willing to lie. Where it read "Epilepsy," he had written "No."

Two weeks later, after having spent the weekend at home, on the way back to Rambling Woods, Rusty asked her father to stop the car long enough for her to run into Salvation Nursing Home and fill out an application.

Her father looked expectant when she jumped back into the car. "Don't call us, we'll call you," she told him as she winked at him.

This time when Rusty's father dropped her off, he looked especially upset. "We can't keep on like this," he told her. "It's time we figured a way out of here."

"Dad," Rusty asked, "do you really mean it? I mean, would you really help me?"

"I would, my girl," he said without hesitating. Rusty didn't remember him ever sounding so determined about anything.

"You could say that Dr. Li in the Admissions building helped me more," Rusty told him. "They can't let the patients from here see any therapists except the ones who work here, so they'd have to transfer me out of Graylock, in your custody, and readmit me to the Admissions building."

Rusty looked hard at her father. He would have to get notes from Dr. Li in admissions. He'd have to fight with the doctors and the staff at Graylock. He'd have to effectively convince them that Rusty could only get well if she could be admitted again and see Dr. Li. He'd have to sign papers accepting all the responsibility for whatever happened. It was up to him again. Rusty wondered if he believed in her enough to do it and if he was strong enough to carry it off. She watched her father's gray eyes carefully as she spoke, for any hint of a doubt. But there was none.

When we get you discharged from Graylock, instead of signing you back into the Admissions building and we walk out of this building," Daniel Russell said triumphantly, "we just keep walking. We'll just keep walking home. . ."

Rusty's father did everything right. Rusty escaped Graylock on Thursday and as soon as she put her bags down in the living room, the phone rang. When her mother answered, Rusty knew by the affectation in her voice that it was someone important. Neither she nor her father dared to breathe.

Covering the mouthpiece on the phone, her mother whispered, "It's Salvation Nursing Home. They're asking to speak to a Miss Barbara Russell."

Rusty grabbed the phone and said hello.

"Would you be able to begin Monday morning?"Mrs. Gordon, the directress, asked, "or must you give two weeks' notice at your current place of employment?"

"I can start Monday," Rusty replied, puzzled. She had put no place of employment on her application so she wondered if the woman had made an error. Until she saw the sheepish grin on her father's face.

"What did you tell them?" she asked him after she'd hung up.

"I didn't lie," he protested weakly. "When they called yesterday I just said you weren't home and when they asked where you could be reached, I answered, "Rambling Woods." He laughed when he added, "I guess they thought you worked there."

❖❖ ❖❖ ❖❖

Daniel Russell was sixty-eight but he looked eighty-eight. Life had beaten him; time had worn him down.

As soon as Rusty got the job at Salvation, he handed her the keys to his car and told her, "Get a license. I don't want to drive anymore." She had her license within a couple of weeks.

Rusty had known her dad was no fireball but now he seemed so listless and lethargic that she worried about him. She thought maybe that last bit of effort he had put into helping her escape had used up too much of his energy. The week before, he had gone to the doctor and found he had a clot in his leg, but nothing else seemed to be wrong with him physically. So Rusty had been helping him put his legs up on the small tattered ottoman and applying warm soaks to his calf three times a day. After all, she was doing as much for the old people in Salvation.

Every day now Rusty was going to work and loving it. Taking care of people who couldn't help themselves gave her a feeling of self-respect she never had before. Getting paid for it was a bonus. She was happy. She was still taking her Dilantin and phenobarbital but had stopped taking the Elavil and Mellaril, and her seizures were well controlled.

Often Rusty and Arlene went out driving. Rusty was enjoying her freedom and new station in life and Arlene was thrilled to have her old buddy back. They talked and giggled and stopped in old parks and graveyards, using Rusty's father's car as they had their bicycles in the old days.

Usually the girls took turns driving. One night, after a long and pleasant ride, Rusty and Arlene pulled into a gas station. It was time to switch drivers. Arlene got behind the wheel. She quickly put the car in gear, missed first gear and went in reverse. She backed right through the plateglass window of the gas station into the office. Rusty was stunned. She worried that if the police saw her license they might notify Rambling Woods and she could be scooped right back in. She was in trouble.

The car was badly dented but drivable and so after Arlene's

father had offered to pay expenses, Rusty drove the car home.

Rusty knew her fear that her father would find out was not fear of his retaliation but rather fear of upsetting him. Often he looked as though any more trouble would make him give up.

When she reached her corner, she could see several police cars parked in front of her house and another one in the driveway. Shit! she thought. The gas station owner called the cops.

Rusty put the car in reverse, turned around and drove along a dirt road behind her house. There were no lights and it was pitch black but from there she could watch everything that was going on. She waited for a long time, certain that if she went home they'd arrest her. She heard a high-pitched wail, the sound of a woman screaming or a dog howling. She couldn't be sure.

Then suddenly something pierced through the fog of panic in Rusty's brain. The police car in the driveway was backed in. The only reason for that was an emergency. Medical equipment was kept in the trunk.

Without thinking, Rusty jumped out of the car and ran through the backyard to the door. The screen was locked. She circled the garage, heart racing, feet barely touching ground, and as she flew past the police car she saw that the trunk was open-and empty.

At the front door, a policeman stood guard and tried to block Rusty's path.

Huffing and puffing, she tried to explain, "I'm the daughter of . . ." She didn't know which of her parents was sick. "I'm their daughter," she said quickly.

The policeman moved aside and Rusty ran into the living room. The room was filled with neighbors and Rusty scanned it quickly. Finally she saw her mother sitting on the couch. It was her father.

She walked right past everyone into the back bedroom where she asked another policeman at the door, How is he?"

"Fine, fine," the young policeman said.

Rusty moved close to the bed. She looked at her father. Gray skin, dead stare, no response. She had seen people like this before. At Rambling Woods, and at Salvation. She knew her father had had a stroke. He was in a coma.

When the ambulance came, everything was chaotic. The technicians took one look at him and threw him on the small stretcher they wheeled in.

Rusty held the door as her father was carried out.

The next afternoon when Rusty finished work at Salvation, she drove straight to Community Corners Hospital.

Her mother was sitting next to her father with the same expression that Rusty had seen so many times before when she herself was lying in the hospital bed. It was a mixture of bewilderment and suffering, as though she had been forced to carry an overwhelming burden and she would just have to wait her way through it. It was a passive rather than active expression, as though it had been pasted on from the outside rather than projected from the inside.

She glanced up momentarily, then looked back toward bed again without greeting her daughter.

"Hi, Dad," Rusty said as she took her father's hand. "How are you feeling?"

Rusty's father looked at her and smiled the polite smile of a stranger. "Well, hello, dear," he said quietly. "Did you come to collect the rabbits?" He didn't seem to know who she was. Throughout the afternoon as Rusty washed her father and changed his soiled sheets, while her mother watched blankly, he spoke in gibberish and unconnected sentences. And though his limbs could move up, down and around, his mind could only go backwards.

Rusty was glad, in a way, that he had lost contact with reality. The reality, the indignity of his situation would have humiliated him. As far as she was concerned, her father had died the night before. It would be much easier to take care of this stranger, unshackled by the restraints of their history, familiarity and intimacy.

Rusty had by now forgiven her father; she felt neither anger toward him nor guilt over him. Now he was an old man who was dying and needed to be taken care of. Rusty could do it best.

For three weeks Rusty worked her shift at Salvation, went home afterward to have a bite to eat and get her clothes ready for the following day, picked up her mom and drove to Community Corners to spend the night with her dad. The staff often neglected him, knowing that Rusty was coming.

One night when she arrived, her father lay asleep gurgling through an unswallowed portion of food left in his mouth. The dinner tray had been left across the room. Rusty understood that someone had started to feed him, he had dozed and they had left him and gone on to do other things. She began coming earlier and staying later.

Another night she found him with dry caked feces on his macerated buttocks and almost always found him soaked in dark yellow urine. When she complained to the nurses, many of whom remembered her from her own admissions, they inserted a Foley catheter into his penis to drain his urine constantly. But he still seldom got any real care other than what Rusty gave him.

During this entire time Rusty's mother either sat immobile by the bedside or stayed home and got drunk. Then Rusty would have to clean Nona up also before she could go to sleep.

The last night Rusty came in, she found her father tied down tight in bed. The nurse told Rusty that he had gotten more and more confused and they didn't want him to fall out of bed. Rusty, because of her own antipathy toward straitjackets and because of the pathos of the vision of this thin and wasted dying old man, untied him immediately. Then she spent the rest of the night trying to keep the terrified, frightened man who was her father from leaping out of bed.

Several times a nurse came in when Rusty asked, "Can't he have oxygen? I think he's having trouble breathing." They finally brought oxygen and started an IV.

Whenever Rusty tried to convince her father to go to sleep he cried in a panicky voice, "I can't. I'll never wake up." And so Rusty hugged and petted, smoothed and soothed her father throughout the night, as she had done for all the others.

He was confused most of the time, but toward morning, in a moment of lucidity, he asked Rusty, "Do you know Fred?"

Fred, the cat, had lived with them for years. A scruffy ugly old Tomcat with orange-and-black fur. Rusty's father swore he hated that cat but several times in the early morning when he thought no one else was awake, Rusty had seen her father feed Fred and even share his coffee with Fred.

Now Rusty answered her father, "Sure, Dad. I know Fred."

The old man's eyes lit tip and he smiled. "Rusty," he asked for the first time since he'd stroked out, "Rusty, my girl, would you take care of Fred?"

"Sure, Dad," she answered, touching his cheek. "Don't worry about Fred." And with that the old man closed his eyes and stopped breathing.

There's nothing so soundless and still as the absence of breath in the human body. Its exquisite silence radiates outward, calls a halt to time. In that one frozen moment, our universe seems to stop to reorder itself, to accommodate to its loss.

Rusty turned the oxygen off. Then she sat in the chair and put her head back. She remembered the way Fred rubbed up against her father in those early morning scenes. The way the cat looked up at him admiringly. And Rusty understood why the old man's last thought was for the cat. It was simple: Fred expected only to be fed. And Daniel Russell could handle that.

Rusty walked down to the nurses' station, her legs leaden. What she felt must have been written on her face, because as soon as the nurse looked up, she dropped her pen, got up from the desk and began to hurry down the hall toward the room.

"He's gone," Rusty said, and she followed the nurse down the hall.

When the nurse had made certain that Rusty was right, that her father had died, the house doctor was called to double check.

The doctor asked Rusty, "Will you tell your mother or shall I call her?" Rusty agreed to do it.

"Will you please collect all your father's belongings and take them home with you?" the nurse asked hesitantly.

"Sure," Rusty said. It would be no trouble. All her father's belongings fit into the small shaving case that her mother had borrowed from a neighbor.

The following day, Rusty went to the Catholic church in town to ask for help. The priest who answered the door had a bulbous red nose and fidgeted nervously with his black rosary beads. His sparse hair looked uncombed, as though he had just awakened, and though he smiled, he seemed preoccupied and, Rusty thought, somehow guilty.

"My father just died," Rusty told the priest, "and I'd like you to say a Mass for him. But I have no money."

The priest flushed with embarrassment and he muttered and mumbled for several minutes before Rusty could hear him say, "I'm sorry, dear, but I'm not able to grant your request." He gave her no explanation, and after they both stood uncomfortably silent for a while, Rusty just excused herself and left. She wasn't even angry, she was hurt.

One of the neighbors donated a suit and socks, but Daniel Russell was buried without shoes. The priest at the graveside who eulogized him was drunk and so he called him Joseph. Rusty often wondered whether the prayers that were said that day for Joseph were credited to her father's account. Daniel Russell had been a dreamer but he wasn't a bad man. Rusty hoped that in heaven a man was judged by his intentions.

"You finally get out of the nuthouse and your father dies on you?" I wailed. "I can't stand it."

"That was only six months before I met you," Rusty said.

"What an adolescence you had," I moaned. "And I thought mine was rough. All I had was a little rejection. Nobody asked me to join the sorority in school. And of course my divorce which knocked me on my ass because I never imagined anything like that could ever happen. Still, I barely survived a regular life. Again, I ask, how the hell did you do it?"

"With difficulty. A day at a time."

"Considering all the bad things that could happen to you every day, how come you weren't afraid?" I asked.

"Oh, my God, Carol, where did you ever get the idea I wasn't afraid?" Rusty asked. "Did I say that?"

"Not exactly," I answered, "but I guess I figured by the way you live, you're not afraid."

Rusty shook her head. "Wrong," she said simply.

"Then how do you do it?" I asked. "How can you smile when you get up each day?"

She laughed. A real, charming, gleeful laugh. "Well, have you ever done anything that took all your courage, that was so big a challenge that you were not sure you were equipped to face it? That you felt you might not be able to overcome the difficulties? That you just might fail?"

I nodded.

"Well, you know that feeling of victory you get when you succeed, the tremendous high when you feel so good about yourself and your accomplishments that you can hardly stand it?"

I nodded again.

"Well, each day that I stay on my feet all day, each day I can see, hear, feel and smell what everyone else does, and each night that I go to sleep in my own bed, I climb under the covers with that feeling of victory. Sure, I have the fear each day, but I also have the victory." Rusty looked serious. "That's really all anyone can hope for, isn't it, Carol?"

For each of us, a victory each day. What a miracle if we could feel that way. Most of us lived life as though we were married to it; Rusty lived life as an affair. I looked at her, this child really, who'd been through more than I could ever handle, and come out of it so well. I marveled at her wisdom and her courage. I felt humble in the face of it.

A thick winter cover of powdery snow capped the cars and rooftops of the houses as the kids and I drove home.

"That was a great birthday party Gram had for you, wasn't it, Mom?" Lynn asked.

"Great, honey," I said. I was driving slowly, trying not to skid on the slushy streets that were quickly becoming glasslike.

"Wish Rusty came," Jeremy said, leaning forward from the back seat to hug me.

"She had a headache, honey," I told him. On the front seat he had carefully placed a piece of cake from the party to give her when we got home. "But I'm sure she'll love to hear about it later."

Rusty and Jeremy really had gotten very close in the past few months. After all, Rusty was the one who made him breakfast and took him to school each day and Rusty was the one he could talk to when I had yelled or gotten angry with him. Creede always took my side, but invariably Rusty understood Jeremy.

When we finally pulled into the driveway, Lynn and Jeremy immediately jumped out of the car. He quickly threw himself down backwards into deep snow in the front yard. "Jeremy," I hollered, "what the hell are you doing? Get up this minute; you'll freeze to death."

He was lying on his back and waving his arms up and down in the snow. Carefully then he moved each of his legs sideways. Lynn was standing next to me, just watching.

"Jeremy," I said more seriously, "if you don't get up this minute, I'm going to kill you." When he kept moving his arms and legs, I asked, "What on earth are you doing? I swear you look like a little lunatic."

"It's a surprise," Lynn said, smiling. "Just give him a minute."

I tried to move close to Jeremy to scoop him up, but he shouted, "Halt! Please, Mom. Don't mess it up. . . One more minute."

Lynn and I stood shivering in the cold moonlit night until Jeremy carefully stood up. Then he asked quietly, "Now, please, Mom, stand as far back as you can and pick me up." I started to walk closer and Jeremy pleaded, "Mom, be careful. Don't make tracks."

I stood and reached forward as he jumped into my arms. Then he hurriedly covered my eyes with his small hand.

"Now look!" he said, pulling his hand away. His voice was quiet and excited. "An angel!" Sure enough, on the snow-covered front lawn lay the shimmering figure of a small angel, outspread wings and all.

"Wow!" I said, looking into Jeremy's sparkling face. "Where did you learn that?"

He struggled out of my arms and stood next to us in the snow, just staring for a moment before he answered, "Rusty. She said on special nights, in special snows, with special children, if you do that, a snow angel appears. And it did, Mom. It did!"

"Magic," I said as I smiled at him. Then we all walked up to the front door and knocked. When Rusty didn't answer after the second knock, I started to get nervous. I rummaged through my pocketbook until I found my keys, and then quickly let myself in. Jeremy started calling for Rusty right away, but Lynn stayed planted by the front door.

We checked the living room, then the bedrooms and the bathroom. Couldn't find her. When I smelled some thing burning from the kitchen, I started to walk toward it.

"Rusty?" Jeremy called again in a loud voice, but as I reached the kitchen, I knew why she hadn't answered.

She was lying on the floor in front of the stove, out cold. The teakettle was blackened, burned. I quickly shut the gas, then bent to try to wake Rusty. I noticed she had a large bruise on the right side of her head just under her fine blond bangs where she must have hit the stove as she fell.

Lynn had disappeared but Jeremy was standing stark white and quiet, frozen in the doorway. "She'll be all right, Jeremy," I told him quietly. "Really she will."

I tried to lift her up by the shoulders but she was too heavy for me, and as I laid her head back down on the white vinyl floor, her body began to tremble.

And I began to panic. The thing I had been worrying about for months, Rusty's first seizure, and how the kids were going to handle it, all flew through my mind now "You can wait inside if you like, Jer," I said in as calm a tone as I could manage, but even as his large brown eyes widened, he shook his head.

I just knew Lynn was hiding upstairs in her room. I frantically looked around for some blankets to pad the floor so Rusty wouldn't hurt her head, and for something soft enough to put in her mouth. But before I could move, I heard the sound of Rusty's tongue clicking on the roof of her mouth. I didn't know it at the time, but that click was to be my warning in the years to come. An ominous timer which, once set, would give us only seconds before Rusty fell to the floor in a full-fledged seizure.

Now the fingers of her hands curled and her wrists snapped inward. Click, click, and her head shot to the side. Click, click, and her teeth came down hard on the side of her tongue. I shouted at Jeremy to get a pillow just before Rusty's body stiffened in an arch so severe that only the back of her head and her heels supported her. After long seconds, her body collapsed. Soon she stiffened again.

Jeremy was crying as he knelt down next to me. "Mommy, is she hurting herself?" he asked as Rusty's head came down hard again and again on the kitchen floor. There had been no time for him to get the pillow.

"Rusty can't feel what's happening now," I told him. "It's like she's asleep." I tried to move him away from her thrashing arms but his worry kept him glued to one spot.

After several minutes, Rusty lay quiet and pale. The clicking had stopped and only her eyes, under her eyelids, still twitched.

"Is she all right now, Mommy?" Jeremy asked quietly.

"I think so," I said, putting my arm around his shoulder. He reached out and held Rusty's limp hand tightly.

"Is it over now, Mommy?" he asked after several minutes.

"Yes, honey," I told him softly.

"Good," he said.

Then Jeremy lay down on the kitchen floor next to Rusty and put his small arm around her neck, while we both waited for her to wake up.

CHAPTER 14

Maybe I really should have worn a headdress. It must have been easier in primitive times. The Vision Quest. The transformative journey. The path wasn't brightly lit or marked with big green signs like a modern thruway. In fact, I finally figured out that I'd have to sniff like a bloodhound or track like an Indian scout in order even to land on the path, never mind reach my destination. I'd have to check for the smashed leaves and listen for the broken twigs of the women who'd gone before me. Rusty was one of them. They had faced their shadows, they had grappled with their illusions.

I had spent the whole day calling several doctors I had worked with, doctors I had heard of, doctors others had recommended, but without regular hospitalization coverage or cash, no one would see Rusty. These paragons of virtue I had looked up to–was it possible that money was their motivation, not healing and helping? I couldn't believe it. My faith was waning.

Dr. Jeff Lamberta was my last hope. He was a new doctor in town, an internist, who was not yet well established. I had met him a few times while working at the hospital and hadn't been impressed with him. He seemed competent enough, that wasn't the problem; it was his constant good humor that had put me off. And the way he dressed. He was a real fashion plate, always wore the latest styles. dark hair combed in place, and even in the middle of the night, he never seemed to need a shave. It was absolutely inconceivable for me to think of a doctor who spent so much time caring for himself being capable of really caring for others. I didn't expect much when he answered the phone.

"Dr. Lamberta, you don't know me," I began, a little less breathlessly than I had on the previous forty phone calls, "but I'm a nurse and I have this problem. There's a twenty-year-old girl who has epilepsy and her seizures have just gone out of control and we need help. She's had eleven grand-mal seizures in just about as many days and we can't get a doctor to take care of her." I was about to continue with the hard-sell routine except that he cut me off.

"All right," Dr. Lamberta agreed, "bring her to my office this evening and I'll take a look at her."

"We don't have any insurance but Medicaid," I told him apologetically. And then I held my breath.

"I didn't say anything about payment," he said.

I hung up and went flying down the steps, faith renewed, to tell Rusty. "Whoopie," I hollered, landing in the living room, "we have acquired a real live physician and one whose main concern wasn't even money. There are still miracles in this world."

Rusty was sitting quietly on the couch, and when I plopped down next to her, she looked over at me and smiled. "Aren't you happy?" I asked her.

She put down the book she had been reading and said, "I do

appreciate your trying to help me. It's just that I've been to enough doctors not to think of them as miracle workers."

I hoped she was wrong.

The last two weeks had been difficult. Partially because of a lack of imagination on my part. After Rusty's first seizure, I was sure we'd have time to recover, get our balance and get on with normal living, before it happened again. By the expression on Rusty's face when she first woke up, I should have gotten the clue that she knew something I didn't, but it took me a while to catch on. So we didn't devise anything special, and both of us tried to ignore the fact of her seizures for a while. I was trying hard not to make a federal case out of them because I didn't want Rusty to feel bad.

During the first week, most of Rusty's seizures had come in the middle of the night and so we had managed to escape the questions of the kids while we both continued to work. But by the second week, the seizures started hitting her with the force of a boxer's punches in the final round of the Golden Gloves championship match. She was hardly on her feet before she was knocked out again. We knew that something had to be done fast.

The plan inside my head was pretty simple. First, a good doctor to prescribe the right medicine. Acceptance by me of Rusty's epilepsy would certainly erase the effects of all the previous prejudices she had had to endure. And, of course, emotional support until we could get through a temporary period of crisis and then the eventual return to normal life, everything solved perfectly. In other words, a happily-ever-after story.

I called Salvation and told them we both had a virus and we'd be out of work for a few days. Rusty increased her Dilantin from three to four times a day and added one-half grain of phenobarb three times a day. It didn't seem to help.

I had even called to make her an appointment with my favorite shrink so she'd have someone to talk to in case anything special was bothering her. Both of us knew that stress could trigger seizures, in the same way stress could aggravate an ulcer.

Dr. Nelson was a marvelous psychiatrist who had the added advantage of having been a general practitioner for more than ten years: a man who knew well both the body and the mind. I figured he'd be perfect. He was a heavy, messy, gentle man, and his dress was abominable. Polka dots and plaids and all the wrong colors together. But his large dark eyes held a look of compassion so profound that I never really saw anything else. I met him when I had worked at one of the state psychiatric hospitals during my nurse's training and his caring and understanding so impressed me that when I had personal problems and was getting divorced, he was the one I went to for help.

When I called him with Rusty's problem, all he said was, "She doesn't need an appointment with a psychiatrist. Not yet anyway." And then, "Epilepsy is a physical disease, Carol. Before she sees anyone, her seizures need to be controlled. Just think about it. If when you woke up in the morning, you didn't know whether you were going to make it across the street, up a flight of stairs or through the day without falling on your face, would you have psychological problems or would any fears you had be justified? Get her to a doctor and get those seizures controlled." A really smart man, Dr. Nelson.

Most of the patients had gone by the time Rusty and I got to Dr. Lamberta's office that night. The one old lady who was still sitting on the Early American couch in his waiting room looked as though she had been sitting so long that she had become a fixture. She had one arm in a cast and a bandage over her forehead. Rusty and I sat on the two chairs across the room. The receptionist, a tall, good-looking woman, was talking on the phone and so hadn't acknowledged us when we came in. But as soon as she hung up, she smiled at us and asked, "Are you one of the doctor's special patients?"

Rusty looked embarrassed, and I was sure she thought that the receptionist was referring to her inability to pay. "My name is Carol," I told the receptionist, "and this is Barbara Russell. I talked to the doctor earlier and he said we could just come in tonight."

The woman laughed good-naturedly and explained, "That's what I meant about special patients. Every day for the last two months, there have been several patients waiting for the doctor when my appointment book says we're finished. Whenever I've questioned them, they've told me that they've talked to the doctor and he told them to just drop in. Whenever I ask the doctor about it, he always says, 'I had to see them, they're special patients'. It's gotten to be a joke around here. The doctor usually has more specials than regulars."

Rusty had just started to relax when the receptionist called us into the office. Then, as I watched, her whole body tensed. "Come on, Rusty," I said, grabbing her hand and pulling her off her chair. "It's only an examination, not an execution." By the way she looked at me I knew she didn't believe it.

Inside the clean white examining room Rusty perched on the hard narrow table while I sat in the small metal chair in the corner. She had said very little since we had left home, and now, because of the silence, we both could hear Dr. Lamberta talking and laughing with another patient. Without thinking, I found myself smiling. "It must be that lady with the broken arm," I said to Rusty, trying to take her mind off the waiting.

"Must be," was all she answered.

When the doctor finally opened the door and came inside, I could tell by Rusty's expression that he wasn't what she had expected. I was grateful that she looked relieved.

My previous impression of Jeff Lamberta had been all wrong. Now he didn't seem vain. There was something about the tentative smile and his lowered eyes that made him seem humble. He gave Rusty a broad grin when he walked over to the table, saying, "I hear you've been having a little trouble lately staying on your feet." He had hit just the right note. Rusty smiled too.

"I've been through this before," she told him quietly, "and no one's been able to do much about it. I hope this time won't be like the others."

"Let me have a quick look," he told Rusty, "and then we'll go inside and you can tell me what the other times were like."

He did a basic neurological examination: he checked her pupils, looked into her ears, made her close her eyes and touch her nose. He asked her to jump on one leg, then the other. Eyes closed, walk a straight line. She seemed okay to me. He weighed her–116 pounds. After he took her blood pressure, he asked us to meet him in his office.

We sat and talked for a long time. Dr. Lamberta seemed very

concerned and listened intently to everything Rusty had to say. I was thrilled, and relieved that now we'd have someone who really wanted to help Rusty get her seizures controlled. I was certain we were well on our way to finding the solution. When we finished, he suggested we increase her medication from a half-grain of phenobarbital to one grain, three times a day, keep the Dilantin at three a day, and add a new medication called Mysoline, two times a day. Then he told us that we should see a neurologist for further testing. The neurologist he suggested was Dr. Aaron Schlunk and Dr. Lamberta assured us that they would work together to make sure Rusty got the best of care. Things were looking up.

But in the car on the way home, Rusty seemed upset.

"What's wrong?" I asked.

"I hate to put you through all this trouble," she said sadly.

"No trouble," I said, smiling. "You're not heavy, you're my brother."

"Lucky for me you have such a sense of family," she said, trying to smile. "But seriously, you didn't take me on as a patient."

"I really don't mind helping out a friend," I assured her. When she still didn't cheer up, I added, "Besides, I didn't holler when you helped me with my kids, when you did everything around the house plus every bit of ironing, and ran all the errands that I didn't want to. Now it's my turn. And nursing's what I do best."

"But why are you willing to do it?" she persisted.

I wasn't used to Rusty being so tentative, surprised by her obvious vulnerability. "Did you see Man of La Mancha?" I asked. When she told me she hadn't, I explained, "In it, Don Quixote, who's this crazy kind of hero, has this loyal sidekick Sancho. One day somebody asks Sancho the same question. And do you know what he answers?" I laughed and in a loud voice sang, "Because I like him.. I really like him..."

Rusty smiled but said, "I'm serious."

I pretended to pull myself together and with mock solemnity said, "I probably owe it to you from my last life. You must have helped me then."

"Not good enough," she insisted, but her mood had lightened.

"I'm just virtuous," I teased. "In fact most people refer to me as 'too-good Carol'."

"Forget it," Rusty laughed. "That, I can't buy. My brain shorts out but it doesn't shut down."

"All right," I said, "if you won't accept anything else, I'll have to tell you the truth."

Rusty was waiting expectantly.

"You make me laugh," I told her.

This time Rusty called Dr. Nelson. "Do I have to stop working and driving the car?" she asked him.

"Only when you're not fully alert," he told her.

"But what if I have a seizure?" she asked.

"You'll probably be fine at work. And seizures while driving are far less frequent than heart attacks. Don't stop functioning while you're able to," he insisted.

It was funny about Rusty's consciousness. Just before a seizure and for a short time afterward, her level of consciousness would shift and she'd get confused. During those times her eyes held a look of bewildered uncertainty and innocence Jeremy had lost by the age of two and Lynn never had.

Once in my life I saw a picture that captured it in a National Geographic: a child from a cannibal tribe who had never been exposed to civilization. The child was naked and wore a ring of blood around her mouth from the raw meat she had just eaten. But the expression she wore was anything but primitive, it was transcendent, angelic. If was absolutely undefended, without a sense of guilt or evil, or shame. How old are we when we learn those feelings? I wondered. The picture was a ghost of a time in a faraway garden before Adam and Eve ever sinned. I was touched by it. Of course, as the child stared at the camera, it stole that look.

But most of the time, Rusty was as alert and capable as ever and so it was a real juggling act for me to break off the need to protect her when she was no longer confused and to move in to help her when she was. Often the change occurred in minutes and without warning. I was constantly on the alert, in the same way I listened for my kids to cry at home, or watched an irregular monitor in the hospital.

For several days after we saw Dr. Lamberta, Rusty had no seizures. We both went back to work and Rusty seemed fine. I thought the medication increase that Dr. Lamberta bad suggested was working. I began to relax again.

"How about a visit to the museum?" I asked Rusty and the kids as we sat in the living room on Saturday morning. "How about a trip into the city, dinner, and dinosaurs?"

Jeremy jumped up and clapped. "I want to see the dinosaurs."

Lynn said, "Could we see the Indians again?"

I nodded and turned to Rusty. "What do you think, kiddo?"

She smiled. "I've never been to a museum," she said. "It sounds like fun."

And so we packed everyone in my car and took off.

Rusty seemed perfectly healthy and happy. The kids and she walked so fast through all the rooms, running from one exhibit to another, that it was almost impossible for me to keep up with them.

At the dinosaur exhibit, when Rusty reached out to touch the bleached white bones of a large mammoth, Jeremy whispered, "Watch it, Rusty. That thing will fall on you if you make his rib loose." Rusty smiled. I laughed at the thought of the dinosaur collapsing from one touch like a house of cards. Lynn smiled. And the guard at the door looked grim.

We went to see the stuffed bears, the carved wooden Indians in full warfare regalia, the stuffed tigers and lions, and then on to the old weapons room and the jewelry rooms-and finally I wailed, "No more. I can't tolerate another minute of this."

"But it's fun," Jeremy insisted.

"It's interesting," Lynn told me.

"It's really an adventure," Rusty added.

"Well, I've had enough of fun, and interesting things and adventures," I said. "One more minute and I'll die on my feet."

"That would really mess up an otherwise perfect day," Rusty

told the kids. And so we left the museum.

On the way to the parking lot, we stopped and bought chestnuts from the silver cart outside. And pretzels, and hot dogs, and ice cream.

It was cold out. I kept having to rub my arms and flex my fingers to keep them from getting stiff. But Rusty and the kids raced each other to the car and so by the time I caught up they were rosy-cheeked and sweating.

Everyone fell asleep on the way home. I drove the long dark expanse of highway in the silent night, and thought about what a lovely day it had been. As though Rusty had read my mind, with eyes still closed she said, "Thanks, Carol. Today was great."

The following week Rusty was sick again. We piled into Creede's blue station wagon and drove the half-hour to Dr. Schlunk's office. Creede had offered, as I knew she would, to help in any way she could, once Rusty had gotten sick. And Rusty was really sick now. Sometimes, though, she didn't have a regular seizure, she just wasn't as sharp as usual. Occasionally a grand-mal seizure would follow, but at other times the period of confusion would just pass.

Rusty had been missing pieces of my conversation all morning, and I knew that meant an alternation in her level of consciousness. It wasn't that she couldn't hear me, it was just that what I said sometimes didn't register in her brain . . . or she couldn't speak. Today, at least the doctor would be able to view her symptoms firsthand. Creede drove carefully, only occasionally looking over at Rusty, who was sitting between us on the front seat. I chatted nervously, casting knowing glances across Rusty to Creede each time Rusty didn't answer a question or comment on what I had said. I was worried that if Rusty went into seizure now, Creede would lose control of the car. It had been foolish of us, I thought, to have her up front, but Creede would have it no other way.

"We can't keep treating her as though she's going to have a seizure anytime. We can't act as though we expect it," she had told me that morning. "Unconsciously, people live up to others' expectations." Rusty had been in the bathroom at the time, getting ready, and I didn't argue with Creede because I was having a heart attack, all my attention focused toward the bathroom, waiting to hear the sound of Rusty's bead hitting the tile floor or the bottom of the shower.

"Negative expectations, bullshit," I whispered to Creede. "It's just good common sense."

When we arrived at the new brick medical building, I was still muttering to myself over Creede's stubbornness even though she had been right and Rusty hadn't had a seizure. But as we walked up the slick marble steps to Dr. Schlunk's office, Rusty seemed uncertain in her gait. She wobbled.

"Are you okay?" I asked. I tried to stay on the same step as she so I could watch her carefully.

Creede, who insisted on walking behind us, reassured, "She'll be fine." Rusty was silent. When I looked over my shoulder at Creede, she warned again with her eyes to say no more.

Dr. Schlunk's office was small but elegantly furnished. Four dainty gold-and-green velvet chairs lined the bamboo walls on which hung several small delicately painted Chinese prints framed in gold. He obviously had a successful practice.

Creede led Rusty over to one of the chairs as I walked up to the sliding glass window to announce our arrival to the receptionist. There were no other patients waiting.

After I knocked on the pane several times and got no response, I walked back and sat in one of the chairs next to Rusty. When I asked again, "Are you nervous?" and she didn't even nod, I was even more upset. Creede shook her head, obviously giving up the hope that I could ever be cool, and then began gaily to rattle off some fairy tale about gremlins and goblins. It made me crazy when Creede treated her like a child, but Rusty watched her, rapt, her face mirroring each expression of Creede's. I was sure then that Rusty was picking up the feeling and not really even hearing the words.

I wondered where Dr. Schlunk was and if the new medicine that Dr. Lamberta had given Rusty was making her spacey. Maybe she's so frightened, I thought, that she's just paralyzed. Still, some nagging feeling warned me that she was going to "flip out," as she called it, and the doctor we had traveled to see was going to miss it.

Suddenly the door in the corner of the room swung open and a tall man with curly dark hair and wire-rimmed glasses appeared. His blue shirt sleeves were rolled to the elbows and his brown baggy pants badly needed pressing.

"Hi," I said, walking toward him. I pointed behind me. "This is Barbara Russell. Dr. Lamberta sent us."

The man looked as though he couldn't quite grasp what I had said. His eyes were as uncomprehending as Rusty's. Then without warning he turned and walked back through the door as I stood staring after him. "Come in," I heard him say from somewhere in the bowels of his office. "Come in and bring her with you."

He was weird. My head was shaking with disbelief as I walked over and grabbed Rusty's hand. Creede sat back in her chair and said calmly, "Just call if you need me."

Rusty followed me like a blind person, bumping into the wall when I turned the corner too quickly. I found Dr. Schlunk hiding out in a tiny examining room. It was painted in high-luster white enamel, and held only one examining table and one tall white metal cabinet. I led Rusty over to the narrow table and patted the top, indicating that she should sit. She managed to hoist herself up more clumsily than if she was well and seemed to be balancing on a see-saw.

As Dr. Schlunk got close, I could hear Rusty's tongue click, and so I whispered to him, "I think she's going to have a seizure."

He looked as though I had spilled hot water on him, he jumped back so quickly. "When?" he asked hoarsely. I looked at him carefully. I couldn't believe he was a neurologist; he actually looked panic-stricken. Suddenly his expression changed–I thought because he had read mine–and he stood taller and took a deep breath. Then he gave me a false confident smile and said caustically, "You just let me know exactly when."

Dr. Schlunk was standing directly in front of Rusty, who was sitting on the end of the table. He picked up his little steel reflex hammer and tapped gently on her right knee. When she didn't react, he tapped harder. Then he tapped one more time, too hard. I winced but Rusty still didn't react.

"Didn't you feel that, dear?" Dr. Schlunk asked. Rusty didn't answer. So he took a pin and pricked her right hand, right arm, and then her cheek on the right side. Nothing. When he pricked the left cheek, he drew blood. I wanted to smack him. I'd seen neurological examinations before, but none seemed as brutal. My hands and teeth were clenched but I resisted saying anything because I hoped there was some method to his madness. Still, I hated his tableside manner. I didn't know whether he disliked sick people, had a lousy disposition, or was just pissed because he had to see someone who couldn't pay a large fee and he had to do it because another doctor had asked.

Dr. Schlunk stopped and looked hard at Rusty. Then he walked over and pulled a cotton ball out of a container in the medicine cabinet. Just as he was bringing the cotton up toward her face, I could see her eyes roll upward.

"Oh, come on," Dr. Schlunk said, annoyed, as Rusty's head started to pull toward the left and tilt back. Then he roughly rubbed the cotton ball he held across Rusty's open eyeball. I was about to embark upon a monumental tirade, when I saw Rusty's thumbs curl, fingers fold over and wrists snap in. I grabbed for Dr. Schlunk's arm and hissed, "She's going to have a . . ."

Before I could finish, he had drawn his hand back as though to pitch a fast ball, and come forward with a slap to Rusty's face that almost knocked her off the narrow table.

The next few seconds were a blur and a buzz. Rusty fell backward in a full-blown seizure, her body banging, crashing and sliding. Dr. Schlunk ran from the room and I screamed "Creede!" before I noticed that she was already standing across from me–Rusty between us–our bodies positioned like guardrails to keep Rusty from catapulting and landing on the hard tile floor.

When the seizure had passed, Creede asked, "What the hell happened?" Her fair skin was flushed and her hair a mess. She had taken most of the beating because Rusty's body was closer to her side of the table. "And where the hell is that doctor?"

Then from the next room we both heard a man's frantic voice shouting into a phone, "Dr. Lamberta stat!" and then, "Jeff? Jeff? This one's for real. I thought the tests were negative!"

Creede and I stared at each other, shocked. At the same moment we both realized that the entire time he was examining Rusty, the

Great Doctor Schlunk thought she had been faking.

"Jesus, Mary and Arthur!" Creede said with disgust.

"What a creep!" I agreed.

Rusty was quiet on the table between us. She had already stopped convulsing when Dr. Schlunk reentered the room and rushed past us to the medicine cabinet. With shaking hands, he reached for a syringe and then fumbled as he broke off the top of the glass vial he was holding. He started to draw up some liquid, when I asked, "What's that?"

"Amytal," he answered curtly.

I knew that was a sedative. "How much?" I asked.

"Seven and a half," he said quickly.

From the table beneath us came, "Click, click," and both Creede and I moved close again, knowing what that meant.

"This will knock out an elephant," Dr. Schlunk said, approaching cautiously while wielding the syringe like a spear.

"It won't touch her," Creede said dryly.

Dr. Schlunk gave the injection and then stood back smugly. But before he had a chance to enjoy his victory, before Creede and I could lift Rusty off the table and put her onto the rug in the next room, she click, clicked once again . . . and was gone.

Thrash, bang, flurry, crash, crack, went Rusty on the tabletop again, and at the same time, Dr. Schlunk was pinned against the white wall by his fear as though by gangsters. I truly couldn't understand him. It always stunned me to realize that doctors were human beings subject to the same fears, attitudes and prejudices as the rest of the world. Invariably that made me feel cheated, as though I'd been ripped off. Rusty was strong in seizure but you couldn't get hurt unless you stood directly in the way of one of her flailing limbs.

Creede and I just braced ourselves on either side of the table until the second seizure was over.

"Should we call an ambulance?" Dr. Schlunk asked breathlessly. But I couldn't even answer him, I was so angry.

"Forget it," Creede said. "Give her a few minutes and we'll walk her out."

By the time we got home an hour later, Rusty still wasn't quite right. She had walked, as Creede told Dr. Schlunk she could, but hadn't answered any of the questions we asked. Hadn't talked at all in fact. I tried to sound cheerful, though I was disappointed, and Creede told more stories, which Rusty seemed, by her expression, to enjoy, but everything was strained. When we began to undress Rusty to get her into bed, she looked as though she didn't recognize either of us. I was afraid that she would fall down the stairs if we tried to take her up to the bedroom and so Creede and I decided to open the couch in the living room and have her sleep down there for the night.

Finally when Rusty was undressed and in bed, she spoke. "I'm hungry," she said in a voice harsh and sharp. She looked angry. I was afraid that she would choke on anything we gave her so I offered, "How about a milk shake?" She nodded.

Creede sat down on the open sofa bed. When I brought Rusty the shake she grabbed it roughly and didn't say thank you. She just gulped it. "I want a cigarette," she demanded. I was surprised. It was so unlike Rusty to talk and act this way. I wasn't sure whether it was the injection of Amytal she had been given or an altered state of consciousness brought on by the seizures. Creede was watching her warily.

I went through Rusty's pocketbook until I found her cigarettes and lit one for her. "Hold this over the ashtray; please," I told her, "so you don't set fire to the covers." A look of anger crossed her face, but she said nothing.

Then I sat on the bed next to her, across from Creede, and watched as several small sparks hit the covers as they missed the ashtray. Creede said, "Rusty, look at what you're doing." And again I saw that strange look of anger cross Rusty's face. Creede and I tried to chat as we watched Rusty carefully, but she seemed oblivious of our presence.

"I want another cigarette."

"No" Creede told her. "Wait a little while until you're more awake. Until that medicine wears off a bit."

But Rusty reached for her pocketbook and grabbed the pack of cigarettes. I pulled them away. She tried to grab them back and I quickly pulled them away. "I'm going to throw them away if you don't stop," I told her. Rusty's eyes narrowed and her lips tightened. Quicker than a snake's tongue, her hand shot out and she almost had the pack. I stood, angry myself now, unreasonably feeling betrayed. I turned around and tossed the cigarettes into the trash.

But almost before the pack reached the pail, Rusty jumped for my back. And just that quickly Creede was on Rusty. For the next few minutes I wasn't sure what was happening. Creede now had Rusty back on the bed, facedown, pinned with her arm bent behind her. "Apologize, or I'll break it," Creede warned.

"Creede, don't . . ." I begged. "She doesn't know what she's doing. She's not thinking clearly."

"Say you're sorry," Creede insisted, bending Rusty's arm hard, "or you'll not have a chance to use this arm ever again."

"Creede, please!" I yelled. "Leave her alone. She's not thinking right."

Rusty's face was deep into the mattress; I could hear her whine, but she wouldn't talk. Creede, still holding her tight, still almost atop her, her knee in the small of Rusty's back, repeated, "Apologize." When I tried to get closer to talk to Creede, she told me, "No matter what her frame of mind, she can never be allowed to lay a hand on you without knowing that there'll be consequences. She doesn't need the ability for abstract reasoning to understand that. Every cell in her body will know by the time I'm finished with her. There are certain behaviors that are not acceptable on any level. And this is one of them. She must understand that. And you must realize that epilepsy is not the cause of this."

Creede was right in essence but I wasn't sure she was completely right. I knew epilepsy didn't cause the aggression, but with Rusty's lowered level of consciousness, the confusion and the sedative Dr. Schlunk had given her, I couldn't be positive how much of the situation Rusty could understand. If someone had just grabbed my cigarettes and tried to throw them away, when I didn't understand why, I might have been angry too. But this was no time to fight with Creede.

"I know, Creede," I told her, "but after being away all those years, she's learned to deal differently than we do."

"I'm sure you're right," she said, "but then she's in for some culture shock." With that, Creede twisted Rusty's arm so hard I could almost hear it crack.

Finally Rusty started to cry. "I'm sorry," she said, "I didn't mean it."

"You will never do it again," Creede said. "Is that understood?"

"I won't," Rusty said quickly.

Creede let her go, helped her up, and after wiping her tears, held her.

"You must never hurt like that," Creede said softly, "because afterward, when you are no longer angry, you will dislike yourself for it." Creede tousled Rusty's hair as though she were a small child, and then added, "This won't be mentioned again. Okay?"

Rusty lay down then, and within minutes was fast asleep. Creede and I sat talking for a while, wondering what was really happening. "I have to get us some books." I said.

Creede looked over to the couch where Rusty lay. "I'm afraid, my little friend," she said, "the answers we need aren't to be found in books."

When she was leaving, she hugged me. "I'm here," she said simply. And I was very glad she was.

The next day, early in the morning, Dr. Lamberta called. He told me that he had spoken to Dr. Schlunk.

"He's a jerk," I said, before he could say anything else "Why would he even think her seizures weren't real?"

"Psychogenic seizures have to be ruled out whenever a seizure disorder is being diagnosed," Dr. Lamberta explained. "And because none of her previous EEG's showed up positive, seizures due to psychological reasons had to be considered." He hesitated for a moment before he added, "Especially because of her previous history."

"There's no way her seizures aren't real," I told him. "I know that just by watching the changes in her consciousness."

"Dr. Schlunk agrees," Dr. Lamberta said gently. "Now, we have to find out why she's having them. I'd like to admit Rusty to the hospital for a few tests," he said.

"What kind?" I asked.

"An EEG and possibly a cerebral angiogram," he answered.

I was pacing up and down in the kitchen. From where I stood I could see Rusty sleeping on the sofa bed. I moved behind the wall and said softly, "She had EEG's."

He interrupted me. "The reports I received from Community Corners and Rambling Woods were negative. I would like to have a sophisticated EEG done, a sleep EEG, to see what we can uncover. Now that she's been having so many seizures, something might show up."

"And why the angiogram?" I asked.

"Just to make sure that all the blood vessels in her brain are normal," he explained. "I'd hate to think anything else besides the epilepsy is wrong, but we can't know without the tests."

I had never thought of that. "I'll ask her," I told him.

Dr. Lamberta hesitated and then said, "We will probably want to do a lumbar puncture while she's in, to make sure there's no infection or hemorrhage."

"Okay, I'll ask her," I repeated. I wanted to make sure that this time she would be included in the decision about her treatment.

Before he hung up, he added, "By the way, Dr. Schlunk wants her medication increased again. Tell her to take four Dilantin, and to increase the phenobarbital to one full grain four times a day. And we're going to increase the mysoline to three times a day."

Before I talked to Rusty, I checked with Dr. Nelson again. Dr. Lamberta was certainly kind and competent but it was Dr. Nelson I had known for years. It was Dr. Nelson I trusted implicitly. He agreed that some testing should be done but was as infuriated with Dr. Schlunk as I had been. "Carol," he said firmly, "I dislike judging a person I don't know, but a neurologist who is questioning a diagnosis should not have slapped her as he did. If she had had an aneurysm, he could have ruptured it. That is not good medicine."

"We haven't got money for another doctor," I said helplessly. Before I hung up, I had to ask, "Why would Rusty's previous EEG's have come hack normal? I thought epilepsy showed up on electroencephalographs."

"Not always," he explained. "An EEG records the electrical activity of the brain in much the same way as the EKG or electrocardiogram records the activity of the heart. That electrical activity is traced on paper. But the neurons or brain cells that generate this activity are very complex and only partially understood. These cells, acting normally, can produce a normal EEG. But that doesn't mean that five minutes later those same cells won't act up and produce, possibly, a positive EEG, indicating, in some cases, epilepsy."

"Can you make that any clearer?" I asked him.

He hesitated while he thought about it. "When the lights in your home go out–is it the wires that are defective, has the switch been turned off, or have you blown a fuse? Brain cells can be structurally perfect, and even the transmission can be fine, yet something causes a blackout. What is that? We don't always know. Until we know more about the brain, there is always the possibility of error. And machines can only offer gross measurements; the human brain is more sophisticated than any of them."

I wanted to understand more. "We still don't know what causes most cases of epilepsy?" I asked.

"We have some knowledge," he said. "We know that birth trauma, with lack of oxygen to the fetus, has some effect. And injury to a certain part of the brain by stroke or accident. But in the majority of cases the cause or causes remain unknown. Each of us is potentially epileptic. When shock treatments are given for depression, patients without epilepsy do convulse. In most of us, the threshold for seizures, that is, the susceptibility of our nerve cells or neurons to disorganize, is relatively high. People with epilepsy have lower seizure thresholds, but even a perfectly normal child or adult may have a seizure if his temperature gets high enough. That doesn't mean that he has epilepsy. So you see that there are many things to consider."

"How can I know what to believe, then?" I asked.

"You must remember to consider everything. Blindly believe nothing. A person cannot be reduced to only what we can observe or trace. Use a different kind of vision, Carol," he said. "The mind can only look, but the heart can sometimes see."

I sat down on the sofa bed next to Rusty and watched her while she slept. She looked so much younger to me since she'd been sick. And more vulnerable. Without her glasses, her long dark lashes on her pale white skin, she could have been as young as Lynn. I reached up and wiped her bangs from her forehead. Like Jeremy, coming up from sleep, Rusty's mouth made sucking sounds–in memory of a baby thumb and comfort?

Rusty was fine when she woke up. She didn't remember much of what had happened at either the doctor's office or at home. What she did remember, though vaguely, was that Creede had tried to break her arm. She didn't know why. When I explained it to her over breakfast, she kept shaking her head in disbelief. Finally she said, "I am sorry, whatever good that does."

As I poured her some coffee, I saw that while I'd been talking she had hardly touched her breakfast. The bacon and eggs I had cooked had been moved around a bit to look as though they'd been eaten, but most of it remained.

"You hate my cooking?" I teased.

Rusty made a face. "No, that's not it," she said. "My stomach has been feeling weird and I haven't been hungry. Maybe it's all the pills."

"Feeling weird how?" I asked.

"Full or something. I almost always have indigestion lately. The fullness climbs all the way up into my throat a lot of times." She stared down at the pills in front of her. "Eight pills a day probably fills me up," she added.

"Eleven," I said. When she looked puzzled, I told her about my conversation with Dr. Lamberta.

She swallowed her pills and her stomach growled. "The little man who dwells in my belly and is in charge of inventory is probably running around like a crazy person looking in his encyclopedia for the composition of the new medicine," she said, then added more seriously, "Carol, if they keep this up, I'm going to rattle when I walk."

"You haven't told me whether you're willing to go to the hospital for testing," I said. "Dr. Lamberta wants us to call him back this afternoon." I knew I was pushing her but I was certain that if we could get some "good medicine," Rusty could be seizure-free once and for all.

"You know how much I hate hospitals," she said sadly, "but in case there is something wrong that can be fixed, I guess I owe it to you and the kids to get it fixed."

"What about you?" I asked. "What do you want to do for yourself?"

"If I really had a choice, a free choice, I mean," Rusty said, "I'd like to be locked in a closet until this passes."

"Great attitude," I said sarcastically. "A form of passive suicide, right?"

Rusty frowned and shook her head. Then she said gently, "No, Carol. Nothing like that at all. In fact, I'm almost positive that the pills, the tests or the treatments will kill me far quicker than the seizures. And even if they don't kill me, they can take my life."

"I don't get it," I said. "You're that afraid of the pain or the treatment?"

"No," she said, "I'm that afraid of the consequences of my seizures. And the diagnosis of the doctors. Every time something happens where I hurt myself, they decide I'm crazy. They can lock me up and throw away the key. They can take my life, not just kill me."

"Can you go this once," I asked, "just to make sure nothing else is going on?"

Rusty nodded. "Yes," she said, "but let me tell Jeremy and Lynn about it...."

I really would like to take them sledding just once before I have to go into the hospital," Rusty insisted. "And I really don't want to drive right now. Couldn't you just take us there?"

"What is this," I teased, "a takeoff on the Last Supper? The Last

Sleigh Ride?"

Rusty tried to smile. "I'm going to be in the hospital for days," she said. "No real air, no trees, and no kids. Before I go, I really would like to do this with them."

"You've got it," I told her.

Even I had to admit it was a gorgeous day. The snow, just fallen, was cold fluffy white cotton; it didn't even feel wet. And there was lots of it.

I had stuffed Jeremy into his blue snowsuit with so many sweaters underneath that he could hardly move, but I didn't dare let him get sick.

Lynn struggled into a red nylon jacket from the year before, and I made myself a note to buy her a new one. The kid never asked for anything.

Rusty just wore a sweatshirt and jeans. "You'll freeze to death," I told her three times, and finally she relented and put another sweatshirt on top of the one she was wearing.

The park was filled with people that day, but Rusty found a special hill, away from everything and everyone. The kids dragged the new red sleds my parents had given them the Christmas before and Rusty pulled her own. It was a plain wooden one that she had kept since she'd been little.

For three hours Rusty and the kids dragged their sleds up to the top of the hill, jumped on them and rode down. First, each of them alone, then two of them on a sled, finally all three piled on and rode, screeching down the hill together. They tried to terrorize me by riding up to where I stood and then falling in a heap at my feet. They were laughing so hard, the tears from their eyes froze on their faces. Finally they agreed to come home.

That evening, I made them all hot chocolate and then we lay around watching TV until it was bedtime. It had been fun for them and it was great for me to see them happy. I wondered if we'd ever have a day like it again.

CHAPTER 15

They did the EEG first. Rusty was taken from the main hospital to another building and placed in a chair next to a technician in white who sat in front of a large noisy machine. She didn't feel really well and was bothered when the technician stuck the electrodes with all the goo onto her scalp, without acknowledging her or apologizing for what he was doing. She remembered how embarrassed she had been the first time she had had this done. It was while she was in high school. Because her parents had no car, she had been forced to take the bus home. She had been absolutely humiliated that they hadn't let her wash her hair afterwards; it had been pasted to her head all the way home, so everyone could see.

Now it seemed to go quickly; in fact Rusty slept through most of it. And the technician didn't have to flash any lights to get his reading. Sure enough, this EEG came back "abnormal" in the temporal areas.

They did the spinal tap, or lumbar puncture, next. In Rusty's bed in her room. A doctor she didn't know, Dr. Moreno, introduced himself the morning after Rusty's admission and told her he would do the test. He explained that the fluid which surrounds the brain flows through the spinal column. If there is infection or blood around the brain, it would show up in the spinal fluid.

Smitty, a pretty black nurse who usually worked the surgical floors, would help him. Rusty didn't much care for Dr. Moreno. His dark hair was greasy and when he shook her hand, she saw dirt under his fingernails. Not great for a guy who's looking for an infection, she thought. But she had faith in Smitty. They had met the day before when the young nurse had come to explain the test to Rusty. She was bright and sympathetic. Rusty didn't tell her she had had other taps, because she wanted to hear the information again. The last time, it had been a disaster. Rusty had limped for weeks. One thing that Rusty thought important was that whenever she asked a question, Smitty didn't try to evade it. Rusty had learned that the things which had endangered her most were those that were unspoken.

On the day of the test, Smitty came in before the doctor. She brought with her a large sterile canvas-covered tray which she placed on Rusty's overbed table. She was immaculate. Even her hair looked starched. And her voice was soft and easy. It helped Rusty relax.

"This will only take about fifteen minutes," she explained as she helped Rusty into a clean white hospital gown. "It shouldn't be too bad. Of course there'll be some burning when the local anesthetic is injected into the skin on your spine, but after that there shouldn't be much discomfort. If you feel pain, please let us know. Afterward, you'll have to lie flat for about eight hours so you don't get a bad headache, and you should drink a lot of fluid."

Rusty walked into the bathroom, combed her hair and brushed her teeth. She got back into bed just as Dr. Moreno entered the room. He said hello to Rusty and was about to open the sterile tray when Smitty, holding up a small package, announced, "Doctor, I got you this brush for your hands because I knew you'd want to scrub before you started." Rusty smiled as Smitty thrust it into his hands and added, "I'll open the tray and get Barbara set up while you're at the sink." Then she smiled a wide white-toothed smile.

As soon as Smitty heard the water run, she walked over to the table and carefully unfolded the white canvas to expose the shiny stainless-steel tray. Then she came over to Rusty.

"Lie on your side," she said, helping Rusty turn, "and bend your knees to your chest." She placed a small pillow under Rusty's head and added, "Try to keep your chin tucked against your chest. That helps separate the vertebrae in your spine and makes it easier to insert the needle."

Dr. Moreno inserted the needle without too much difficulty, and because of the local anesthetic, Rusty felt only pressure. It seemed to take much longer than fifteen minutes, but Smitty explained that was because the spinal fluid was dripping into the three small tubes rather slowly. She bent down and whispered, "The spinal fluid's clear," and so Rusty was pretty sure even before Dr. Lamberta told her that she didn't have an infection and had no evidence of hemorrhage.

That night when I visited Rusty, she seemed sleepier than usual. I stayed for a long time just wiping her forehead with cold washcloths and petting and patting her arms. She was in a private room, so no one objected to me being there even after visiting hours. It helped that I was a nurse, although right now I felt pretty impotent, and all that kept repeating itself in my mind was, "I'm sorry you have to go through this again." But instead of saying that to Rusty, all I could manage, like my mother, was, "Did you have anything to eat today?"

She was still lying flat in bed. "Nothing but pills," she said groggily. "I tried some Jell-O and ginger ale but it made me sick. Besides, every time I take a sip of anything, there's a pill attached to it."

Before I left, I carefully shaved Rusty's fine blond hair off her neck. She was going to have the angiogram the following morning and the doctors needed a sterile field to push the catheter into the carotid arteries. This test forces a liquid contrast medium, which shows up on an X-ray, through the arteries and veins in the brain to show any blood-vessel abnormality.

The next morning, while Rusty was lying on a stretcher in the hall, Dr. Hesin visited her and said, "This test is too painful to stay awake. We'll give you something to make you sleep."

Rusty was grateful, because when she closed her eyes, the lights in the operating room spun brilliant luminous webs into surrealistic pictures as Dr. Hesin threaded the thin plastic catheter into her carotid artery. Rusty was amused by all the colors and patterns. Bright reds and blues flew toward and then away from her face, distracting her. And as the thick liquid dye flooded through the blood vessels in her brain, Rusty was dreaming about a galaxy full of shiny red, silver and green stars. And so she hardly felt the burning.

I stayed with Rusty that night too. And though she had no grand-mal seizures, she was hard to arouse. I was worried about that. Any irritation of the brain from testing could cause a lowering in the level of consciousness. I constantly checked her blood pressure and her temperature to make sure there was no leaking–or bleeding into the brain, no swelling that could cause increased pressure. Often I checked the dressing on her neck where the catheter had been inserted, to make sure her artery wasn't leaking-to make sure that she wasn't bleeding. Several times I shook her awake harder than I should have to make sure she could swallow. Internal bleeding or swelling could cause her throat to close.

All through the dark quiet hours of the long night I kept a tight hold on her hand, trying to squeeze my wishes for her to get well in through her pores.

In the morning, before I left, Dr. Lamberta came in on rounds. "You can go home tomorrow if you like," he told Rusty. "Everything's negative but the EEG, and so now we just have to wait until the medication takes hold."

"It looks like it's taken hold," I told him. "She's zonked most of the time."

"We can't be sure that's not still some kind of seizure activity," he explained, "and if it is the medication, she'll get used to it. In time her body will adjust and her tolerance for it will increase."

I left thinking at least we had ruled out any concrete structural damage in Rusty's brain. If it was seizure activity, I hoped it would pass soon. And if it was the medication, I hoped that her body would soon learn to tolerate it. Because while I truly never minded caring for Rusty, and really didn't see it as an inconvenience, I did miss her conversation. I wanted desperately to have all of Rusty back, complete with her wit and her wisdom.

Creede drove when we picked Rusty up the next morning. I had called in sick to work again, and talked to Mrs. Frick about giving Rusty a leave of absence. She seemed hesitant when she agreed. As we checked out of the hospital, Rusty could hardly walk and she didn't have much to say. "It's the remaining seizure activity as well as the medication that's making her groggy," Smitty said. "In time that will pass."

"I hope so," I said as I held Rusty's wobbling body and led her across the concrete parking lot into Creede's car. When Creede saw Rusty, she frowned. "It's the remaining seizure activity as well as the medication," I told her, as I'd been told.

They had again increased her Mysoline. That meant twelve pills a day.

When the kids came home, Rusty was sitting on the couch. Jeremy ran over and kissed her hello, and she asked, "How was school?" She seemed almost normal again.

Lynn sat with her till late at night watching TV and though Rusty didn't speak, things seemed okay. Until she got up to walk to the bathroom. Then she was so off balance both Lynn and I had to grab her to keep her from falling. "Is Rusty drunk, Mom?" Lynn asked while we waited for her outside the bathroom.

"No, honey," I told her. "It's part of the epilepsy or the side effects of the medication she has to take that makes her seem like that."

"Is she going to always be like this?" she asked.

"Jesus, I hope not," I said.

But if, at the time, I'd had a large crystal ball that enabled me to see the future, I would have made some requests. For Rusty I would have bargained for a magic shield to protect her, to help her defend herself against the onslaught of demons and doctors and death.

And for myself, one fairy godmother who would offer me three wishes and promise on Zeus they'd come true. My first wish would be for all the world's medical knowledge, and for my second, I'd wish for the wisdom of Solomon translated into the jargon of Freud. My third wish would probably have bent her wand, because it would have been for the patience and endurance of Job.

But instead of allowing us the easy way out, Life in its wisdom whipped up a plot that forced us to use the tools that we had. We had

Rusty's courage, my single-minded belief in her, Creede's love of us both and the help of a few other people who cared. Most of the time, that was magic enough.

That night after the kids were in bed, Rusty had another seizure. A bad one this time. It lasted too long and when I called Dr. Lamberta he suggested, "Do you have any injectable Amytal at home?" He had ordered some before and I had one vial left. "Give it first, and if it doesn't work, call an ambulance," he said. I gave it and in a few minutes she relaxed.

After she had slept for an hour or so, she awakened absolutely alert. And devastated that it had happened again. "See what I meant?" she asked, almost in tears. "See why there can't he promises?"

"No," I said, "I can't see. I've fed people and cared for them when they haven't been able to use their arms. I've been their arms. I've helped people walk when they couldn't stand. I've been their legs. I've fought for them when they needed me. I've been their voice. It's a privilege, really, to help like that. And it's the closest thing to God that I understand. So I can't see why this is any more of a problem."

Rusty was sitting on the couch looking down at her hands as I spoke. When she lifted her head, she smiled weakly and said, "Have you ever had to be somebody's brain before, somebody's mind, somebody's perceptions?"

I shook my head. "No," I said, "but I understand the responsibility. I won't take it lightly."

Rusty ran her hand across her cheek to wipe away a falling tear. "Thank you," she said softly.

I reached over and hugged her. "It could just as easily be me in this fix," I told her. "It really could. We're not so different, you know."

That night Rusty slept in my bed and I kept the gauze-wrapped tongue blade within easy reach on my night table. I lay awake thinking about all the months before when Rusty was fine, when almost everything she did and said was so clearheaded, confident and wise. And suddenly I knew how tenuous wisdom was.

Penny stopped by the next morning on her way home from work while Rusty and I were asleep. I had gotten the kids off to school and then gone back to bed. By the time I woke up again and came downstairs, Penny had already disappeared but there was a stack of new books on the kitchen table neurology books, The Physician's Desk Reference, psychiatry books, a medical dictionary and two books by rebel psychiatrist Szasz. And a note:

Carol,

Didn't want to wake you. I've been searching through libraries and bookstores for weeks and this is all I've found. Not a lot of reading material available on epilepsy but I got what I could. Hopefully that will give some clues about whether Rusty's confusion and staggering are due to the medications or the seizure activity. I also brought some books on conventional psychiatry and treatment which I figured might help you tell Rusty what they look for in case she gets sentenced again. The name of that game is Prescribed Behavior. Anyway, the books by Szasz should help you keep your sanity. I love his titles. The Manufacture of Madness and The Myth of Mental Illness. Both positions, the conventional and his, are simplistic, but if you're selective, I think there's some valuable stuff here.

Mr. Gragone's been good at night so after I take care of him, I've had a chance to read most of these. The one clear conclusion I've drawn is that even today, so much still remains to be learned about the brain and its functions, that the doctors are still treating her with pills of myth and magic.

Hope the books help.

Love,
Penny

P.S. My father is getting better, I think. He got out of bed yesterday and made clam chowder for me and the kids. It wasn't bad except for too much rosemary.

Rusty tottered into the living room. "Want to see?" I asked, holding up one of the books. I couldn't figure out why she was so sharp and balanced right after a seizure and then after a while she started to stumble and get somewhat confused again.

Rusty walked up to the table and looked. When she saw the titles of the books, her expression changed to one of distaste. She shook her head and asked, "Can I move them over by the couch?"

"Sure," I said. "Can you eat some breakfast?"

"Only hot chocolate," she said, taking the books off the table.

In the following weeks, Rusty began to stay awake most of the night. She spent long hours doing dishes and cleaning floors and closets. On the nights I went to bed before her, I couldn't sleep for fear she'd have a seizure and need my help.

Soldiers in battle sleep in the same trench. I insisted that Rusty sleep with me in my bed so that I didn't have to stay awake straining to hear her. This way, when the bed started to shake, I would automatically wake up. So both of us would fall asleep as dawn was breaking, and it did nothing to help my nerves or improve my disposition. One thing I discovered pretty quickly was that my philosophy and theories about myself and the rest of humankind didn't hold up quite as well on a twenty-four-hour basis as I thought they would. Exhaustion often taxed my compassion.

Creede came over one day when Rusty had begun to repaper the cabinets and rearrange the dishes. Rusty was more confused, more often than before, and she rarely walked straight anymore.

Creede and I were drinking coffee and I wasn't yet fully awake. "Why don't you rest for a while?" I asked Rusty.

"I have to move around to stay awake," she said. "I feel better when I'm moving." But as she held the pile of dishes to carry over to the cabinet, she teetered and wobbled as though drunk.

"Don't do that now," I told her, afraid that she would drop the dishes, break them and then cut herself on the pieces as she fell.

"Let her do it," Creede said firmly.

"But she'll hurt herself," I hissed at Creede.

"If that is what's meant to be, that is what will be," Creede insisted. "You can't command her to stop living in order to keep her alive."

Rusty hadn't seemed to be paying attention, but she had overheard us. She turned toward me and smiled a crooked smile. "All these precautions are like hanging garlic around my neck to ward off evil spirits," she said. "If we don't know what's causing the seizures or why, how do we know that what I don't do will prevent them?" She shook her head, lost her balance and almost fell. "Yep," she mumbled, looking amused, "just like hanging garlic around my neck."

CHAPTER 16

I needed some help. Rusty was still having at least one seizure a day and I couldn't leave her alone to go to work. Dr. Lamberta had sent several requests for nursing assistance to the Department of Social Services but all of them had been refused. So after I sputtered and fumed at home for a while, I decided to do battle in person. Hand-to-hand combat has always been more effective for me: nobody recognizes a soldier in the mail.

Now I sat, body tensed, ready to spring, on a small folding chair on one side of a dingy room. Across from me sat the representative of the federal government I had come to challenge.

"We can send someone for three hours each day," the stragglehaired young welfare worker said proudly as he shuffled through the pile of papers on his desk.

"What is that?" I asked. "We don't know when she'll have a seizure and need help."

"I'm sorry," he said simply, not looking at all sorry.

"It's going to cost you a lot more to institutionalize her, than to leave her home with me and send someone for eight hours a day to see that she's okay," I said.

"We have no slot for that," he said, thumbing through a large black loose-leaf folder.

"What the hell do you have slots for, if not when it's needed?" I asked, frustrated.

He just shrugged.

"Well, I'm not going to work and leave her alone in a house by herself during this crisis, and I'm not sending her back to a nuthouse when she's physically sick," I said, exasperated. I was almost resigned and ready to leave when I had a stroke of genius.

"Hey," I said, trying to change from a werewolf to a beautiful maiden, "maybe you can pay me for the eight hours as a nurse, just until we can get through this period."

He shook his head from side to side. "No slot," he repeated.

I almost growled at him, "Forget about slots, what about help?"

He seemed for a minute to crumple, to fold in on himself. Suddenly he brightened. "Are you married?" he asked hopefully.

Oh no, I thought, not this, not now.

"Answer," he said like a Gestapo chief.

"No."

"Kids?" he asked, rubbing his hands together.

I looked at him suspiciously. "What has that got to do with it?"

He looked so gleeful, I suspected he was going to try to get them away from me because I was a single mother trying to bring them up in an environment he felt was unacceptable. "I have a conventional mother and father who take care of them often," I said in defense.

"How old are they?" he persisted.

Now I was panic-stricken. Whom to betray? Rusty or my own children? I applied my usual magical moral hierarchy. My children were healthy. "Eight and five," I answered.

"Wonderful, wonderful," he said happily as he rummaged through a lower drawer on the left side of his desk.

"Not so wonderful," I said. "They're just regular kids."

He looked puzzled, smiled tentatively and then waved an application in front of me.

"What's that?" I asked hesitantly. I was sure it was a child-abuse form that he wanted me to sign in order to indict myself.

"A slot," he said triumphantly.

"A slot?" I felt as though my IQ had dropped fifty points since I'd begun.

"You're an ADC mother!" he said as though discovering oil, "and therefore you're eligible."

"Wait a minute," I said. "I'm a what?"

"You're head of household and you have two young children,we can't let them go hungry." he said, looking proud.

"But I work," I said haughtily.

"Not anymore," he said just as haughtily. "Not if you want to keep your friend out of the nuthouse."

It was a gray day and it was drizzling. On the drive home I struggled with my feelings about being on welfare. Every one of the conventional stereotypes was deeply implanted in my bone. I just knew it was wrong somehow, immoral in some sense. I was certain that by the following day I would be lazy, raggedy and messy. That monthly check from the federal government would certainly and insidiously eat away at my motivation until I no longer wanted to learn or work ever again. I would just waste away on drugs and booze in an overly populated house with one shiny Cadillac in the front yard. Expecting the entire working population to support me as though it was my due because I was wearing a banner of need across my chest. I got completely carried away and almost cried at the loss of myself. . . my integrity, my ethics, my life. And then I got a great idea. I'd just make a deal with the Great God of Universal Funds to give me a low-interest loan. I wouldn't really be on welfare; I'd pay them back the rest of my life as I worked. Besides, I was saving the federal government tons by keeping Rusty for them until she got well, when she'd pay them back for the rest of her life too.

Suddenly I realized that alongside the myth of the Prince on the White Horse or Doctor Deity loomed the myth of the Welfare

Recipient. And I had bought it and swallowed it whole. I was too compulsive to be lazy, and my mother would haunt me to death before she'd allow even a modicum of messiness. I wasn't moving from the house I lived in, and on the meager stipend welfare was giving all of us, I was lucky if I could put gas in my VW, much less buy a Caddy with the government's money.

The myth was nonsense. I had worked my whole adult life, and though at times supporting the kids had been difficult, I did get a sense of satisfaction from it. But now it was more important for me to be home. I wanted to spend more time with Jeremy and Lynn. And as for working at Salvation—Lenny was still the hero of the day-room, he had almost enough to buy another pinball machine, Marta had been discharged and, thank God, Mr. Gragone's diabetes had stabilized and he was almost ready to go home, otherwise I would have been stricken with guilt. So now there would be no more horses tied to my limbs, each pulling in a different direction. I would finally have enough time to really watch Rusty, to study her seizures, to read, research, and study about epilepsy. Dammit, I thought, I'm going to figure out a way to help this kid ... and maybe as an added bonus, the entire population of people with seizures. I couldn't believe there wasn't something more that could be done.

Jeremy and Lynn were still in school and Creede was with Rusty when I got home. "Freedom," I sang as I walked in the front door. "No more working on the chain gang. . ."

Creede looked up from her book and greeted me. "And did Social Services offer to send in the troops?" she asked dryly.

I shook my head. "Something better," I said; then, "Where's Rusty?"

"She's in the bathroom," Creede told me. "Just took a shower and washed her hair."

I made a face and breathed out hard. Then I hissed, "What's the sense of you being here if you're going to let her drown?"

Creede looked annoyed. "Why don't you just build her a rubber room?" she asked caustically.

"I may be overprotective," I told her, "but you're just the oppo-site."

"Good," she said. "Maybe between us she'll have a chance."

Just then Rusty came stumbling into the living room. She looked like a newly hatched bird with her wet blond hair sticking out like feathers, but I had to admit she looked happy.

"How was it?" she asked me.

"Freedom," I told her happily. "They wouldn't send anyone, so they said I could stop working and take care of you."

Rusty frowned. "What about the bills?" she asked. I was surprised she was so alert. Maybe they were right, maybe her body did get used to the medication, I thought.

"They put us all on welfare," I told her. "The bills will be taken care of." Rusty sat down holding her stomach as though she was in pain. "What's wrong?" I asked. Rusty shook her head. "Tell me what's wrong," I repeated.

"You and the kids are going to have to be on welfare because of me?" she asked.

"Hey, quit that," I ordered. "I've been looking for a way to stay home with my kids for years without having to get married. Stop taking credit for the things I discover."

Creede added, laughing, "It'll do her good. She never has been able to budget."

But Rusty was upset and nothing we said would make that any better. She was just sitting now, staring at her cup of hot chocolate. And as I continued to tell her and Creede how happy the kids would be knowing I would be home all the time now, I could see that Rusty wasn't listening. My heart skipped a beat. "Rusty?" I said; then more loudly, "Rusty," as I poked her arm, "would you please concentrate?"

She nodded and squinted her eyes as though she was confused, but she still didn't answer. "Click, click," I heard her tongue, and quickly turned to Creede. But before we could lay her on the floor, her thumbs curled in, her fingers folded over, her wrists flexed. Click, click. Eyes up and to the left. In an instant her head snapped back, her back arched and she hit the floor. The chair went flying.

I flinched and held my breath, as though she was a glass pitcher falling onto brick. I could almost see her shattered, scattered body in pieces all over the floor. But she stayed intact.

For several minutes she was still. Then, like a mechanical soldier fallen on his back with motor running, her arms and legs jerked in the exaggerated movements of a formal march. Cracking elbows, cracking heels, cracking head, until the motor stopped and she was still again.

"Rusty?" Creede called, kneeling next to her. But she didn't answer.

That evening Creede decided we should all go out to eat at Burger King. I didn't think it was a great idea. Rusty was still only half with us, she was confused and ataxic, weaving and wobbling, but the kids were thrilled, so I gave in. "She's as alert as she's going to be for a while," Creede insisted. "And you aren't doing anyone a service by not carrying on as normally as possible." She put her arm around me. "Life must go on, you know."

What she said was incomprehensible. As far as I was concerned, life was going nowhere until Rusty got better. Because there was nothing to say, I just followed them all into the car. Lynn sat up front with us because she looked a little nervous, but Jeremy sat in back with Rusty, chattering happily as though nothing at all was wrong. Every once in a while he would speak very carefully, as though talking to a younger child, when he wanted her to understand. But he seemed not at all afraid or upset by her.

After we got there, we all stood in line, suffering the inquisitive glances of the people around us, yet managing to get our burgers and drinks. Then Creede led us all over to a corner booth, right in front of the large plate-glass window. She nudged Rusty into the booth first.

"What the hell are you doing?" I asked, panic stricken. "She'll flip out and shatter pieces of the glass and her body all over the parking lot." I tried to whisper, but panic tightened my vocal cords, so I didn't really succeed. The kids were waiting, standing next to me.

"No, I don't think so," Creede said. "I think she'll be just fine."

"Creede," I hissed, "I won't let you do this. Just be a little careful."

"Sit down," she said quietly, and I noticed that Lynn was staring down at the floor and Rusty and Jeremy were moving their heads when each of us spoke, as though watching a tennis match.

I sat down. "Aunt Creede won," Jeremy said. "Rusty's going to be fine."

As the kids ate, Creede leaned over and said to me, "Stop worrying. I think her subconscious will get the message that 'flipping out', as you so aptly describe it, just could be dangerous to her health."

"That implies some control," I said, annoyed.

"Who knows where control is?" Creede shrugged. "This way we cover all bases." Creede took a huge bite of her hamburger, complete with raw onion, and added, "Besides, we can't keep her in a buoble. That's no better than the way she was living."

Rusty was sitting next to Creede just watching what was going on. She hadn't touched her food. "Eat," Creede ordered, helping Rusty out of her bulky winter jacket, "and drink some of that shake. You're getting skinny."

As soon as she said it, I knew she was right. Rusty had gotten thin and I hadn't even noticed. Still, each time she took a bite of her hamburger, I was so afraid she would choke that I instinctively leaned toward her. By the look on Creede's face, I was pretty sure that if I didn't get it together, my body would be the one flying through those plate-glass windows.

Later that evening, Rusty obediently stood on the scale. When it registered under one hundred pounds, I wasn't sure it was right. "Get off so I can see what I weigh," I said, and when it registered the same hundred pounds for me, I knew we were in trouble. I never weighed more than ninety-eight. The scale had registered over, not under, and Rusty had lost sixteen pounds in the last few months. "You'd better start eating," I said, "or soon you'll be just a flashing beam of light."

She laughed, but I was worried now.

"Why don't you go up and lie down?" I suggested. "You seem tired."

Rusty looked up as I spoke, but her gaze was uncomprehending. I repeated what I had said and she gave me a half-smile and nodded. When she turned, she tettered as though she had lost her footing; then she managed quickly to regain her balance.

I followed her to the base of the stairs, pretending to have to get some towels from the utility room, and watched as she began to climb. I held my breath until she was halfway up, and then breathed out slowly. She was one step from the top as I opened the door to the laundry room. Before I walked in I turned once more toward Rusty. She hadn't moved. "Rusty?" I called, but she stood frozen, her back toward me.

Rusty's feet left the step, a wooden springboard, her spine in an almost perfect arc as she dived toward the hard dark wooden floor as though it were the clear blue water of a bottomless pool.

"Should I hold the tongue blade or call emergency?" Jeremy asked as he stood next to Rusty's thrashing body. It seemed he had appeared within an instant of Rusty's fall. And in that same instant I had heard the slam of Lynn's bedroom door.

"Let's just wait and see if it passes," I told Jeremy. He knelt next to me. "Rusty hates any fuss and she hates to go to the emergency room. Besides, if she comes right out of it, she doesn't need any of that." Unless, I thought, she's fractured her skull this time. After a few minutes Rusty's body stopped shaking and she lay as still and quiet as death.

"Is she okay, Mom?" Jeremy asked, leaning over to touch her cheek. He pulled the tongue blade out and held it.

"Rusty?" I called, but she didn't respond. Then Jeremy and I heard the "click, click" of her tongue at the same time. Jer tried to put the tongue blade back between Rusty's teeth but her jaw was already locked.

"Oh look, Mom," he said, holding up the gauze-covered tongue depressor. "Now Rusty will bite her tongue or choke." He frantically tried to push it past her clenched teeth.

I pulled back his hand. "Never force anything into Rusty's mouth when her teeth are already clamped," I told him. "You'll cut her gums or loosen her teeth. And remember to watch your fingers." Jeremy's eyebrows were knit. "Don't worry, babe," I said, as Rusty's arms and legs stiffened and relaxed and then stiffened again. "Since there's no blood now, her tongue's probably in the clear. The muscles in her tongue will probably keep it up and back in her mouth. As soon as she stops seizing, well turn her on her side a little so she won't choke on her saliva."

Jeremy nodded; then he jumped up to grab one of the pillows from the couch. Together we managed to get it under Rusty's banging head. And we waited. She went from one seizure to another but her color stayed pink. Still, after ten minutes I had about decided to call the police for a rescue ambulance. Then, as quickly as they began, the seizures stopped and Rusty lay quiet and still again.

When I was certain she was all right, I left Jeremy holding her limp hand and went upstairs.

Lynn's books were open on her desk but she was lying facedown on the bed with her pillow over her head. I poked her on the butt. She sat up. "Is Rusty still alive?" she asked nervously.

I nodded. "Most times seizures look more dangerous than they are," I explained.

"Or sound?" Lynn asked, covering her ears. "I thought she got smashed when I heard her crashing down the steps."

"I know," I said, touching her hair. "It must have been scary for you."

Lynn began to cry. "Mom, don't be mad at me for not helping Rusty," she said. "It is scary for me. But why can Jeremy stand it and I can't?"

I sat next to her and put my arm around her. "Lynn," I said, "different people handle difficult situations in different ways. It's not right or wrong. And a person can't help being afraid if that's how she feels. You know that feelings aren't right or wrong. They just *are*." When Lynn looked a little better, I asked, "Can you explain to Mommy just what it is that you feel afraid of?"

"Maybe Rusty will get sick when I'm home alone with her and if I don't do something right and she dies, then it's because of me. It's my responsibility then," she said.

"And how does hiding from it help?" I asked, puzzled.

"Cause if Jeremy learns what to do and we're both here, then it's his responsibility because he's done it before," Lynn explained.

I bent over and kissed her forehead. "Lynn," I said, if you ever are alone with Rusty when she has a seizure, you can always call the police. And in any case, the responsibility is not yours or Jeremy's. It's mine. And Rusty's."

"But if I know what to do, I'll have to do it. So it feels like my responsibility," she insisted.

"And so it's the responsibility, not Rusty, that you're afraid of?" I asked.

Lynn nodded. "I don't even know Rusty's really sick," Lynn explained, "because I've never seen her be sick. It's just somebody else saying she's sick. When I see her, she's okay, so it's hard for me to believe. But I do like her so much it worries me to even think that if I saw her sick, I might feel different."

I looked at Lynn and smiled. "Rusty feels the same way about it," I told her. "Because she's never seen herself in seizure, it's hard for her to believe it too."

"All clear," Jeremy shouted from the foot of the stairs. "Rusty's sitting on the couch. I helped her and she's good again." He sounded triumphant and I knew that after all my talking, the difference in Lynn's and Jeremy's reactions still bothered her. There was no way for me to explain just then that besides the difference in their personalities, the difference in their ages was important. Jeremy, at five, still trusted me completely, still figured that if I was around there was no danger that I couldn't handle. He also knew little about responsibility and death. It seemed a lack of understanding on Jeremy's part, not lack of character on Lynn's.

"Stop worrying," I said, messing up her hair as I got up. "There are a lot of things you can handle better than Jer. You're doing fine."

Each day seemed to blend into the next, with no structure at all. Everything began to revolve around Rusty and her seizures. Most days now, Rusty had long periods of fogginess and confusion. I don't know whether the eyes are windows to the soul, but I do know that they are windows to consciousness. When Rusty's brown eyes were dull, I knew my words would never penetrate. At first, like a lunatic, I'd talk louder. But an increase in the volume of my voice didn't propel my words any deeper into her brain or make my meaning any clearer. It was just shouting in a foreign language.

When I finally understood that, I'd sit Rusty on the couch next to me and position her as I would a rag doll. I'd brush away the blond hair that had fallen in her eyes, straighten her sweatshirt, and pat her here and there as I did when trying to reassure my children. Then I'd show her beautiful pictures to try to enter her brain without words. A soft sunny day with a flowing clear stream, tall trees, green grass . . . maybe that could tell her of my feelings or let her know my mood.

One day when she was particularly out of it, like Annie and Helen Keller, I wrote "I love you" with my fingers on her palm. Tactile sense was one of the last to go, I knew from my patients in coma. She looked up at me, puzzled first, and then she smiled. A touching, childlike, funny smile. Then she grabbed my hand, and on my palm with her finger, she traced a happy face. I hugged her tight, and cried.

One night after the kids were asleep, I took a long relaxing bath, bubbles and all. I made the water especially hot, hoping it would relax some of my tense sore muscles. Through the bathroom door I could hear Rusty cleaning and puttering around the living room and kitchen. Restlessness, I remembered, another side effect.

A few days before, I had been reading some of the books Penny had brought. The more I read, the more confused I got. As I had looked up each of the medications in the new PDR, The Physician's Desk Reference, I had noticed that the list of side effects or adverse reactions took up more space than the good the medicine was supposed to do. In fact, I was stunned to see "sudden death" and "convulsions" listed as warnings of toxicity under several of the medications that Rusty was taking. I was even more surprised to find that other medications she took could cause restlessness or sedation, tremors, difficulty swallowing and stomach discomfort including severe indigestion and loss of appetite. Those were side effects but they were also symptoms of certain kinds of seizures according to the books on epilepsy I had read. Most of them were also Rusty's complaints. But what was causing them? The epilepsy itself or the medication?

I planned, after my bath, to go up to bed and continue to read. I just knew that if I could get a handle on what was happening, I could make some suggestions that the doctors would listen to, and maybe that would speed things up. After all, I had known Rusty before she was sick; I saw her for hours each day, so I could observe her seizures and the changes in her levels of consciousness. I knew her better than they did and so I had a more accurate baseline. I dried my hair, turning off the dryer several times in order to listen for Rusty. Then I got into a pair of fresh jeans. Both of us had gotten used to sleeping fully dressed in case we had an emergency in the middle of the night.

When I walked out of the bathroom, Rusty was half-hidden in the hall closet. She was organizing again. "Call if you need me," I told her. Then I went upstairs.

I was deep into one of the books on epilepsy, concentrating hard on the auras of seizures, or warnings for epilepsy, when I heard a strange noise. "Rusty?" I called, and when there was no answer, I got out of bed.

Rusty had fallen facedown in the closet, her flailing arms tangled in coat hems and boots, as she thrashed in the narrow space. Maneuvering with difficulty, I grabbed her by her feet between seizures and pulled her onto the livingroom rug. Then I got a pillow and put it under her head.

This time, as I knelt next to her, I felt something different happening. There was a brutal intensity to these seizures. My heart started to beat fast. My palms were wet. I had felt this way before, during a cardiac arrest at the hospital, but never before with Rusty.

Once, a patient of mine at the hospital had been declared dead, and I just knew he wasn't. He was an old man who had been burned in a barbecue fire and there was no chance for his survival. But the doctor had put him on a respirator and had hooked him up to an IV to keep his blood pressure up. Sometime in the early morning, I checked his vital signs and found them absent. He had no blood pressure, no audible heartbeat, no visible respirations. When I had asked the doctor to come up and check him for me, he and another nurse agreed the man was dead. "I don't believe he's dead, doctor," I kept insisting. Finally the doctor grabbed me by the shoulders, shook me hard and yelled, "Get control of yourself. What are you basing your judgment on?"

Then, while the doctor was at the front desk writing out the death certificate, I was in the old man's room scratching the bottom of his feet, pinching his belly. As a last resort, I walked to the top of the bed, put my hand on his forehead and told him, "You've got to breathe, or they're going to put you in a refrigerator." And it was true. The morgue.

That did it. He breathed. I couldn't explain it, even to myself, but I had known that man's consciousness was still in his body, in that room.

And now, as I watched Rusty, I felt with the same certainty that her consciousness was slipping away. Not in the temporary sense of loss of consciousness in seizure but permanently. Now I was getting more panicky by the minute. I tried to calm myself. But her breathing wasn't right.

"Rusty," I said, "Rusty, listen to me . . ." She was hammering her head on the floor as the force of the seizures kept moving it off the pillow. "Rusty, don't be afraid," I continued softly, leaning very close to her ear. "It will be okay. I promise, this will pass." I touched her cheek. I felt so helpless.

With my heart in my throat, close to tears, I knelt back and just watched as Rusty's body flailed and banged. Her skin was getting dusky. I took a deep breath and tried to think what to do. I put my hand on her chest and I could feel the pounding of her heart as though I was touching it. What could I do?

Suddenly I remembered Rusty's story of Dove: *When the will is suspended, somebody has to care enough to bend it toward life.*

"Goddammit, Rusty, you're not dying while I'm around," I swore. "No way."

I put both my hands on her heart, closed my eyes, and with all the will I had, I tried to drag the energy up from the center of my body and force it down through my arms and hands into Rusty. I didn't pray. But every part of me was pushing forward, was straining hard and thrusting whatever will I could into Rusty.

I had been stalling until then. Trying to wait out Rusty's seizures so I wouldn't have to take her to the hospital. But it was almost twenty minutes now, any longer would be dangerous. I called Dr. Lamberta. "Get her to the emergency room," he said. "I'll call them and order something."

I called the police, who would call an ambulance. Creede was at work so I called my father to come and stay with Lynn and Jeremy so I could go with Rusty. I had told both my mom and dad about Rusty before she moved in. I knew they would help any way they could. It made me feel better.

My father had thrown his pants over his pajamas, covered his tangled night hair with a hat, and run over. When I let him in, Rusty was lying quietly in the middle of the living-room rug. Her eyes were closed, her long lashes resting on her very pale, smooth skin. She looked like a child asleep. My father stood above her, his head bowed, hat held over his chest, a gesture of mourning and of respect. Then suddenly, as though something from outside had grabbed her by the shirt front and shaken her like a rag doll, Rusty's body began again. Another grand-mal seizure.

My father knelt beside her and put his right hand under her banging head. "Don't do that, Daddy," I told him. "You'll get hurt."

He looked up at me and said gently, "I'd like to think that some of my pain will take some of her pain away."

CHAPTER 17

Rusty was angry by the time I got to Greenvale Hospital that morning. "Why was I admitted?" she asked me.

"Nothing we did at home seemed to stop the seizures, and even in the ER, after they gave you a shot, they wouldn't stop. When they called Dr. Lamberta and told him, he decided to keep an eye on you for a few days," I said. "Besides, I think they want to do another test."

Rusty sighed and ran her fingers through her blond hair. "Carol," she said slowly, "all the tests have already been done. Again and again, in fact. Nothing ever shows up."

I walked closer and held her hand. "That's not true, Rusty," I told her. "You said that all your other EEG's had been normal and yet the one they did here wasn't. Patients in state institutions just don't get the same kind of care that private patients do. As long as Dr. Lamberta's willing to help us, we really should take advantage of it."

Before Rusty could say any more, Jeff Lamberta entered the room. "Hi," he said. "How are you this morning?"

Rusty tried to smile. "A little sore," she said, "that's all. And pretty unhappy about being here."

"I know," Dr. Lamberta said seriously, "but you can't continue with your life outside until we can get these seizures under some sort of control." He turned around and grabbed one of the straight-back chairs to sit on. I moved around to the other side of the bed. "Rusty," he continued, "I know you've been through a lot of this before and I know that you're pretty tired of it, but there's one more test we'd like to do before we release you this time."

Rusty frowned. "Who's 'we'?" she asked. "And why do we have to do more tests? What is it we're looking for?"

"There's a Dr. Rosenberg, who's a neurosurgeon I've consulted," Dr. Lamberta told her quietly. "I've told him your history, and about the frequency of your recent seizures. He suggested a pneumoencephalogram and offered to come to Greenvale to do it for you."

"What is it for?" Rusty asked, "And how is it done?"

Dr. Lamberta looked down at his folded hands. "I'd rather let Dr. Rosenberg explain it," he said. "He's an excellent specialist and is much more familiar with the procedure. His explanation would probably make you more comfortable."

Rusty made a face and mumbled, "It'll probably make you more comfortable . . ." Then she caught herself and said, "I'll settle for what you tell me. I know you; I don't know him. And I prefer truth to comfort."

For a minute Jeff Lamberta looked uncertain; then he seemed to make a decision, because he took a deep breath and began. "Well, first," he said, "the test is done to discover tumors in the ventricles of the brain or in the pituitary gland." He looked at Rusty to see how she was reacting. Then he went on, "You'll have to fast for about eight hours before, and the test will take a couple of hours. You'll probably be strapped into a motorized chair and then rotated in various positions after air is injected into your spine."

Rusty interrupted him by asking, "Rotated how?"

"In a somersault fashion to help the air reach the ventricles in your brain," he said. "Then they'll probably take more X-rays. They'll also start an IV in case of emergency and probably keep a cuff on your arm to monitor your blood pressure."

I tried to break the tension I could feel by saying, "This, Rusty, is what's known as informed consent."

"It sounds more like some kind of medieval torture," she shot back. Then she looked at the doctor. "Is it dangerous? And painful?"

Dr. Lamberta got up and walked closer to her. When he reached for her hand, even I was worried. "Occasionally there can be a reaction from any kind of procedure. With this test it's not unusual to experience nausea, sometimes vomiting, and a headache afterward. But they'll probably give you a sedative first. And pain medication, if you need it."

Rusty looked thoughtful for what seemed like a long time. Then she asked him, "Do you think I should have it done?"

Dr. Lamberta looked troubled. "We've increased your medication and it still hasn't controlled the convulsions. I do want to be sure that there's nothing going on that we don't know about. God knows there's enough about epilepsy itself that we don't understand. But I want to be certain to rule out anything else."

"Okay," Rusty relented, "get the doctor and schedule the test. And then get me out of here. Deal?"

Dr. Lamberta nodded his head and shook her hand. But when he left the room, he didn't look happy.

Rusty's chin rested on a small pad and her head was strapped into a viselike contraption that reminded her of one the ophthalmologist used to examine her eyes. When she looked sideways, she could see the shiny steel of the long needle as Dr. Rosenberg lifted it off the sterile tray next to her. He was a very thin, very tall man and so when he walked behind her and spoke, his voice seemed to come from above. It gave her confidence. "I'm going to insert this needle into the subarachnoid space," he explained, as though he expected her to understand.

She felt the needle on her spine as he pushed it through the skin. Rusty thought he must be a very good doctor because there wasn't much pain. She had had spinal taps before and some of the needles felt like hatchets going in. Not this time, though.

"I'm going to remove some fluid now," he explained, and Rusty thought the Valium they had given her must be working because she didn't particularly care what he was going to remove. She heard Dr. Rosenberg's voice again: "Now I'm going to inject a small amount of air."

Rusty's heart, like the frantic fluttering of birds' wings, was first to warn her. Then some part of her drifting consciousness stopped and listened like a small deer at a waterhole; her body like his stiffened, sensing danger. But it was already too late. The air bubble, like a grenade thrown into a parched forest, exploded first and then lit up the whole terrain of Rusty's brain.

"She didn't do well," Jeff Lamberta told me in the waiting room. "When they injected the air and tried to lower her head, she lost consciousness. Her blood pressure dropped and her pulse got thready and weak. Then she vomited. They managed to stabilize her after about a half-hour, but she started seizing."

"Where is she now?" I asked, wanting to see her.

"In the recovery, room," he said, "and later I'd like to move her to intensive care."

"Oh, Jeff, don't do that," I pleaded. "They won't let me *special* in intensive care. And it can't be good for the other patients in there if she's throwing seizures all the time."

"I want her watched carefully," he told me, "and I want all the equipment available in case anything else goes wrong."

"Like what?" I asked him.

"Like an arrest," he said. Then he left for the recovery room.

Creede had picked up the kids, brought some flowers for my table and started supper by the time I got home. But I was too upset to eat. There had been no beds in intensive care and so when Rusty was brought out of the recovery room, she was put on the second floor in a private room.

"Is Rusty okay?" Lynn asked as she sat down next to me on the couch. I reached over and ran my hand over her head and down her long brown hair. It comforted me to see her bright brown eyes and her rosy-colored skin, to know how healthy she was.

"I don't know, honey," I said trying not to sound morose. "She wasn't doing too well when I left."

Jeremy, who had been doing headstands in the corner of the room, turned himself, with a thump, right-side-up and ran over to me. "Don't worry, Mom. Rusty will be fine soon. She sure will, I know it."

Creede sat down on the floor next to the couch and grabbed Jeremy around the waist, pulling him down onto her lap. "That's what I like, Jeremy. Certainty," she said. "But may I ask where you received your information?"

"Sebastian told Mr. Bibble," he said earnestly.

Lynn looked down at Jeremy and said emphatically, "This is a real problem and Rusty's really sick."

"I know that," Jeremy said, getting upset, "but Mr. Bibble . . ."

"Oh please, Jer," I said leaning my head back on the couch, "try to understand that sometimes things don't work out the way we want them to. And maybe Rusty won't get well, and maybe Mr. Bibble makes mistakes sometimes."

Jeremy looked crushed. "You don't believe Mr. Bibble knows . . ." he began.

But before I could answer, Lynn leaned forward on the couch and hard-whispered, "Jeremy, Mr. Bibble isn't *real*. I told you this is a *real* problem."

Jeremy hit her and then ran up the stairs, furious. "Mr. Bibble is *too* real. Ask Rusty. And he said Rusty will be home when Santa Claus comes," he called down. Then he ran into his room and slammed the door.

Lynn rested her head on my shoulder. "I guess he's too little to understand," she said wisely.

Creede got up and walked over to the stove. "I don't know, Lynn, whether that's so. He knows something is wrong. And something from inside of him tells him it will be okay by Christmas. That means he understands as much as any of us . . . and maybe knows more."

Lynn went upstairs to talk to Jeremy, and Creede began to put the food on the table. "Stop moping or you'll do no one any good," she said to me. "Call Lynn and Jeremy down for supper, try to eat, then go back to the hospital and see if you can do anything for Rusty. I'll stay here with the children tonight."

Rusty had been seizing almost constantly, for sixteen hours now, with only a few minutes between one convulsion and the next. These were wild, head-wrenching, back-cracking arches that shook her body and the bed so badly that the metal rails rattled like Armageddon.

I stood next to her bed, first petting and pleading, then shaking and commanding her to wake up. Several times during the night, Dr. Lamberta came into the room, checked Rusty's pupils, listened to her heart, gave her an injection of phenobarbital or Valium and just stood by the bed shaking his head.

The last time he came in, he looked concerned.

Status Epilepticus is the official diagnostic term used for recurrent unceasing seizures, and the big dread with epilepsy. It's a medical emergency; life-threatening. All I knew was that it seemed impossible for a heart to keep pumping with such force at such speed for any length of time. "She'll die of exhaustion if they don't stop," I said aloud.

"It's possible," he agreed, "but her heart seems to be holding up so far." He gave her another shot of Valium and her seizures grew milder but still didn't stop. One time she wet herself; another time she bit her tongue. Her skin was getting warm and flushed. She was dehydrating.

"There's no way to start an IV right now," Dr. Lamberta said.

"How much longer can this go on?" I asked him.

"I can't tell you that." He put his hand on my shoulder to try to reassure me.

Finally, after he left, I sat back in the high vinyl chair and closed my eyes. My back hurt from leaning over the rails for so many hours and my feelings of impotence and frustration made my eyes burn. I had a pounding headache and desperately wanted some miracle to stop Rusty's seizures just long enough to give her worn-out body a chance to rest. Even with my eyes closed I could keep track of her seizures by the beat of the side rails. Every time the noise stopped for a few seconds, I checked to make sure her chest was moving up and down, to make sure that she was still breathing.

Then sometime in the early morning when the tension of listening to the rattling rails had scraped my skin raw and left my nerve ends exposed, Smitty, who was working on the floor, came in and offered to watch Rusty while I took a break.

It was cold out. Dirty, hard snow covered the ground and the tall black trees looked naked and lifeless. But as I walked across the hospital parking lot, the rising sun pushed its way through the heavy dark clouds, turning everything golden. It was the beginning of a new day and I was sure that if Rusty's seizures didn't stop, she'd never see another.

It began to snow again, wet, large flakes that covered the sidewalk and sprinkled over me. As I walked around the building I thought about how much I expected from life. A guarantee each day that there would be a tomorrow for me. I acted as though I had signed a contract and paid for it. And when the day appeared, I passed judgment on it. Often, as though catalog-shopping, I reacted as though the Universal Warehouse had delivered the wrong item. If there were problems or difficulties that day, I complained as though I had been sent damaged goods.

Who was I to treat Life with such arrogance? What right did I have to behave as though each new day was my due? What did I offer Life that made me valuable enough to even keep on the books? I felt humble that morning, and grateful. And terribly lonely for Rusty.

On the way back to the hospital, I stopped at my car to get a book to read. As I opened the door, I heard a peculiar whine from underneath. I bent down and looked. A small brown-black-and-white beagle puppy sat shivering near my front wheel. "Get out of there," I said. "I could have run you over." He wagged his stiff little tail and came zooming out. He began to yip and bark, a very squeaky bark at that, and ran in circles around my legs. Then he sat in front of me and shivered. I looked around for his owner but didn't see anyone, so I started to walk toward the hospital. He followed me. "Go away," I told him, waving my arm. "I don't even really like dogs." But he wouldn't go. He just ran ahead of me and then stopped, sat and shivered. Finally I picked him up and brought him back to my car. "Stay in there so you don't get killed," I told him as I set him on the back seat, "and I'll take you to a shelter later."

As soon as I got off the elevator and walked onto the floor, I knew something had happened. I began to run down the hall toward Rusty's room. I could see the red crash cart outside her door and I could hear the strained voices of the nurses.

I stopped short at the door, afraid to know. But then the sound of the regular beeping of the cardiac monitor reassured me.

"Did she arrest?" I asked Jeff Lamberta, who was standing at the head of Rusty's bed. When he nodded, I added quickly, "Is she all right now?"

"Well, she's stopped seizing," he said as he looked at her in bed. She looked pale and she had an IV.

"I'm sorry I left, Jeff," I said, but he waved my apology aside.

I thanked Smitty and told her she could leave. Then I straightened up the room. When I'm nervous, I clean.

Rusty finally opened her eyes. Both Jeff Lamberta and I were hanging over the rails staring at her.

"Hey," she said hoarsely, licking her dry lips, "don't you have anything better to do?" Then her eyes closed and she whispered, "What happened?"

Jeff explained as much as he could before he left to get some sleep. When I was alone with Rusty we didn't even speak. I felt terribly guilty that at the very moment she needed me most, my own needs had gotten in the way.

She lay for a long time, her eyes closed, and when she opened them she just seemed to stare into space. Finally I leaned over and held her hand.

"You wouldn't believe the dream I had, Carol," she said, her voice almost echoing in the thick silence.

"Only tell it if it's entertaining," I teased. "I'm not up for anything too heavy."

She smiled a sweet and gentle smile. And then she said, hesitantly but not particularly to me, "I was someplace black as night for a while. Then several small dots of light, like stars, poked through until there were so many that everything was filled with light. I was inside it, peaceful and happy.

"I saw a child, about three, and I knew it was me. I was running across a field, my feet barely touching. My father was there. He picked me up and threw me into the air, and I was flying, happy and excited, then, all around, I could hear a voice I knew was his. 'Go back, Rusty,' he said, 'it's not time.' I wanted to stay. But before I could tell him, I felt myself falling and I was back in this hospital bed.

"Dr. Lamberta and you were looking down at me, but I didn't want to let the memory or the feeling go."

Rusty had a look of longing in her eyes I'd never seen before. Like the look of a mother who'd been separated from her child too long. I could feel my eyes fill.

Years later, as I worked with patients in intensive care and with terminal patients, I was to see that look and hear stories eerie in their similarities to Rusty's. Later, other accounts were documented and they became known as 'near-death experiences.' Statistics supported the people with credentials who reported their findings. But nothing made me believe more than the common look of longing on the faces of my patients. That look was truth unveiled.

When I bent to kiss Rusty good-bye that morning, she was starting to doze, but with a sleepy voice she asked, "How was your walk?"

"How did you know?" I asked her.

"I saw you outside," she said, not opening her eyes.

"You couldn't have. You were in bed," I told her, surprised.

"Well, it seemed like I could see you from up high," she said slowly and hesitantly. "Like a camera, better than my usual sight. And even if my body was in bed, the part of me that would know it was me–even if I had plastic surgery–could see what was going on in here and outside," she said, turning toward me. Then, "Carol, why do you think my father said, 'It's not time'? What do you think I'm supposed to do yet?"

❖❖ ❖❖ ❖❖

"There it is, Mom," Jeremy shouted. "There's our tree." Lynn, Jeremy, Creede and I had been out for hours looking for Christmas trees and none that we saw seemed right. Most of the best ones were gone because it was Christmas Eve.

"Really, Mom, look!" Jeremy said, standing in front of a large Scotch pine that was leaning against the wire fence.

"I don't want to spend a fortune, Jer," I said. "It looks pretty big."

An old man dressed in raggedy khakis with a dark green knit hat pulled low on his forehead was standing next to us. "You can have it for ten," he said. "Don't want to have to burn it. Cut it myself down in Pennsylvania and trucked it here too. Just as soon have you take it as burn it."

"Please, Mom, please?" Jeremy begged.

I walked closer to look at it, and Creede pulled it forward so we could see the back. "All the branches are gone on this side, Mom," Lynn announced. And they were.

But Jeremy was insistent. "It's still good, Mom. Honest," he said excitedly, "it's just wounded."

We rode home through the snow-covered streets with the tree tied to the top of Creede's blue station wagon. When we began to set up the tree, the trunk was crooked and the stand was broken. While Creede tried to balance it and it kept falling to one side, I said, "I know, Jer, it's only got a limp." We were all laughing now. Creede and I sawed the bottom straight, then while Lynn and Jeremy painted ornaments, Creede and I wired the stand until it was sturdy.

We played Christmas carols on the stereo, ate more popcorn than we put on strings, and had as much tinsel knit into our hair and clothes as we put onto the tree. We used so many lights that we needed four extension cords. Afterward we hooked at least a hundred gold, red, silver and blue ornaments on the wilting branches. Then Creede made gingham bows and tied them as carefully onto the tree as onto a child's pigtails.

When we had finished I turned off the lights in the living room, and all of us sat on the floor watching the tree.

"Look, Mom," Jeremy said, "it s winking at us."

Lynn was mesmerized. "Can we put our presents under the tree now, Mom?" she asked.

"Okay," I said. "Just remember to put the ones for Rusty up front because we don't want her to have to struggle to get them."

Dr. Lamberta had said the day before that I could take Rusty home for a while. She had stopped having grand-mal seizures but was still having some sort of seizure activity. Dr. Schlunk had increased her medication to thirteen pills each day and he impressed upon me that it was important for her to take them. I promised I would make sure she did.

"See?" Jeremy said, turning to Lynn as he finished decorating the tree. "I told you Mr. Bibble said Rusty would be home for Christmas."

He looked so happy and we'd had such a nice night, I didn't have the heart to tell him that Mr. Bibble had only been half right.

Rusty could hardly stand as I tried to dress her Christmas morning, and it was even more difficult for me to get her to walk. The kids were waiting excitedly at home with Creede for Rusty because of the big surprise they had planned. I wondered whether she would even know what was happening.

It was quiet as we opened the front door. Creede and the kids had lowered the blinds so that only the tree lights shone. The packages, in brightly colored paper, were stacked high, waiting to be opened. Alongside, was our surprise: one small brown-black-and-white beagle puppy wearing a red satin bow, lying fast asleep.

When Jeremy hollered his greeting, the puppy opened his eyes, and for a minute the confusion in his eyes matched Rusty's. Then he shook his head hard and his ears went flopping.

"Look, doggie," Jeremy yelled, "here's Rusty! Surprise!"

The puppy ran over and began jumping up and down in front of her, wagging his tail, and Rusty smiled. Creede and I sat her down on the floor, the kids and the dog surrounding her, as I tried to wrench her out of her heavy jacket. But her eyes were fixed on the puppy. Then with one enthusiastic leap he jumped forward and landed on her chest, pushing her backward. When she fell, she laughed and so did the kids.

"What's his name?" Rusty asked slowly. "What do you call him?"

Lynn was the one to approach this time. "He's for you, Rusty. He'll keep you company. So you can call him anything."

The morning I was to get rid of him on my way home from the hospital, the shelter was closed. And once Jeremy and Lynn saw him, I knew we were sunk. "Just like Lassie," Lynn had said. "If Rusty is in trouble, he can go for help."

"Not a bad idea," Creede had said. And so we kept him.

Now Jeremy started to wrestle with him and the Christmas packages went flying.

"Jeremy," I hollered, "cut it out!"

I went over and grabbed the frisky puppy by his collar. "And you," I said, "whoever you are . . . Sit!"

Rusty crawled over and sat down next to Jeremy and the dog.

"Hi," she said, and she lifted the puppy with difficulty onto her lap, but he quickly jumped off.

"He's your dog," Jeremy said, putting his arm around Rusty's shoulders. "Yours and Sebastian's. So you can call him whatever you want."

Rusty smiled and looked at me questioningly. "Really?" she asked. "He's mine?"

When I nodded, she looked pleased. Then she looked at Jeremy and Lynn. "What about Sebbie for a name?" she asked, looking amused. "Sebastian will be proud to have someone named after him."

"Sebbie!" Jeremy called. "Sit! And give me your paw!"

Jeremy was trying to push the puppy's bottom down onto the floor at the same time he grabbed the poor dog's paw.

Rusty shook her head hard; she seemed to be trying to clear it. "Jeremy," she said slowly, "Give me your paw must sound awful to a puppy. If he gives you his paw, what will he use?" Then she held out one hand and placed the puppy's paw into it with her other. "Friends?" she asked. "Friends, Sebbie?"

Sebbie's tail started to wag madly and he reached up and washed Rusty's face with his tongue.

CHAPTER 18

My mother should have had eight children and my father should have been a philosopher. Instead, when the "Help Wanted" ads appeared in the Cosmic Chronicle, they both applied to be my parents. What a coup for universal order when they accepted the job.

"Daddy, what should I do?" I asked as I sat across the table from him after supper one night. My mother was puttering around the kitchen cleaning up, the kids were inside taking a bath and Creede had offered to stay home with Rusty.

"About what, baby?" he asked, as though nothing special had been going on the past few months.

"About Rusty and her seizures," I said, and when he still looked puzzled, I added, "It's been months now that she's been sick. I've had to stop working, you've given us money, I've left the kids here much of the time. How long do I have a right to sacrifice everyone else for Rusty's epilepsy and my commitment? How long do my burdens have to be carried by everyone else too?"

My father was carefully paring the skin off an apple. Cutting around and around, keeping the skin in one piece. "A family is one unit, Carol," he began. "One member doesn't carry a burden–if that's what you choose to call it–alone. An oak bench is too heavy

for one person, it becomes light for three. Then it's no longer a burden, it's simply a commitment."

My mother turned to look at me. "I'm the kind of woman," she
asked, "whose own grandchildren are a burden? How can you talk
like that?"

"I don't mean anything by it, Mom," I explained, again amazed
by her ability to misinterpret–or reinterpret. "I just know how tired
you are, and this makes so much extra work, I feel bad."

"Everybody's tired," she said simply. "Everybody works. That's
life." Things were so clear for my mother. For me, there had to be
reasons, analysis, arguments. For Mother things just were.

"Daddy," I said, "I guess what I'm asking is, do I have a right to
make a commitment for all of us?"

He smiled at me. "You've made it," he said gently, "and we as a
family can only offer support." He held out a section of his apple and
I took it. "Rusty's sick," he added, "she needs us and she's a human
being like the rest of us. So, what's your question again, baby?"

❖❖ ❖❖ ❖❖

Penny had asked that I work a case for her. Her father had gone
into uremic crisis again and she had to be with him. Since Mr.
Gragone had been discharged from Salvation, Penny had been doing
private duty in one of the local hospitals. Her present patient was a
little old lady, Isabella Malton, who had just suffered a stroke and
was senile as well. She needed a private-duty nurse because one
night when she thought she was a bird she had struggled to a standing position on the bed and was ready to fly into the air, when one
of the staff nurses found her. Her family couldn't stand when the
floor nurses put her in a Posey restraint and tied her in bed to keep
her from hurting herself so they called the nursing registry and
Penny was hired. She loved Isabella and so she wanted to be sure
while she took care of her father, Isabella would be well taken care
of. When she asked if I would do it, I explained that because I was
on welfare, I couldn't work. Then she explained that I could work
under her name and just be another welfare cheat. We hadn't really
had enough money and I was so tired of Brand X food that I sacri-

ficed my scruples and accepted. I'd have to pay for this later, I figured.

As I walked onto the medical-surgical floor, the old familiar smells made me aware of how much I had missed real hospital nursing. I thought how much easier this night would be for me.

There were four patients in the neat new hospital room. Isabella was in the bed closest to the window on the left. She was a tiny little thing, with long braided white hair and pink fragile skin.

"Well," she said, looking me over as I introduced myself, "you're not Penny, but you look bright enough. I guess we'll be fine."

"I hope so, Isabella," I said, laughing.

Isabella and I got along well through that night. I washed her and straightened her bed several times during the shift but she refused to close her eyes and go to sleep. When I asked her why, she told me that when you get old enough the time of day doesn't matter. And the weather doesn't matter. "It doesn't matter if it's dark and rainy outside," she said, "as long as it's light and sunny on the inside."

I enjoyed her and she knew it. She loved having the company to chat with and so she spent the night gossiping with me about her roommates. The woman across from her had heart trouble. Next to her was a woman whose diabetes had forced an amputation of a gangrenous leg, and across from that woman, right next to Isabella, was a woman with terminal cancer.

Sometime around four in the morning, Isabella dozed off and I sat back in my chair, thinking. The woman with the heart attack would probably be fine if she watched her activity, monitored what she ate, and tried to cut down on her stress. She could heal and have a relatively normal life. And the woman whose leg had been amputated could get a prosthesis and learn to walk on it. She would have physical therapy to help, and her family and society's support. She was mentally alert and most organizations made allowances for handicapped persons. She would he fine. Then I looked over to the woman lying in the bed next to Isabella's. Her illness was terminal. Still, I thought, she's medicated and resting comfortably. There are skilled people to take care of her and a clean bed in a new hospital. And medical insurance would pay for it. Certainly it was terrible that there was no cure for her illness, but at least there eventually would be an end to her suffering. And in the meantime, her family spent hours each day at her bedside. Even though I was upset with myself for thinking it, at this point, any of them seemed better off than Rusty. For her there was no place, no kind, skilled nursing, no family support, no public acceptance, and her altered state of consciousness and her seizures could go on for eternity. It exhausted me just to think about it.

When the hall lights went on, Isabella woke up. Smiling. As I gave her morning care, she announced, "I'm senile, you know."

"Oh, I'm so sorry," I said in my most compassionate voice. "That must be awful."

Isabella held her finger up and looked at me wisely. "You're not thinking, my child. Senility is a gift from God." When I looked puzzled, she explained, "What else allows an eighty year old woman to look into the mirror and see a twenty year old girl?"

That night had been easier than all the nights in the previous months. Still, by the time I got home, I was exhausted. Creede had stayed with Rusty because she had continued to have at least one seizure a day. The kids were at my mom's.

As soon as I walked in the front door, I knew it had been a bad night for Creede and Rusty too. The sofa bed in the living room was open and both of them were sound asleep. I knew that Creede would never have slept with Rusty downstairs unless Rusty had been sick. I tapped Creede lightly on her shoulder. "What happened?" I whispered.

"That was some night," Creede moaned. "Something new is happening." When I raised my eyebrows and looked puzzled, Creede explained, "She wasn't quite right. And then suddenly she jumped up and crawled toward that window faster than I could run. Went right through it." Creede pointed to the window, now covered with tape and cardboard.

"Did she hurt herself?" I asked.

Creede nodded, sat up and lifted Rusty's arm. There were small scratches on it, but nothing more. I could also see that Creede had tied Rusty's wrist to hers. "I wanted to make sure that while I slept she wouldn't crash through any more windows."

"Did you give her some extra phenobarb?" I asked.

Creede shook her head. "Didn't need to. After that seizure passed, she fell asleep and hasn't awakened."

Rusty hadn't moved but I could see by her regular breathing that she was fine. Creede untied her wrist and handed me the rope. "If you want to get any sleep," she said, "you'll make sure she's safely anchored to you so she can't go anywhere without your knowing it. Otherwise you're liable to wake up to a heart-stopping crash." I nodded and let Creede tie us up.

Before I could fall asleep that morning, I lay awake a long time. I was angry at what was happening. That there seemed to be no help for someone in Rusty's situation. What rights had we? Were other people in the same boat? And where were they? How did they live their lives around someone in a bad period of seizures? I needed more information.

Later, I made a thousand phone calls to try to find an epilepsy support group, but the ones that I reached were fragmented and just beginning, and could offer me little help. No counseling except private therapy was available, and the information on the medical aspects of epilepsy had to be handled by a private physician. They were aware of the problems, they told me, and they were starting to apply themselves to them.

"But what do people do if they have no money and can't get their seizures controlled by medication?" I asked.

"Research funds are available for difficult cases if they're interesting enough," one woman from an epilepsy institute told me. "You can try Calvary Neurological Center in New York. Or one of the other teaching hospitals."

I wasn't ready for Rusty to be an experiment.

I began, even more obsessively, to read neurology books. What was this new kind of behavior that Creede had described? I wondered. What would cause Rusty to jump out of bed and crawl toward a window? Now, as I read, I was surprised to find out how many seizure types there were. And how many people had combinations of two or more. Finally I found what I thought I was looking for. Under the heading "Psychomotor Seizures or Partial Seizures with Complex Symptoms" I read:

At the beginning of a seizure of this type, the person may become dizzy for no apparent reason, or confused, or afraid or angry. He may experience strange sensations-a ringing in his ears, spots before his eyes, changes in the way he sees colors. Often the person doesn't lose consciousness but his consciousness is altered. There can be distortion in his sense of time, he may become disoriented and not know where he is; familiar surroundings may look strange to him. Also, some of his movements may become automatic and repetitive. These seizures can last from minutes to hours and often progress to a grand-mal seizure. The area of damage or disturbance, in this case, is the temporal lobe.

That's where the EEG that Dr. Lamberta had done at Greenvale showed spikes for Rusty! Now that I knew what category to check in one of the other books, I found that temporal-lobe epilepsy could also include twilight states which could last for hours or days, in which the person can carry out a series of complex actions, even take a journey and have no memory of it. The types of epilepsy filled two pages and the list of symptoms was staggering, everything from disruption of the heartbeat and all the other automatic functions, to distortions in sense perceptions as well as thought disorders and hallucinations.

How can any one figure out what's happening? I wondered. And then I saw the warning. "If the intermittent nature of these disturbances is overlooked, an incorrect diagnosis of paranoid schizophrenia may be made." Such a small sentence, so few words, but if it's made, I thought, it hangs like the sword of Damocles over the person's head for life.

It was two days later that I was forced to run to the books again. Rusty was sitting on the couch with me and though she often fell asleep spontaneously during our conversation, she was less confused than she had been for a while. It was during one of those naps that I decided to make some tea.

I was in the bathroom when the kettle began to whistle and as soon as I got out I turned it off. But it was too late. Rusty was in seizure again. It passed rather quickly, and so while she slept off her postictal (postseizure) state, I leafed through a book on epilepsy. Under "Triggers" I found that almost anything can set off a seizure, depending on the irritability of the brain cells at that time. Flashing lights, high-pitched sounds could sometimes do it and . . . my teakettle! I got up and threw the whistle in the garbage. Rusty was sitting up by the time I'd finished, and seemed to feel okay. "Want some hot chocolate?" I asked.

"Thanks," she said, smiling.

I was pouring boiling water when the phone rang, so I couldn't pick it up right away. By the third ring, I reached for the receiver . . . but Rusty was already in another seizure. While Rusty slept this time, I turned down all the bells on the phones.

By the next afternoon, Rusty was staggering again very badly and yet she insisted on taking a shower. I argued with her about it. "No way," I told her. "I'm not going to pick your slippery wet body off the bottom of the shower. Wash at the sink."

She agreed reluctantly and when I wanted to stay in the bathroom with her, she refused. Several times while standing at the sink she lost her balance and had to grab onto the wall. Finally, trying to respect her wishes, I said I'd leave if she let me put a towel around her waist and anchor her to the legs of the sink just to help her maintain her balance. She agreed. The tub was right behind her. "Sit if you feel dizzy," I said. "Just loosen the towel on one end." She nodded and I went into the kitchen to allow her some privacy.

I was standing at the kitchen sink washing dishes, looking out the window at the backyard, when the rescue whistle blew. I was glad that Rusty was home with me so I didn't have to worry. The whistle blew a second time, and I was listening for a third blast, which would indicate a fire rather than an emergency, when I heard what sounded like Rusty crying out. By the time I opened the door, I had already heard the crash of glass and plaster.

God watches over children, drunks and Rusty, I thought later as we sat in the emergency room waiting for a skull X ray. Rusty had fallen back into the tub in seizure, and her head had broken the handle off the ceramic soap dish inserted in the tile wall. Now I knew the triggers for her seizures were teakettles, telephones and rescue whistles. I wondered how I was going to convince the fire department to send up smoke signals rather than blow high-pitched sirens. Maybe I'd just buy Rusty some earplugs.

I couldn't live constantly worrying about Rusty breaking her head. I was getting frantic thinking that by the time this bout of seizures passed, Rusty would be damaged for life. I sat for hours that night and the next day trying to figure out how to cut out some of the danger. Finally I called Creede and told her. We had to come up with something other than nailing her to a bed, something that would spare Rusty but not immobilize her.

The red football helmet lay on the kitchen table. Rusty turned her back on it. "You'll have to wear it," Creede said, "or we can't let you walk around."

"I hate it," Rusty told her, pouting.

"Rusty, wear it just for a while so your head doesn't get broken . . ." I pleaded.

She looked at me as though she was ready to give in, but then she added, "I hate red. I never wear anything red. I look terrible in red."

"Now she wants a designer helmet," Creede said dryly. "I often ask myself why I associate with such lunatics."

"Creede," I said, "it's easy enough for us to get her a color she likes."

"I think you're both nuts," she remarked. But she went to see what she could find.

Two hours later Creede was back. She placed four helmets on the kitchen table and went into the utility room. When she came back she was dragging Rusty with her. "There you are, your highness," Creede said. "Pick your crown."

There was a plain white one, a silver one with black trim, an orange one with a green letter, and a bright gold one with a royal-blue bolt of lightning right in front.

Rusty smiled at Creede and didn't hesitate for a minute. "I want this one," she said, choosing the gold.

"You'll look like Flash Gordon," I told her.

"Or a representative for the electric company," Creede said, but I could see that she was pleased.

When Jeremy came home and saw Rusty in her helmet, he was jealous. "Rusty gets everything," he said, and he stormed upstairs.

Lynn just shook her head. "He's really crazy, Mom," she said.

Rusty followed him upstairs and I could have sworn she walked with more confidence. It hadn't occurred to me that breaking her head might have concerned her as well as the rest of us.

When Jeremy came downstairs, he was smiling. "Sebastian told Rusty to let me wear it when she's laying down. And he even said that when Rusty gets better I can have it."

"All's well that ends well," Creede said, hugging him.

Sebbie was driving me crazy. He got into everything. That day he had managed somehow to get into the cabinet under the sink, grab the container of Comet with his teeth, and chew it apart in the living room. Wet from his saliva, the powder had bleached large spots out of my brown carpet and my dark green couch. I wanted to kill him but instead I just threw him out of the house. Later, because of the kids' pleadings, I put him in solitary on the front porch.

He was a sweet puppy actually, and he was wonderful for Rusty. Often I wondered what went on in *his* brain. Dogs were so attuned to anger, they ran or crouched or hid from it. In all accounts of ghosts, I'd heard, dogs were noted to whine and slink away. Their instinct was infallible in protecting them from danger. Yet, whenever Rusty fell in seizure, no matter how much flailing and banging her body did, Sebbie would always try to play with her. One time Jeremy summed it up just right.

"Sebbie knows there's nothing to be scared of when Rusty's

being sick," he said, "and he knows too that if he plays with her, it's like when I hug her. She'll come back quicker."

I didn't have the guts to get into a philosophical discussion about where he thought she'd be coming back from, but by the way he had said it, I was sure he was referring to that part of Rusty that I called "consciousness." Because I wasn't ready to hear his answer, I never asked the question.

Now, while Creede, Rusty and I were in the living room and the kids were safely tucked in bed, I thought of how much my life had changed in the last months. So many of the answers I thought we had, we didn't. But I was still sure if we could get to a better hospital, with a staff more familiar with seizure disorders, with a more experienced neurologist, we might be able to solve the problem.

Suddenly Sebbie began a relentless howling from the porch. I pulled aside the curtain and looked out. There he was sitting, head up, snout raised, intently howling at the full moon in the dark sky. After I shouted at him a few times, without success, I gave up and sat back down in the living room. "I wonder why animals howl at the moon?" I asked aloud. Everything lately had to be considered a piece in a larger puzzle. I looked for clues everywhere all the time. I had been writing symptoms and theories on everything from Scott towels to toilet paper.

Creede leaned back on the couch. "I imagine that the moon sends off a high-pitched vibration that's out of a human being's capacity to hear. Like some of those dog whistles. When the animal hears it, he responds with a howl in answer."

"Sounds good," I said, "but I wonder what effect, physiologically, the moon has on the human brain. I mean, inevitably when there's a full moon, I get a headache. And I know that people in hospitals seem to be more restless and have more pain. And in psychiatric hospitals, patients act out more. Human bodies are mostly water, about seventy percent, I think. It seems to me that if the tides rise and swell during a full moon, maybe the brain swells as well, causing the kind of pressure that affects all the areas which control behavior."

Creede nodded, but Rusty was looking off into space, deep in thought. "What do you think, Rusty?" I asked.

She looked over at us and smiled. "It all seems possible. And probably each of those things is a part of the answer. But we won't really know until we understand everything about the tides of life and the currents of existence."

Creede and I just looked at Rusty. With a concept like that, there's something the matter with her brain? I thought.

Yet Rusty had been having both grand-mal and psychomotor seizures very frequently for the last few months and we'd had to increase her medications again. Then they seemed to stop but she had tons of petit-mal or absence seizures where she didn't hear or respond to what was said. I could hardly remember the time when Rusty and I had a long and adult conversation, hardly imagine what it had been like not to be tense as a guitar string, waiting for some crisis.

We lived in sort of a vacuum, the kids going to school, spending weekends at my parents', all of us eating and sleeping when we could. Rusty even began to look different; often her expression was vacant or bewildered as a child's. I never missed Jim anymore, though he had called often, wondering if there was anything he could do to help. I never wanted to go out on a date or to a movie. I never considered the quality of my life. I began to understand the families of my terminal patients or my patients with chronic illness, whose lives were consumed just with getting through each day.

The rules had changed somehow. I was no longer worried about my future. We were stuck in each moment. It had become a test of endurance. Rusty and I only had to weather it. Until this period passed. And experience had taught Rusty that eventually it would pass. So it was just time we had to beat. And ignorance; a common enemy that kept us bonded together. We had to win. It was survival. But at the same time, we needed to do something more than we were doing.

I had been haunting Jeff Lamberta for months about getting another neurologist to look at Rusty. A more experienced, less frightened top neurologist. At a good teaching hospital, I just knew that they'd have knowledge that had not yet been released to the world at large.

Dr. Lamberta was having a difficult time because Dr. Schlunk had not done anything that could be verified as incompetence, and he was the only neurologist on the staff at Greenvale. Staff doctors in small community hospitals have an almost incestuous relationship. Calling in a doctor from outside is like bringing home a mistress to a wife. No fun if you have to live there. But it was no fun for Dr. Lamberta to have to deal with me either. Not to speak of Dr. Nelson and us having no money. In truth, though Jeff Lamberta never said an unkind word about Dr. Schlunk, I had the feeling he wanted another doctor on consultation as well.

Finally he called and announced, "I found another neurologist who's willing to see Rusty. The only problem is that we can't have an appointment for weeks yet. I tried to get in touch with the neurology department at Calvary but there were no openings for some time, so I tried Hillsdale. It's as good as Calvary for neurological problems, and Dr. Levitz, the doctor I spoke to, is a well-known neurologist."

"Thank you for both of us," I said.

It was spring and Jeremy had a holiday from school. Lynn had stayed over at a friend's house the night before and wasn't coming home till late.

"I'm going to catch a fish," he told me, but when he came out of the utility room he was carrying the crab net. I didn't question him; it didn't seem important.

Rusty was sitting on the floor in the corner of the living room, crying. "Hey, Rusty," I said, sitting on the floor next to her, "why the tears?"

Her bottom lip quivered and big tears rolled down her cheeks. She tried to stop them by sniffling hard, but her chest heaved again and again and the tears kept coming.

"It's all right to cry, Rusty," I told her. She drew her legs up in front of her and put her head down on her knees. I petted and smoothed her hair. "Don't try to stop the tears, honey," I encouraged. "Can you tell me why?"

But she couldn't. Her big brown eyes searched my face for long minutes as though trying to get me to understand. Then, like a small trapped bird, her eyes darted all around the room. I could see she was alert but now I knew she *couldn't* speak.

I pulled her close to me and just held her as I had Lynn so many times when something hurt too deep for words. "It'll be okay, Rusty. Really, honey. It will."

But right then I felt like a single buoy in a boundless ocean.

When she had spoken the day before, she seemed confused and was inappropriate when she did respond. Now she seemed very young again, and I was afraid of this new development. So much of the time her symptoms did remind even me of symptoms I'd seen in the mentally ill. She listened to things I couldn't hear, smelled things I couldn't smell, talked in sentences I sometimes couldn't understand. She looked fearful without a reason I could find, got angry expressions without provocation from external things. God only knew what was going on. I didn't.

Jeremy brought his tackle box and gear down to the water and then came back to the house. He had taken Sebbie with him on a leash and had tied him to one of the trees near the canal. "I'm taking Rusty down there too," he told me. He grabbed her hand and tried to pull her up. She struggled till she was standing, and Jeremy held tight to her hand. "She likes it outside," he said.

"Don't sit her too close to the water," I shouted after them as they walked down the path to the canal. "Remember, I can't swim."

"Mommy, be serious," Jeremy shouted back.

I watched out the window as Jeremy sat Rusty against a big tree. Then he carefully removed her gold helmet and placed it next to her on the grass.

"Jeremy," I shouted from the window, "what are you doing?"

"Letting Rusty get some air," he hollered back, and even from where I was I could see him frown. "She's only on the grass," he added.

I ran around the house spring-cleaning. The puppy had chewed everything in sight and so as I dusted I tried to color in the teeth marks on the furniture with dark furniture polish.

When the phone rang and I answered it, Nona asked, "How's she doing, Carol?"

"Not great," I said.

"I was just wondering," she continued. "I need some groceries and I don't want to have to bother the neighbors."

"You'll have to bother the neighbors," I said. The woman drove me mad, especially since right now I could even feel a bit sorry for her. Still, the only time she called, it seemed to me, was when she wanted something. And another need right now was like a too-big wave: if it hit me, it would drown me.

When I finished cleaning, I leaned out the window to shake the bathroom rug. I was surprised to see Jeremy's hands flying in animated gestures as he talked to Rusty. And I was more surprised to see that she seemed to be answering him.

"Lunchtime," I called out later, and Jeremy came running.

"Can me and Rusty eat outside, like a picnic?" he begged. "I might miss a fish if I come in."

Okay," I said, "but bring her in first so I can give her her pills."

"I'll take them to her," he said quickly. "It'll be faster."

So I gave Jeremy Rusty's pills and a picnic lunch, and sent him back down to the dock.

During the next few weeks, Rusty miraculously seemed to improve. Each nice day she and Jeremy went down to the water, and on the other days the kids and she played games in their rooms. Rusty's confusion seemed to be clearing a lot and she wasn't having as many seizures. It still amazed me that right after a seizure, when she really came to, she was much more alert than before. Lately the periods of clear thinking were getting much longer. And her balance was much better. Often now when Lynn came home from school, Rusty and she would go upstairs and I'd hear loud music playing. I didn't want to embarrass Lynn by asking, but I was sure that Rusty was teaching her to dance.

I was beginning to trust again.

Creede and I were sitting at the kitchen table, looking over color charts of paints. Rusty was upstairs resting. I had decided to do the house over in pastel colors, and Rusty and Creede said they'd help me paint. The kids were lying on the floor in the living room, Lynn was tape recording stories for Jeremy to listen to when he was alone in his room, when my mother called.

"You have to tell your son not to make fun," she said quietly. "It's not nice . . ."

"Ma," I said, "what are you talking about?" I knew I was in trouble. My mother loved my kids to death, but whenever Lynn or Jeremy had done anything wrong, they became *my* son or *my* daughter.

"Lettie from across the street called," she said, "and told me that Jeremy had all the children on the block lying on their backs jumping around with sticks in their teeth." My mother sighed. "And your daughter just stood by watching." When I didn't say anything, she added, "Don't yell. Just talk to them, honey. Most of the time they're good children."

When I hung up the phone, I must have looked as upset as I felt, because even Creede looked puzzled.

"Jeremy," I said firmly, "get over here. Lynn, you too."

They both came over and stood in front of me, nervous and expectant.

"Jeremy," I said solemnly, "I'm surprised at you. I thought you cared about Rusty–then I find out that you have all the kids lying on the grass imitating her. Why would you do that?"

As I watched, Jeremy's little face dissolved in tears. "I don't believe *you*, Mom," he said, his bottom lip quivering. "I thought *you* loved me." He turned and ran up the stairs.

I looked at Lynn questioningly. "Mommy," she said, her head down, "he was trying to teach the kids what to do when somebody has a seizure. Would you be mad at him if he was showing them how to fix a broken leg?"

When I went upstairs to apologize this time, Jeremy said, "It's okay, Mom. You just didn't understand. Parents don't know everything. Nobody knows everything."

"Next time, don't use a stick, Jer, only use something soft so it doesn't cut," I said, touched by his acceptance of me. "People with seizures can't swallow their tongues, and you'll only hurt them."

"Sure, Mom, he said smiling, "I'll tell the kids tomorrow."

One night, after the kids were in bed, I was on the couch reading and taking notes. Rusty, in her gold helmet, was sitting on the floor leaning against the livingroom wall. I noticed she wore the same expression as a football player who'd been pulled from the game and was sitting on the sidelines.

"What's up?" I asked from my perch on the couch. She had been very alert for the past few days and hadn't had a seizure in almost a week. "What's troubling you?"

"My life," Rusty said. "I'm tired of being nonfunctional."

"You're functional," I told her, laughing. "More than I am anyway. You did all the laundry, washing, drying and folding. You scrubbed three floors and waxed them. You painted part of the porch and repapered all the closets."

"That's not what I mean," she answered glumly.

"All right," I said, "give me your idea of a fully functioning human. I'll be your fairy godmother." I held up the pencil I was using and waved it like a wand. "Begin, my child," I said. "Wish for anything."

Rusty sat with her chin in her hand, thinking. She looked pretty funny wearing a sweatshirt, Bermuda shorts and a gold helmet. "First," she said, "I'd like to be able to run barefoot in the grass and be sure I could stay on my feet. I'd like to be able to go outside alone, without this on," she continued, pointing to her helmet, "and feel the sun and wind in my hair again. I'd like to get into my car and be able to drive anywhere and be sure I'd get back without hurting myself or anyone else. And I'd like to completely remember everything that happened in any day."

"Yes, yes, my child," I said, pointing my imaginary wand, "you have made fine wishes but with some you are burrowing into the deeper reaches of wisdom. So this may take a little longer. But please don't stop. . ."

Rusty smiled and continued, "I'd like a place of my own filled with things that I'd bought with money I'd earned from going to work every day." When I looked hurt, she quickly added, "So I could invite you and the kids over."

"That's better," I said. "Who wants to be a fairy godmother who grants a wish and loses a roommate? It's sort of a conflict of interest, you understand." I could see Rusty liked the idea that with all the trouble she felt she was causing, I still wanted her to live with us. "And now, for the big jump," I announced, "the wish that only *I,* as a fully ordained white witch, can fulfill. A wish that is bigger and better than all others . . . the kind of wish that can turn a frog back into a prince, or princess, as the case may be. Your *last* wish, my child."

"A credit card," Rusty said.

"A credit card?" I squealed. "You waste your big wish on a lousy credit card?"

"Well," Rusty said seriously, "if I had a credit card, it would mean that they had checked my past and there was nothing wrong with it and it would practically guarantee me a future. Because no one would give a person a credit card who wouldn't be around to pay them back."

After almost a month of relative peace, the thunderbolt hit again. Worse than before. Lynn was upstairs, and Jeremy was sitting on the couch with Rusty when she began to complain about a funny smell, stood up, and crashed to the floor all in an instant.

Jeremy went quickly to get the tongue blade, and between seizures placed it gently between her teeth. But when he turned to get the pillow from the couch, Sebbie jumped on top of Rusty and licked her face. I ran over, grabbed him, and almost threw him into the utility room. "Mom," Jeremy called, "Rusty's getting a funny color."

It was true. Her skin looked bluer than it ever had. I quickly tried to turn her sideways, but she was stiff as a board.

I rushed to the phone to call Jeff Lamberta. And while I was arguing with his answering service, Sebbie got out of the utility room. He playfully ran over to Jeremy and Rusty and grabbed the exposed end of the tongue blade with his teeth, growling as he shook his head back and forth so hard that his ears went flying. "Let go!" Jeremy told him, slapping the puppy's bottom. But Sebbie was having a great time playing with Rusty and the tongue blade. I was trying to figure out whether this whole scene was a comedy or a tragedy.

"Jeff," I said when he answered the phone, "Rusty's not breathing right."

Jeremy was now behind Sebbie with his small arms wrapped around the puppy's middle. But while Jeremy tugged hard at Sebbie, the puppy tugged hard at the tongue blade. When Rusty relaxed, both Sebbie and Jeremy fell back on the floor.

"I'll be right over," I heard Jeff Lamberta say before he hung up.

When Jeff arrived, he insisted Rusty be taken to the ER for intravenous medication. And when I objected, he promised that as soon as she came to, he'd release her.

I watched from the doorway as the ambulance techs carried Rusty out and Jeff Lamberta followed.

Lynn came downstairs, and when I explained what had happened, she began to cry. "Why are you so upset?" I asked. "It's happened before. Rusty will be all right."

"But before, it wasn't my fault," she sobbed, "and now it is."

Just then, Jeremy wandered into the living room and saw Lynn crying; he was twice as upset. "Don't listen to what she says, Mom," he said. "It's a lie."

"What's a lie?" I asked.

And then there was silence.

"What have you done?" I asked them both. By the look on Lynn's face, I knew we were in trouble.

Afterward, I sat for a while, trying to compose myself. It was always better if I tried to get myself together before I talked to the kids if I was angry.

Finally, after an hour, I went up to Jeremy's room. "Why did you throw Rusty's pills away when I trusted you to give them to her?" I asked sitting next to him on his bed.

"I'm not going to talk if you're not going to listen, Mommy," he said stubbornly.

"You're going to get a slap if you're fresh."

"Mom," he said slowly, "I'm talking about *listening* not saying I'm bad before you know."

"Okay," I said, "tell me."

"Down by the canal, Sebastian told Mr. Bibble..."Jeremy began, and I sighed. "You *promised*," he reminded, and when I nodded, he continued, "Sebastian was going to go away. He was going to take a knapsack and leave Rusty. He said there was too many earthquakes and he couldn't live like that. He said that he was taking Rusty's dreams and finding a place where he could sing."

"Jeremy," I said, "I don't know what this has to do with the pills."

"Mom, listen," he said, with his hands raised, palms up. "Sebastian said that he was tired of cleaning up. That his life was in danger because the pills dropped on his head. They even broke his fine china. But worse than that, he couldn't sweep fast enough to keep them out of the way, so he was always tripping–"

"Jeremy," I said seriously, "it's dangerous for people with epilepsy to not take their pills. We were lucky that Rusty still took her morning and night pills. Not taking pills can make them so sick that they can die."

"But if Sebastian would go away, then Rusty would die any-way," he reasoned. "She can't live without the dreams or the feelings in Sebastian's box."

"Never again, Jeremy," I warned. "I don't care what Sebastian and Mr. Bibble say. Do you understand? I'm your mother. . ."

Lynn was more upset than Jeremy. "Lynn, next time, tell me sooner if anything like this is going on. It wasn't, but could have been, dangerous."

"I knew Rusty should take her pills, Mom," Lynn explained, "but she got so much better when she didn't take them that I thought maybe Sebastian and Mr. Bibble were right."

I frowned. "You too?" I asked.

"You know what I mean," she said. "I thought maybe Rusty knew something we didn't. But when she got sick again today, I got afraid."

"Never again," I warned her too. "I'm your mother . . ."

And the assumption that because I was older, I was wiser, combined with the title "mother," and its inherent arrogance, blinded me to a truth that they could see clearly at the time. A truth that would take the rest of us much longer to discover.

CHAPTER 19

The day we went to see Dr. Levitz, the neurologist, he examined Rusty in the office and then sent her to the waiting room while he spoke to me. "If we do a myelogram and find something, we have a problem. If we don't, we have as big a one. Because no regular hospital will keep Barbara for any length of time. As long as she continues to have so many grand-mal and temporal-lobe or psychomotor seizures each week, you'll have to consider placing her in a supervised environment."

Dr. Levitz was a decent kindly gentleman with balding head and wise blue eyes, and therefore had the sensitivity to look embarrassed when he told me that. There were no facilities available for people with epilepsy whose seizures were temporarily out of control. Without money there was no kind of supervised environment but a state psychiatric facility.

He did what he could. He increased her pills again. Now she was taking four Dilantin, four grains of phenobarbital and five Mysoline each day. She was down to eighty-eight pounds.

I was in a spaz, panicked again that we were going to wind up having no alternatives but the one I had sworn against.

When Dr. Levitz suggested another test, I fought him at first, but when he patiently explained our options, I gave in. I was hoping it would at least give us time, and maybe some small clue. Again, while Rusty resisted, I was putting all my nickels on medicine and Dr. Levitz.

After her second appointment with Dr. Levitz, and the report of a negative EEG that was done in his office, I had the nagging feeling that he was against a wall. And now he seemed to believe that many of her seizures were psychologically based. He hadn't said anything specific but I felt his attitude change. It was only a look, or the slight irritation in his voice, but it bothered me. Rusty hadn't said anything about it, but when Penny had stopped over one day, she had.

"Of course he'll start to believe it's psychological. Especially if he can't do anything with his magic treatments and pills," she said. "It's tough to find out you're not a magician. Or even that when you're trying, some of the answers still elude you. Because if they admit there's something going on that they don't understand, they have to admit that if it happens to them, they won't be able to do anything about it."

So one day when Rusty was particularly out of it, I took her over to see Dr. Nelson at his office. He would know. He was between sessions and asked us right in. Usually he smiled and chatted and looked very happy to see me. But now he looked concerned and upset. He quickly found his ophthalmoscope and examined Rusty's eyes and ears. As he did, I told him my fears that Dr. Levitz believed Rusty's seizures were being caused by some deep-seated psychological problem. He was furious. "She has retracted eardrums and turgid eye grounds," he said. Both these signs were indications of changes in the intercranial pressure.

"Take her home and put her to bed," he said. "I'll call Dr. Lamberta myself . . . and Dr. Levitz. Maybe together we can find a medical center that can offer some treatment."

Creede and I drove Rusty to Hillsdale Hospital two days later. "I don't really want to do this," Rusty said quietly. "I really don't."

"But Dr. Levitz believes that maybe the myelogram will show something that the other tests missed," I told her. "And we have to be sure, don't we? He's supposed to be one of the best neurologists around." A myelogram was another test like the puenmoencephalogram. Only instead of injecting air into Rusty's spinal column, the doctor would have to inject a contrast medium, a liquid that would show on X-rays. Its purpose was to try to find a tumor in a different location from the other tests. A tumor we could treat.

When we arrived at the hospital, Rusty insisted we leave her in the lobby.

"Why?" I asked. "I want to come up with you."

"I want to take responsibility for myself," she insisted. And I knew it was because she really didn't agree with the way I was doing it. "I can answer any questions they ask, and when they explain what they want to do, I want it to be my choice whether to accept it or not," she added.

Creede was pretty quiet. Which meant she was stumped. She just went out to the car and came back with Rusty's bag and my large hatbox hair dryer. Rusty had refused to go without a dryer and the smaller one had broken when she fell the last time. So I lent her mine.

"Can I just help you carry this upstairs?" I asked, feeling terribly guilty about subjecting her to more tests and then abandoning her, whether she wanted me to or not.

"I'll manage," she said, trying to smile. There was a silence between us as though we had argued. Then she added, "Really, I will be fine. Go home to Lynn and Jeremy, will you? I don't like them to have to come home to an empty house."

I nodded. Whatever was happening with Rusty was getting me crazy. The night before, when we had made the arrangements to bring Rusty to Hillsdale, she was in space. She didn't recognize anyone, couldn't understand what we were saying and couldn't respond enough for us to get a fix on her. Today, we drop her at the hospital and her brain is spinning like Einstein's. Right then, I was so exhausted I was glad for the few days' vacation.

That night the kids were upstairs, and I was lying on the couch trying to relax and enjoy not listening for the crash of a helmet. But I was nervous. The after effects of the pneumoencephalogram had been so severe at Greenvale . . . and a myelogram wasn't much better. Instead of turning her in a chair, they'd put her flat on her stomach. But they'd still have to tilt the table down to get the dye into her head. And if she started to seize again, and again, I couldn't think about it.

Suddenly I heard something. Then someone was pounding on the door. I got up and opened it.

"I signed myself out," Rusty said as she staggered in. For a moment I was relieved. But then our lack of options flew back into my brain and I panicked. "How could you do that to me?" I hollered. "It took so much to get you in. We talked to so many people, pulled so many strings."

"I know," she said, her head down, "but I just can't go through any more tests. I can't let them practice on me anymore."

I looked at her forlorn expression and then plunked myself down on the couch. "How did you get home?" I asked.

"I walked."

"Jesus, Rusty," I moaned, "that's at least twenty miles, how did you make it?"

Rusty smiled her mischievous grin. "Took the parkway," she said. "It's quicker."

Then she went out to the porch and came back carrying the big blue hair dryer. "Here," she said as she moved toward the couch, "Your hair dryer. I didn't forget it."

I slumped down on the couch. "We're in a terrible fix, buddy. We're in big trouble." Then, remembering that she was the one who was sick, I asked, "Why did you do it, kid?"

"Try to understand, Carol," she said. "I know that you, Creede and the doctors are doing what you believe is right, and I do understand that you're doing it for me. But instinctively I know all this is wrong. Every time I take more medicine, every time I have another test, it almost kills me."

"Well, what are we going to do now?" I asked her.

She sat down next to me on the couch and reached for my hand. "Just lock me in a closet," she said sadly, "and leave me alone until all this passes.

"But I can't just do nothing," I told her. "I couldn't handle it if something terrible happened."

"Look, Carol, at least when I was in the nuthouse and they were tying me up and putting me in solitary, making me take drugs that I knew were bad for me, forcing me to eat through a tube, I knew who my enemies were. I was angry at them, furious with them for all the indignities. But now I don't know who the enemy is. I know how much you care about me and how much you want to help me get well. That disarms me. I can't be angry. I can't fight back. And the only one I wind up hating is me for disappointing you." She put her head down as she told me, "Carol, the pain of a few fractures and a black-and-blue body is nothing compared to the kind of guilt I'm feeling. Do me a favor, and don't care about me so much." When Rusty looked up, she looked straight into my eyes. "Please stop trying to save me, or you'll wind up knocking me off."

I was crushed. I had been able to be sensitive only when I wasn't doing the damage. "I'll try," I said. "I promise I'll do the best I can." And that promise was made to us both.

Dignity is such tender territory. And medicine is such a brutal tool.

On the first really beautiful sunny day, Creede came to pick both Rusty and me up to take us to the beach. Rusty was especially foggy that day, couldn't keep her balance at all, and I wasn't thrilled to be going out, especially to the beach.

We must have had to walk a mile, barefoot on the warm sand, while Creede sang happy songs. "Stop acting as though you're crossing the Sahara," she told me.

Rusty smiled at me as though sharing a joke.

"Smell this wonderful air," Creede said to Rusty, who was staggering forward between us. "It's the healing energy of the ocean."

Rusty fell. Creede helped her up and dusted her off like a child. "Pay attention," she told Rusty, and to me, "Put your arm through hers. It will help hold you both up.

"Creede," I moaned, "why did you insist we do this?" I hadn't slept well for a lot of nights and so I thought she was crazy. But she was also a big help with Rusty so I couldn't refuse.

"We must maintain some semblance of normalcy. And normal human beings do go out sometimes and do walk along the beach on beautiful days," Creede insisted,

"I don't," I told her. "I like the weather indoors. The only thing different I do in the spring and summer is open my windows wider."

"You, my girl, are no example of a normal human being," Creede said dryly. And Rusty laughed.

Finally we were allowed to sit down by the water. We watched as one huge wave folded over the other in constant succession. The noise was deafening.

"I can't hear myself think," I shouted to Creede across Rusty.

"That's good," Creede shouted back. "You do altogether too much thinking. Stop trying to figure life out. Just get out and live it. Life is not a picture you can frame."

Rusty lay back down on the sand and soon fell sound asleep. The waves had slowed to a rolling few with just an occasional swoosh. Creede got up and walked around Rusty to sit next to me. "What will you do if she doesn't get well?" she asked softly.

"Oh, I don't know, Creede," I said. "I never even thought of that." I turned my head and looked down at Rusty. She looked so young and healthy with her blond hair swept off her face and her dark eyelashes making shadows on her sunburned cheeks. "I just know she'll be okay again. It's just a matter of time."

"During that time, you're willing to put your life on hold?" she asked.

"It's not on hold," I said, smiling. "I'm living it, the only way I know how."

Creede nodded. "Funny, but it never occurred to me before now, that it could continue," she said. Then, "I worry about you, my little friend."

"Don't," I said, reaching up to pull her hair. "I'm fine."

For a long time we sat silently. The sun was setting when Creede woke Rusty. "Open your eyes for a look at nature," she said as she helped Rusty sit up. "We have to go soon," she added, "but before we do, I'd like to give you something."

Rusty's eyes were questioning. "I'd like to give you the horizon," Creede said, pointing toward it.

"That's not yours to give," I said, laughing.

"Why?" she asked. "Whose is it?"

"Besides," I said, "what is she going to do with it?"

Creede raised her eyebrows as though I was being absurd. "Your turn," she said.

"Me?" I said. "There's nothing here for me to give her."

"Look again," she said, reminding me of Jeremy and Mr. Bibble.

"Okay." I laughed and with a grand-gestured swing of my arm said, "Rusty, I give you every seventh wave."

"Why every seventh?" Creede asked.

"I figure every wave is too much for anyone to handle," I told her.

"Have you anything to say?" Creede asked Rusty.

Rusty smiled her wacky drunk smile and giggled. "It must be the medicine," she said, "but this sounds funny."

Then we all laughed. On the way back to the car, Creede ordered, "Dig your feet deep into the sand. Pretty soon the tide will come in to wash the footprints away. She put her arm around Rusty's shoulder and pulled her close. "Each of us needs to leave our mark," she said.

Since Rusty had talked to me on the night she signed herself out of Hillsdale, I tried to mind my business and leave her alone. I didn't want to be her jailer. I didn't want her to be my pawn in fighting for justice. I didn't want to be strong at her expense. And yet I so wanted her to have a chance at life. A chance to be well. I tried to allow her freedom so as not to cripple her.

Though Rusty had very few seizures in the next weeks, and none of them grand mal, she was still very ataxic. She often lost her balance. Slowly the amount of medication she was taking started to really bother me. I had been struggling with it all along, but now it began to sink into my faith-ridden brain that she had actually done better when Jeremy had thrown away her pills. Still, I didn't see much choice but to keep giving them, because withdrawal from them could mean Status Epilepticus and possibly death. At the time, blood-level tests for anticonvulsant medication weren't available routinely and no one had suggested we have them done.

Rusty tried to do even more around the house and also began to help her mother again. She insisted on calling a lot of the shots, and

I had a hard time dealing with it. There was always truth in what she said, always right on her side, and yet like a note in a song that throws the whole melody off, Rusty's perceptions were just a little off. My biggest conflict was over her decision to drive. I didn't use muscle, I just told her I wished she wouldn't.

"But I'm not having any seizures," she told me.

"Still, you're staggering from the medication."

"Well, it's because I stagger so much when I walk, that I want to drive," she said.

"That doesn't make sense," I insisted.

"If it's the medication that's making me stagger, and I have to take it my whole life," she asked, "I just have to adjust to the fact that I can't walk and I can't drive?"

Trying not to control Rusty's behavior was pitted against wanting to keep her from being hurt. Sorting my priorities was becoming a Herculean task.

Then Rusty had three accidents in a short period of time.

"It wasn't my fault," she told me after the first one. "I was stopped at a light."

"Well, at the very least, you're too unlucky to be driving, then," I said.

The second accident happened because Rusty was in a bind again, and as far as she was concerned, it was unavoidable. A large Irish setter had run out in front of her and when she stepped on the brakes to stop, the car behind her hit her. "He was tailgating," she insisted, "and the insurance is going to pay for my damages, so I couldn't be wrong. Anyway, did you want me to kill a dog rather than get the back of my car a little banged up?"

"Well, from now on, it has to be your responsibility," I told her. "I can't take responsibility for what you do if you're not going to listen to me."

She smiled her funny drunk smile and said, "You can't take responsibility anyway, even if I listen to you. If I do it, I'm responsible."

"But you're not acting responsibly," I told her.

She gave me her cocky look. "No," she said, "I'm not doing what you want me to. That's different."

I began to treat Rusty the way I did my kids. That meant I was alternately kind and understanding and then firm and authoritative. The constant stress was making me pretty irrational. One day I'd speak softly, the next I'd yell. And of course, I'd read. The more books I read, the more divergent the opinion of the experts was. So each week, I had a new theory. Rusty was often confused by my reactions because I had forgotten to warn her when I had changed lanes. "Why didn't you tell me?" she would say.

"I did," I'd answer. And if I had just read a book in which a large emphasis had been placed on psychology, I'd add, "Your not remembering is just a defense. Hearing is the last sense to go–you know that. People in comas near death who recover tell how they were able to hear."

Rusty would defend with, "Well, maybe I heard you, then, but I forgot. So it can't count."

One night after Rusty had gone to bed, I was lying in bed reading and came across a passage by T. S. Eliot:

Half of the harm that is done in this world
Is due to people who want to feel important.
They don't mean to do harm but the harm does not interest them.
Or they do not see it, or they justify it
Because they are absorbed in the endless struggle
To think well of themselves.

When I read that, I wondered about all the doctors, psychiatrists, social workers and nurses who were treating or had treated Rusty. And I wondered about myself. Then more quickly than Rusty forgot things, and without her reasons for forgetting, within minutes that passage slipped from my mind.

The third accident was the worst. It almost totaled Rusty and her car.

"Don't forget you have an appointment with Dr. Levitz," I reminded, "and Jeremy's sick, so I can't take you."

"I'll get there, don't worry," she told me. She was now insisting on taking responsibility for herself most of the time and I was tired enough to allow it.

"Remember,"I told her, "no hitchhiking."

Rusty nodded. Creede was supposed to take her but she'd worked two shifts and was asleep. So rather than break her appointment and disappoint me, Rusty again took the car. This time she was hit on the parkway, and her car turned over. "But it wasn't my fault," she said again. "The insurance company is going to pay to have my car fixed."

That night in the emergency room, I told her, "I don't think you should be driving right now. The insurance company is not going to pay for a new head when yours gets squashed like a pumpkin." Her whole body was black and blue.

After several attempts to reason with her, one day when she tried to get into the car, I blocked the door.

"What are you doing?" she asked.

"Stopping you," I shouted.

She stared at me both puzzled and angry but didn't push me aside. "Move, Carol," she said. "Please. I'm all right."

I wouldn't budge and neither would she.

Finally I threatened, "You can't live here anymore if you get into that car." I was afraid that she would hit someone and then she wouldn't be able to live with herself. Or hit something and she wouldn't live.

So she listened to me and didn't get into the car. Instead she ran upstairs and staked out in Lynn's room like one of the original pioneers. She put a chair against the door and refused to come out. When, after a half-hour, I couldn't convince her, and I had to go to my parents' for Sunday dinner with the kids, I called Creede. I asked her to try to talk some sense into Rusty and then I left the house.

After dinner, when Jeremy and Lynn had gone out to play with their friends, I explained to my mom and dad what had happened that morning, and told them that Rusty had locked herself upstairs in Lynn's room.

My dad decided to call her. "Rusty," he said when she picked up the phone, "tell Poppy what's wrong." I watched his expression of concern intensify as he listened for a long time. Twice his eyes filled and he shook his head. Finally, in a soft reassuring voice he said, "Don't worry about it, baby. Nobody is going to take you away." Then he hung up.

But during the time Rusty and my father were talking on the phone, Creede had been trying to get into the house. When Rusty didn't answer her knocks or shouts, Creede had shattered the front window and walked in. She had been so worried that when she found Rusty was all right, she was furious.

"Stop playing games, Rusty," Creede shouted as she glowering in the doorway to the bedroom. "One day you're going to cry wolf once too often."

Rusty was confused and surprised. She hadn't heard Creede at the door and didn't know what she was doing there. When she figured out that I had asked Creede to check on her, she felt betrayed and angry. "I'd just love it if everyone would stop getting their kicks from pushing me around. I want all of you to get the hell away from me and leave me alone."

Before Creede could stop her, Rusty grabbed Sebbie, jumped into her car and drove away.

When I got home I called her mother's house. I still didn't understand what had gone on and was angry that she had taken the car. "What happened now?" I asked testily.

Rusty hesitated before she said, "Up till now, I trusted you implicitly and allowed you to make all the decisions. But as my head cleared, you never asked my opinion about what I felt was best for me. That's frustrating. I'm not objecting to your nursing opinions but there are other situations that you seem to think aren't important. Like, I can't just sit around and do nothing between doctor appointments and hospital stays. I need to do things to fill up my time. I can't just sit on the couch and read, I don't have the attention span for that now, I'm too hyper. Or too sedated. Sometimes I can't sit down and sometimes I can't stay awake. You're always worrying that I'm going to hurt myself, so you stop me from doing everything."

"Well, don't act as though I've got nothing to worry about," I said. "You have fallen, you have hurt yourself and we practically have a hot line to the police station."

Rusty was quiet for a long time; then she said, angry now, "Why don't you just admit you've had it? Why don t you just say you can't deal with it anymore?"

"Okay," I snapped, "I can't deal with it anymore." I was tired of feeling punished for trying to help.

I could hear Rusty take a deep breath. "Then don't. When I'm well again, I'll call you."

"A familiar line," I said teasingly. "Don't call us, we'll call you."

"I'm serious, Carol," Rusty said. "If you care about me at all, wait until I get back to you."

I had just enough time to realize she meant it. "Rusty," I said before she hung up, "promise you'll take your pills?"

"I Promise," she said. "Give me some time. I'll call you."

I held the phone in my hand for a long time before I could put it down. Then I walked into the bathroom and automatically turned on the water to wash my face. But as I looked at myself in the mirror, my throat started to hurt. Suddenly, from the deepest part of me came a cry, a wail, and with it came the tears.

CHAPTER 20

My childhood was crammed full of hero stories. Before I went to sleep at night, my father would read me one. While my mother hustled around the kitchen each night cooking us a marvelous meal, my father would tell me one. There was, of course, Robin Hood. And Jesus–a different kind of hero. But my favorites were the manhood rites of the American Indians. I loved those stories.

After I was grown, one day as my father and I sat talking I

reminded him of those stories. "You know, Dad," I said, "I always thought of myself as Robin Hood, or Jesus or the young Indian brave."

"Yes, baby," he said, smiling. "All of us do."

"Daddy," I said, "you're missing the point. I'm a woman. I should have thought of myself as Maid Marian, or the Indian squaw."

He smiled at me. "No, Carol," he said gently, "you're missing the point. When you see a leader, you tell them leadership stories."

But now, the last thing I felt like was a leader. Robin Hood had helped the poor, Jesus had healed the sick and raised the dead, and the Indian brave had found enough answers to make him a chief. After Rusty left, all those stories poked fun at me.

It was summer, vacation time, so the kids went to their father's for a while, and I began to try living alone. The year Rusty and I had lived together had taught me a lot. I had been so certain about so many things at the beginning. I had been so sure good doctors would immediately be able to make her well that it was a startling disappointment to find out they couldn't. I had been absolutely certain that if I read enough, studied the books and recorded her symptoms accurately, I could fit the puzzle pieces together. If, at the same time, I loved, believed in her, and was willing to take care of her, well, then, anything should be possible.

Suddenly I could see how pompous I had been in my judgment of Rusty's parents and others whose limitations had caused her pain. I, myself, had hurt her because of my own needs. That made me feel shaky. Most of my life I'd made mistakes with confidence. I had been able to act decisively because I'd trusted my own perceptions. But nothing I had done seemed to be working. Besides, because Rusty's perceptions differed so from mine, I couldn't be sure I was right. Not being able to see another person's view can make all the difference in certainty and confidence.

Now, fighting for Rusty was like fighting with Rusty, and her will or strong-mindedness–the thing that had kept her alive all those years was endangered by my will, my strong-mindedness. To win, in this case, would be only to lose. If both of us wanted her survival.

Because I finally understood that, my need as a nurse to make things better had to be sacrificed. The only way for me to do that was to try to stay away. But I had to do something I felt sure about, so I called the nursing registry and went back to work, taking care of a terminally ill man, Judge Goldstein, who wanted to die at home.

The days flew with me burying myself by working long hours. I washed him and fed him and sat him in a chair. I talked to him, let him tell me how he felt about his sickness, how different it was to feel powerless instead of powerful. We laughed together. Everything I did seemed to make Judge Goldstein more comfortable and that in turn made me feel better again. Before I realized it, a month had passed.

I thought constantly about Rusty. Several times I picked up the phone to call, but remembered what she had said, and carefully put it down again. The last time, it felt so awful, I called Dr. Nelson instead.

After I explained what had happened, I asked him, "Do you think I should go over to see her, or at least try to call?"

"You can drop her a note if you're concerned about her," he said kindly, "but I would try to respect her wishes. She may need the time to break some of her dependency on you. She may need the time to work out how she feels."

"I understand that," I told him, "but what if she's sick? What if she needs me?"

He hesitated. "She's not your responsibility," he said gently. "She told you that. She may need to get through this period by herself. You can't force yourself on her any more than you could force her to get treatment when she chose not to. She's not incompetent, Carol. She's ill."

Judge Goldstein was very sick, getting worse each day, so I began staying with him and his wife and before I knew it, another month had passed. Soon my kids would be coming home from their father's and school would start again. Often I thought about Rusty. And in clear images, I could remember so many of our favorite times. .

One day, remembering the orange and yellow autumn leaves, I even ran outside into the yard and tried to spin around alone, but the air seemed thin, I felt silly, and the only thing I got was dizzy. That day when I went upstairs and looked in the mirror, I even tried to hug myself as Rusty and I had done. But strangely enough, when the mirror showed me with only two arms hugging–the two arms looked all wrong.

Those good times with Rusty seemed like aeons ago. The fun, the carefree times, the healthy times. The picture of Rusty spinning around was now superimposed on the fallen Rusty, and both lay over Jeremy's snow angel.

I really missed her.

Judge Goldstein was dying. Painfully. I called his doctor and asked for some injectable pain medicine to give him.

"Not possible," his doctor told me. "Who will monitor the amount he's getting?"

Dr. Prudden, his doctor, was in his seventies and had been practicing a long time. He didn't like the idea of nurses taking over patient care. "His own pain will monitor the amount of pain medication," I told him. "And I'll keep an accurate record."

"I want him in the hospital," Dr. Prudden insisted. "Patients don't always know what's best for them."

"He knows how much pain he has," I argued. "He knows he's dying and he wants to die at home. What more does he have to know?"

"I insist he be admitted to the hospital," Dr. Prudden said.

"He insists on staying home," I repeated.

Finally, with Judge Goldstein's wife's permission, I called another doctor and asked for pain medication. When I explained the judge's history and explained his wishes, the doctor agreed to make a house call and order the medication we needed.

That night as I sat next to Judge Goldstein while he slept peacefully, I thought how strange it was that this man who had been a judge for so many years, with the power over other men's lives, was so defenseless when it came to his own dying. How each of us has our day, and how each of us will wind up as vulnerable as Rusty or Judge Goldstein. I wondered if there really was any justice.

When Judge Goldstein woke up, he was terrified. "Help me, Carol," he pleaded. His face was deeply lined with pain and fear.

"Is it pain?" I asked.

"Not really," he said, straining to smile. His eyes were cloudy. He was looking far away. "I thought I heard my mother call," he added, and I knew he thought it whimsy. But I had heard that too many times before not to know what it meant.

"Maybe she did call," I said, sitting next to him and holding his hand. "At a time like this, sometimes mothers do."

With difficulty he turned to face me. "Why do you do this?" he asked, and I wasn't surprised because it was a question I had heard so many times before. A question I had asked myself.

"Nursing, you mean? Working with dying patients?" I asked.

He licked his dry lips and nodded.

I got up and got a piece of wet gauze filled with ice so he could suck on it. He had been having trouble swallowing lately and I didn't want him to choke.

"It's important to me," I said. "It allows me to see my future."

"But it must be frightening to see so much death," he whispered.

"No," I told him gently. "Not for me. Not anymore."

He smiled and squeezed my hand.

Later, when he was struggling to breathe, I asked, "Should I wake your wife?"

"Please, no," he said. "Just hold my hand. Let's spare her this."

I knew nothing about Judge Goldstein's past; he knew nothing about mine. At that moment, the only thing that was important was that I was another human being; that was enough to keep him from being afraid.

After he died, I sat for a long time holding his hand. I felt it go from warm to cold. Then I just watched him for a while, letting my thoughts wander. What had his life been like? Did he do good or bad things? And did any of that matter now?

As had happened so often before when I stayed with patients after they'd died, I imagined I could hear them talk. And the things they said were always comforting. Always reassuring. Always: "Everything's fine as it is. Just live. That's all that is important."

I got up and closed his eyes. Then, I gently washed his body, taking time over the bruises and the protruding bones that showed the price he'd paid for life. I silently told him how sorry I was that he had ever had to suffer anything at all, and that I understood what a tough battle he had fought. It didn't matter that I didn't know his particular pain, his particular battle. All of us have them. The feeling I got was the same feeling I had when I watched my kids sleep at night, in total surrender and vulnerability. I didn't have to stand apart then, I could push their hair off their foreheads and go over the things that had happened in the day, either smiling at something or apologizing for some damage I had done them.

Later, after his wife had cried and hugged him goodbye, and we were waiting for the medical examiner, I was sitting alone in the room with him and suddenly I felt energized again. It had happened to me before, with other dying patients, and though I could never prove why, I had worked out a kind of understanding. It was as though someone was moving out of a house they had lived in for a very long time to go somewhere else. There were always things in that old house that were too much of a burden to take. Furniture, nick-nacks that wouldn't fit in the new house or didn't match. But for whatever reason, some possessions were always left behind. Given to a friend or neighbor who was staying in the old place.

Life energy, human energy, can't be taken into death. Maybe it's a gift, and so it's left behind. To a friend.

After the medical examiner pronounced Judge Goldstein dead, I stayed to wrap him in a shroud and to make sure the funeral directors would treat his body with respect as they carried him away.

I had only known him for two months, and I didn't know him well. His death shouldn't have mattered to me. But it did.

❖❖ ❖❖ ❖❖

When Rusty hadn't called me the first month, I thought she was angry with me for being what she saw as controlling, and when she didn't call the next, I was sure she was furious. No news is good news, I kept reassuring myself. I was certain if anything happened to Rusty, Nona would call.

Eventually, when I couldn't stand it another minute, when I

couldn't respect Rusty's feelings any longer, I called her mother. "Can I talk to Rusty?" I asked.

Nona was silent for a long time. I thought she wasn't answering because she was angry with me too.

Finally she said, "Rusty's in Brighton Hall."

"Where's that?" I asked.

"Rambling Woods," Nona said.

It happens when something hurts so bad you can't even cry. It really does happen. Not only with fear. But also when something is so brutal, so unjust, so painful, that you can't stomach it . . . you do throw up. It also happens when a promise you made with all your heart gets broken.

That night, I couldn't sleep. I woke up soaking wet with sweat, knowing I had dreamed, not remembering what. I went down to make myself some tea, and the silence in the house made me feel like a stranger there. I stood in front of the kitchen window a very long time just staring out and let the water from the faucet run full force, filling the kettle and running over into the sink. I couldn't believe it. Rusty in Rambling Woods, again.

The night was still and warm. Light from the full moon hanging in the black starless summer sky shone over all the trees in my backyard. From the kitchen window I could see the shadow of the abandoned tree house. I looked at it a long time and wondered why I'd never had the courage to climb into that damn thing with Rusty and the kids. Even Lynn had gone. But I had always refused. Why? I wondered now.

When the tea kettle boiled, I turned it off. I never made the tea. Instead I walked outside and looked up at the moon. It was still smiling. I roamed down to the canal and sat in the still dark of the dock just staring into the black water for a long time.

The leaves from the trees were rustling as I started back to the house. But just outside my door, I turned to look around the yard again. And all I could see was the tree house. I walked slowly to the bottom of the tree and looked up. It seemed high to me. Then I lifted my foot and put it on the first wooden rung that Rusty had so carefully hammered in, so Lynn wouldn't fall. I tested it. It seemed to hold. I grabbed onto the ropes that Rusty had hung on the overhanging branches and pulled myself up. One rung at a time until I reached the top, where I was smothered and covered with leaves. I bent, stepped inside and I sat. It was very dark and quiet. "Rusty," I whispered, "I'm so sorry. I really am so sorry." Then I put my head on my knees and I cried.

Four days after Rusty had gone home to her mother's house, she had gone for a walk with Sebbie. The puppy ran, jumped and leapt around on the new leather leash she had bought him. Several times she slipped and fell when he pulled too hard, and each time she struggled to hold on.

When the white cat ran into the road and sprinted across Sebbie's path only inches from his nose, he bolted forward, pulling Rusty down once more. This time she fell in a muddy puddle and hit her head hard on the ground. She sputtered through the dirty water that had sprayed up into her nostrils. She could taste the dirt on her teeth. She was dizzy. Her head was spinning and her eyes wouldn't focus.

She wondered how many pills she had taken that day. She was supposed to take thirteen, but one day faded into another and she didn't remember whether she had taken three or twenty.

They made her sick to her stomach; she was almost always nauseated lately so that all she'd been able to eat or drink for months was hot chocolate. And she was getting tired of that.

Rusty rolled over on her back and Sebbie was licking her face. She laughingly pushed him away with her hand and tried to get up. She couldn't sit without falling over. So she rolled over again and tried to kneel.

She was on all fours when Sebbie bolted again and the leash flew out of her hand. Sebbie dodged his way through the traffic and disappeared into the woods across the street.

Rusty spent the next hour searching for him, calling out.

Finally she started home. She noticed, and it amused her slightly and puzzled her too, that several times she tripped on what appeared to be level ground. People passing her stopped and stared. She thought they were looking at her mud-encrusted face and body.

What she couldn't know was that she looked as drunk as a Bowery bum. She staggered when she walked and appeared to be talking to herself. She had a gash on her forehead where she had hit the curb of the sidewalk, and it was bleeding badly. She never felt it.

Rusty's mother was out shopping with a neighbor when she arrived. So Rusty stumbled into her room and got some clean clothes; then she went into the bathroom to turn on the shower. She sang as she undressed, for the moment forgetting about Sebbie, and grabbed the razor out of the medicine chest. She jumped under the hot water. It felt wonderful. She had forgotten the shaving cream and wanted to shave her legs and underarms, so she got back out of the shower to check the medicine chest. No shaving cream. The bathroom was cold, so she decided to use plain soap. She got back under the hot water again and let it warm her shivering body.

Then she started to shave under her arms. The razor was old and dull. Several times she cut herself but didn't feel it. When the cut hairs fell on her chest and belly, she thought they had sprouted there. And so she shaved those too. And cut herself again. When the water spilled down pink, Rusty looked up at the shower head. Pink water, what a gas! And she continued to shave and knick and cut all the way down to her ankles.

She remembered then about Sebbie, knew she'd have to find him, and so she hurried out of the shower to dress.

Her mother, just standing in the doorway, scared her at first, but when she heard Nona scream she was bewildered and concerned.

"My God, Rusty," her mother cried, "Not again. What have you done?" The neighbor was now standing behind her. Rusty grabbed a towel to cover herself and that's when she noticed the blood. She was as surprised as they were. Rusty didn't understand till much later why her mother committed her again.

Brighton Hall was an inpatient facility with open wards on the grounds of Rambling Woods. One institution was state funded and one was funded by the township. Inside, neither looked as though they were funded at all.

Rambling Woods was, at that time, undergoing administrative changes and therefore was not accepting admissions. That's why Rusty was taken to Brighton Hall. The two policemen who brought her in, didn't want to. The psychiatrist who admitted her didn't want to.

"But I can't take care of her, and she has nowhere else to go," Nona Russell told them.

And so Rusty was admitted to Brighton Hall. Within an hour of being there, she fell, broke her front teeth, fractured her skull and was immediately sent to the medical building which served both Brighton Hall and Graylock. It was called Stark Med #7.

Rusty had been in the hospital for more than two months and her mother had managed to visit with her almost every day, even though the doctors said she shouldn't bother, that her daughter wouldn't even know she'd been there.

Rusty was slumped over onto the tray of the geri-chair. She had been tied in so she wouldn't slip down and fall out. She could barely raise her head. When she did, her mother tried to get her to drink some soda–she had always liked soda–but it just drooled out the side of her mouth.

Now Nona Russell got up to leave, crying. She couldn't take seeing her daughter like this any longer.

Rusty couldn't swallow. Rusty couldn't talk. What her mother didn't know was that Rusty was aware of everything that was happening around her. Though her body wouldn't function, her mind did.

Since she'd been here, Rusty had spent a lot of time parked in front of the TV in the dayroom. She began to understand exactly how the old people she had taken care of at Salvation felt parked along the walls in the hall, because here she was exactly like them. For sixteen hours at a time, you're placed somewhere and left until they move you in to lunch or into bed. She had no control over what she did, when she ate, or when she went to the bathroom.

Then, one day, Rusty's head was a little clearer than usual and a voice from deep within her said, "This will be enough, no more."

She remembered reading a story in the newspaper about a young girl who had been raped and whose throat had been cut. The girl had fallen down in the parking lot and could feel herself losing strength, bleeding to death. With the little strength she had left, the girl forced herself to stand. She shoved a piece of her blouse into the hole in her neck, and began with great effort to run to the highway for help. Several times, the girl had gotten so tired that she had wanted to lie down and rest, but she knew if she stopped, she'd bleed to death. Finally she had made it to the main highway, where someone had picked her up and had taken her to a hospital.

Now Rusty had the feeling, with the same certainty, that if she stopped fighting, if she allowed herself to give in and rest even for a moment because she was tired, all her will to live, like blood, would drain out and she would die.

It had been weeks that she hadn't been able to swallow well, so often the attendants didn't bother to take the time to crush the pills and try to get them down. Too often when one of them did try, Rusty choked so badly, they got frightened. That's how her medication was initially cut down enough for her body to begin to work again and her mind to uncloud.

That afternoon, she decided she felt ridiculous sitting in a high-chair and so she began with studied concentration to untie the knots of the Posey jacket that trapped her. It took hours, but then, she had hours with no one watching, to finally free herself. She gently slid down under the tray like bending under a limbo stick, fell to the floor and began to crawl to the bathroom.

Once inside, she tried to pull herself up on the ridge of a sink to see if she could stand.

Suddenly the swinging door behind her opened and the attendant, John, was towering over her. "What do you think you're doing?"

"My nails," she said aloud. And the return of her voice surprised her as much as her sarcasm surprised John.

"Don't move," he ordered. "Wait right there." Then he went to get a wheelchair.

Rusty tried again to pull herself up on the sink, but her legs wouldn't hold her. So she crawled over to the toilet and struggled up to the seat and for the first time in weeks managed to urinate with privacy. She was elated. Forgetting she couldn't stand, she toppled to the floor.

When John got back, she was lying face down, out cold.

Several days passed and Rusty began to feel a little stronger. She noticed that long periods of time had passed that she couldn't account for. But there were none of the post-seizure clues like a bitten tongue or aching muscles. She figured that maybe she had gotten so weak that instead of thrashing and banging when she fell, now she just melted and wriggled like a caterpillar. That idea struck her as funny and so she giggled out loud. Again she was surprised when she could hear her voice. One of the patients who had been pacing back and forth in front of her looked startled by the sound of her giggle. When she stopped and stared at Rusty, Rusty crossed her eyes and moved her arm up slowly. And it did move. She found she could control it. When the woman looked frightened, Rusty laughed again.

The next day, John took her out of the geri-chair and put her into a regular wheelchair. They even allowed her to go downstairs to the dining room to eat again with the other patients. Then they allowed Rusty to get out of the wheelchair, and holding on to them, to take a few steps. What exhilaration she felt to be upright and walking again.

The day I talked to Nona, I immediately called Brighton Hall to try to speak to Rusty. The head attendant on duty had no idea who she was and had no record of her being there. I called Rambling Woods admissions and asked if they had information. Barbara Russell wasn't a patient there, according to their records.

I called the psychiatrist in charge of Brighton Hall. The girl I was looking for, he thought, had been transferred to another building. When I asked where, he explained that patient information was a private matter and therefore confidential. He could tell me no more. I was in tears most of the day, frustrated by my inability to talk to Rusty, to see her now that I knew she was sick.

I called Nona back. She told me, "It's no good, your trying to see her. She won't even know who you are." I was frantic.

As soon as I got off work, I immediately drove to Rambling Woods.

Once there, I still couldn't get any information. I didn't know where to begin to look for Rusty. I left my name with a social worker, explained the situation, told her I was a nurse and asked that she call me as soon as she found out anything. She agreed. I walked back to the car totally frustrated and sick with worry over Rusty.

It was on that wonderful day, that marvelous lucky day, that Dr. McDevitt, one of the world's most wonderful doctors and a very competent neurologist, happened onto the ward.

Rusty didn't notice him until he was standing almost directly in front of her. And then his size alone startled her. It was difficult to keep her head straight, hard to keep it from wobbling, so her eyes focused badly. Still, she could see he was young and fine-featured. He was also immaculate, his black hair shone and his clothes were well-tailored. Then he smiled. It was such a warm compassionate smile, and when momentarily he frowned, it was with concern. His gray-green eyes had a look of intelligence she had seldom seen since she'd been in Stark Med.

"How do you feel, dear?" he asked without condescension. She was always asked that, usually in a tone that indicated the answer should be "Fine."

Rusty instinctively felt Dr. McDevitt really wanted to know. So she began to talk, haltingly at first, then faster, to tell him exactly how she was feeling. The words came, and then the concepts, though those with more difficulty. Webs clouding and tying up thoughts in her mind. He listened patiently. After a few minutes he took her, with his arm around her shoulders, to sit with him on one of the wooden benches. He made her close her eyes and touch her nose. He looked deep into the pupils of both eyes, he checked her reflexes and made her push with each fist, then each foot, against his palm.

Finally he called over Mrs. Zelnick, the head nurse, and asked, "What medication, in what dosage, is this young lady getting?"

She went to get Rusty's chart. "Dilantin four times a day, phenobarb four times a day, Mellaril three times a day, Mysoline five times a day, and Cogentin four times a day," she said as though reading some exotic roll call.

Rusty had been placed back in the wheelchair several feet away from Dr. McDevitt. But even from where she was sitting she could hear him sigh.

"Where are the blood level slips?" he asked the nurse. Drug or blood levels indicate the amount of medication concentration in the bloodstream. It's the only sure way to establish if someone is getting toxic from too high a dosage.

"None were ordered, doctor," she answered apologetically.

"How much does Barbara Russell weigh?" he asked, beginning to sound cross.

"Eighty-three pounds, doctor," she answered, as though happy to have found some of the information he needed.

Dr. McDevitt looked disgusted. "Cut the Mellaril and the Cogentin completely and cut everything else in half."

When the nurse nodded, Dr. McDevitt added, "And for God's sake, check what these patients are getting. She's so toxic you're lucky you didn't kill her."

Mrs. Zelnick sounded defensive when she said, "The doctor ordered it, sir. I just followed orders."

"Ellen," Dr. McDevitt said slowly, emphasizing every word, "just because a doctor ordered it doesn't mean you have no responsibility. What if it killed her? Would you be exempt?"

Mrs. Zelnick looked across the dayroom to see if anyone else was listening; then she turned back to Dr. McDevitt.

"And why," he was asking, "is she on Mellaril and Cogentin? Is either a new drug of choice for epilepsy?"

"She's been diagnosed as paranoid schizophrenic, doctor," Mrs. Zelnick told him.

But he shook his head and said, "How the hell can you tell what symptoms she's exhibiting when everything is so masked by the side effects of the medications?" He was still shaking his head as he was leaving. "Cut that medication immediately," he repeated.

Rusty couldn't grasp all that had happened that day because of the thick fog in her brain.

But from within, down deep inside that secret place which knows, the small and happy voice of wisdom began to yell, "Here goes!"

CHAPTER 21

Rusty was back in Brighton Hall, standing at the nursing station playing with the dial on the black telephone as I walked through the door onto the unit. I stood for a while studying her. How much of her mind was still intact? I wondered. After two months of not seeing her, my heart was pounding as I watched her. Same pale freckled skin, blond hair a little longer. She wore a brown shirt pressed without a wrinkle and the brown and gold striped pants that we had bought together. She turned her head when one of the male attendants spoke and I saw the familiar look of childlike vulnerability, her full lips slightly parted.

"Rusty?" I called softly. But she didn't hear me. I called more loudly, "Rusty?"

She came running. And then she hugged me, buried her head in my neck and cried. I just held on, patting her. She smelled of Estée, even in a nuthouse she hadn't forgotten to wear her cologne. After several minutes I pulled her head back gently and looked at her face. Thinner than it had been, with darker circles underneath her eyes. She looked worse than when she had been seizing constantly. I touched her cheek and she smiled.

"What the hell happened to your front teeth?" I asked. My idea of a loving greeting, no doubt.

She looked confused for a moment; then she smiled and shook

her head. "They fell out onto the floor one morning as I was putting on my shoes."

"Rusty," I said, puzzled, "make that clearer, will you?"

She held tight to my hand as we walked down the dingy hall into a small dirty room that held three painted wooden tables and several straight backed chairs. She led me toward the table in the corner of the room, and when we were seated, she explained. "I guess I was on a lot of medication, because I never felt anything. In fact it took me a few minutes to figure out exactly what had happened. You see, I was sitting on the edge of my bed one minute, leaning over to tie my shoelaces, and the next minute I was lying flat on my face on the floor. When I lifted my head and saw blood, I raised my hand t） my mouth in surprise. No front teeth. I was so shocked that I actually crawled around the floor looking for them under the bed, until one of the attendants came and lifted me up. Rusty pointed to her mouth, to her new teeth, which were larger than her real ones, and said, "later that day, the dentist capped the stubs that were left and some-body explained that I had an akinetic convulsion."

There were several other patients milling around, most just jab-bering and walking in circles, bothering no one. Rusty was sitting, foot of one leg across the knee of the other, deep in thought. Then, looking bewildered again, she asked, "Why am I here? And how did you find me?" And so I explained . . .

A week and a half after Dr. McDevitt first saw Rusty and cut her medication, he ran into the social worker from Brighton Hall. The woman told him about my phone calls and so he went back to Rusty to ask how to reach me. But Rusty didn't want me called until she was well.

Dr. McDevitt explained to Rusty that he was certain most of her confusion and certainly some of her seizures were due to drug toxi-city. Reluctantly, then, Rusty gave him my number.

When Dr. McDevitt called, I was still moping around the house trying to figure out how I could track Rusty down. I remembered Rusty's story about Bell and was terrified that somehow she too could disappear.

The sound of Dr. McDevitt's voice, the idea that I could share my concerns with someone who really cared and understood, made me feel better immediately. When he explained about Rusty and told me where she was, I was thrilled.

"Don't get your hopes up," he warned. "She's still a pretty sick girl." Then he told me he was certain most of Rusty's symptoms would disappear as soon as the high level of medication had cleared her body. "The new blood level test will help us control the amount of medication more accurately," he had said, "so from now on there should be far less chance of toxicity. But it will take at least three weeks for all the drugs to clear. We can't make any assumptions until then. She'll have to return to Brighton Hall for now."

As he spoke, I thought about how I had hollered at Jeremy and Lynn when they first saw the logic of cutting down Rusty's meds. Then the doctor explained that hallucinations as well as seizures could be a symptom of the medication toxicity.

Dr. McDevitt sounded very serious when he added, "If cutting the medications doesn't do the job, you'll have to take her into one of the big neurological centers. Calvary would be one of the best. But let's cross our fingers and hope."

Now I looked hard at Rusty as I stood in Brighton Hall. She was worse than she had been some of the time she had lived with me, but certainly better than when I had sent her away. I wondered for the seven hundredth time why anyone would call medicine a science. Every few years when science found a new theory, the old one was obsolete. So what was science anyway except a new idea?

Rusty was leaning forward now, elbows on her knees, head in her hands, still shaking her head, uncomprehending. As I watched, lines from her tears made glistening paths down her cheeks, but she smiled as she said hopefully, "Can I come home?"

I looked around the room again. There was a young boy sitting on the floor in the corner rocking back and forth. And an older woman playing cards at one of the tables. Each time she turned up a spade, she'd scream and grab her chest. The rest of the time she sat quietly, menacing, daring anyone to come near.

Rusty had taken off one of her shoes and was absently rubbing her foot. She never noticed the blood or the indentation in her heel. I knelt in front of her and started to remove her white sock. When her foot was bare, I could see that the back of her heel was gone. Eaten away, chewed to a ragged hole by a decubitus ulcer, caused by the too small shoes she had been wearing. Rusty looked down at her foot as though it belonged to someone else and said, "I never noticed that before. And I don't feel it."

I looked up at her, surprised by her apparent indifference, and then I motioned to the tall male orderly who was standing in the doorway. Rusty told me that his name was Travis. He was a stocky gray-haired man with roughly pitted skin and pencil-thin lips. In the hours I had been there I had never seen a change in his grim expression. His white uniform was dirty and wrinkled and his shoes were scuffed. On his belt he wore an enormous ring of keys like a zookeeper's.

Travis walked over and took a look at Rusty's heel. He shook his head. "Silly bitch," he muttered, and began to walk away.

I was seething. I wanted to lunge at his back but instead I just cut ahead of him, beat him to the door and stood in front of him. With tremendous restraint I said, "I want to see a doctor." When he shrugged his shoulders, I added, "Immediately."

Some of the patients looked up momentarily; some never noticed that anything was going on.

"Look, lady," Travis said in a softer tone, trying to placate, "all I meant was she shouldn't have let it get that far."

"Travis," I said, almost hissing, "I want to see her doctor. Now."

Travis shrugged his shoulders again and sidled past me over to the desk phone. I followed and listened as he talked.

"Dr. Goodman will be right up," Travis told me, and then he sat at the desk and pretended to busy himself with paperwork.

I waited in the small room with Rusty for over an hour before, steaming, I decided to hunt down the good doctor myself I took the elevator down to the main floor.

I asked several people, as though I was a stranger in a strange land, for directions to Dr. Goodman's office, and they answered as though I had asked my question in a foreign language.

Finally I found his office by carefully reading the nameplates on more than thirty oaken doors in the hospital's basement. I knocked once, and then without waiting for an answer, walked in.

Hunched over one of those old scratched and damaged dark mahogany desks was a man of about sixty with a mane of white hair and a large ruddy-complexioned face. He wore an old blue suit with tie undone.

He looked up from the pile of magazines he was leafing through and asked, "What can I do for you?"

I explained all about Rusty, all that had happened since she had been admitted–jet sentences, with fury like smoke trailing. And then I said, "I want to get her out of here."

Dr. Goodman spoke with such indifference that I wanted to smack him. "She must be released in the care of a guardian," he said very slowly, and then added, "And from what I understand, her family is not exactly banging down the door to try to get her home."

"I'll take the responsibility for her," I told him firmly. "Now, what do I have to do?"

"My dear," he said, "I must ask, what exactly is your interest in this young girl?"

If I said I couldn't stand to let her rot like the rest of the people in the place, they'd think I was some kind of a naive nut myself, and so I said, "I'm her cousin, and a nurse."

"I know from Barbara Russell's history, she has no relatives," he said slowly as he looked at me warily, "and though I always mistrust nobility, I know that blood kinship is no guarantee of virtue. So you'd better stick with nurse. Then he said, "You'll have to go before a release board. They will ask questions, and if they're satisfied, she can go home with you."

He started paging through his magazine again. I had been dismissed.

I was still upset by the time I reached the unit again. A staff attendant, a young kind-faced black woman whose badge said her name was Kiki, was wrapping both of Rusty's heels as she sat on the side of her cot in the large barren ward.

"Could you get her some slippers?" Kiki asked, concerned. I nodded, and when she finished she left.

Now Rusty was lying on the cot, her eyes closed.

"What did he say?" she asked nervously.

I sat next to her. "We'll have to pass the release board," I said as I held her hand, "and then I can take you home."

I could see tears welling up under her eyelashes, though her eyes stayed closed; as she asked, "What about Jeremy and Lynn? Do they still want me there?"

I assured her that they did and then told her as gently as I could, "You can live with us for as long as you're not having active seizures. If you start convulsing again, you'll have to go to Calvary Neurological Center." It was a lousy deal and I knew it. I couldn't promise to keep her home again because with her guilts and my overprotectiveness, we'd wind up fighting again. I was trying to consider my kids too. For the short term we could all deal with anything, but if it wound up being long term again . . . So it had to be a hospital, a hospital for the physically sick. It wasn't great, but it was better than here, better than any state mental institution.

"Okay," she said, sitting up again. "And thanks, Carol. I'll try not to cause any more trouble."

Outside, it was getting bleaker. The wind was blowing hard through the many trees on the vast barren grounds and it had started to rain. In the dusk, the bars on the windows of that big brick building made it look like a prison. I wanted Rusty out of there as soon as possible.

CHAPTER 22

Rusty was home again! What a great feeling for me. Creede and Penny came over to welcome her, and the kids followed her around for hours. In the month that had passed until we could pass the release board, the medication cut had shown its effects. She had had no seizures. She was well again.

It was nice to have Rusty back and not have to listen to the crash of a helmet. It made all of us almost giddy.

That night after everyone left and the kids were asleep, I sat down to talk to Rusty. There had been something bothering me for a long time, and because it was so painful, it had taken me a long time to bring it up. But now I couldn't put it off another minute. Rusty and I were curled on opposite ends of the green couch.

"How did you forgive me for letting you go home to your mother so that she could throw you back into Rambling Woods?" I asked, my voice shaking.

"There was nothing to forgive," Rusty said. "I never blamed you. I could see that you didn't have much choice."

"But when you didn't hear from me all that time you were away, didn't you get angry with me then?" I asked.

Rusty frowned. "No," she said softly. "At first I did wonder where you were, but then it just stayed in my mind that I had made you promise to stay away until I was well. It was better that way." Rusty laughed as she added, "I figured you had just had it, and I couldn't blame you. I really couldn't."

"You're a good person, Rusty." In truth I was touched by her understanding. "No bad feelings?" I asked with wonder.

Rusty was serious. "Only the fear that if you ever gave up on me, I'd had it. I'd never get out of an institution with no place to go. And the doctors there made it very clear that they weren't letting me loose on my own. Rusty smiled and her eyes were full of compassion when she said, "No, Carol, I never blamed you."

The following morning everyone was so excited they were up at dawn. By the time I reached the living room, all of them were dressed. "Where are you going?" I asked Rusty.

"The tree house," Jeremy said.

When I made a face, Rusty said, "I've missed it."

Lynn was tying her sneakers when she asked, "Sure you don't want to come, Mom?" And all of them laughed.

"Sure," I said. "I'd love to."

Rusty, Jeremy and Lynn all stopped what they were doing and froze in place staring at me.

"What are you guys looking at?" I said, smiling. "Something wrong?"

"Poor Mom," Lynn said. "She's getting sick."

Jeremy laughed. "You're really going to try, Mom? Really?" Then he held his stomach and started to howl with laughter.

Rusty walked toward me, and pretending to be serious, said, "You can come, but everything stays as it is."

"What is that supposed to mean?" I asked.

Rusty winked at the kids. "No curtains."

Finally I took a book and leaned on the tree reading while Rusty and the kids climbed and played.

"Glad it's back to normal," Jeremy announced. And Lynn, from up in the tree house, waved.

Another month passed and I found it amazing how quickly the home situation had returned to the way it was before Rusty had gotten really sick. She was flying around the house again, cleaning, washing, making breakfast for the kids. Within the first week she had gotten a job as a private-duty nurse's aide from the registry and I was doing a number of easy private-duty cases. At night after supper, while Rusty played with the kids or got our clothes ready for the next day, I'd sit on the couch and read. Things had worked out. My faith was renewed.

One night during one of those scenes, I was sitting relaxing and reading.

"A mouse!" Lynn suddenly hollered, jumping up onto the sofa. "Look, Mom, in the kitchen."

I pulled my feet up onto the sofa too. "We'll have to set a trap," I told her, "and by tomorrow he'll be gone."

Jeremy and Rusty, who had been playing cards on the living-room floor, looked up at me. Then Jeremy asked, "Do mouses bite?"

"Mice," Lynn corrected.

"Do mice bite?" Jeremy repeated.

"No," I said, staring warily into the kitchen.

"Then why do we have to kill them?" he asked.

"Because I'm afraid of them," I told him. "There isn't a house big enough for both me and a mouse."

"They don't do nothing to hurt us, and because you're afraid of them, we have to kill him?" Jeremy asked incredulously.

"Don't put it like that, Jer," I said. "It makes it sound awful."

"It sounds awful to you too, Mom?" he said, his eyes wide. "But because you're afraid, we have to kill a small brown furry animal that won't hurt us?"

We didn't catch the mouse that night, or the next night either. And three days later, when I was cleaning the utility room, I found a box of birdseed that I knew I hadn't bought. I decided to ask Rusty and the kids about it when they got home from shopping.

But I forgot.

The following morning, very early, I got out of bed to go to the bathroom, and as I passed the window in the living room, I saw Rusty and Jeremy outside.

Jeremy bent down, opened the top of the birdseed container Rusty had been carrying, and as I watched, two small furry brown mice jumped out of the box and ran back into the woods.

The kids had been put to bed, Creede was home "hermitizing" and Rusty and I were reading. Though things had been quiet lately, I was still working on my epilepsy puzzle and the consciousness puzzle and the injustices-in-the-bureaucracy-in-society puzzle. This night my mind was snapping up facts like an alligator. "Hey, look at this," I said, holding out the book on neurology I'd been reading. "You'll be stunned to see how smart your brain is. I mean, look at this diagram and you'll see that the path the electrical charge in your brain takes is exactly the path that this brain has marked."

The brain in the drawing was labeled with the parts of the body that each specific part of the brain controlled. Right down the center of the brain in a line from bottom to top, it read: throat, tongue, face, neck, eyes, thumb, fingers, hand, forearm, et cetera. If an electrical current went haywire and ran the full course of that arc, the parts it would hit were in the exact order of Rusty's seizures. In my mind I could see them: first the click, click of Rusty's tongue, then her face and neck to the side, then her eyes up, then her thumb in, fingers folded over, wrist in, arm up, out she went. God, it was practically a blueprint, and still there were doctors who doubted her. There was no way she could have had this information with her background. Of course, it was possible that some of those doctors hadn't seen this picture either. Anyway, I was at it again. Back on the soapbox. Trying to force more information about epilepsy into Rusty.

Rusty shook her head. "I don't want to read anything on epilepsy," she said, "because I don't want to give my unconscious any new ideas."

"Brother," I told her, "have you been brainwashed. You keep believing that the people who told you that you were somatizing and that you were self-destructive were right." I sat up. "I don't think you are," I told her.

"Well," Rusty said hesitantly, "it will take some time before I'm convinced. In the meantime, I'd rather hear what I have to know from you."

"It takes a big toll on your self-esteem when you credit the things that have happened to you as deficiencies of character rather than defects in the equipment," I said. "Of course, I understand that belief gives you the illusion of having more control over your seizures, when in truth it's your brain shorting out, and it's not within your control. Certainly you can make sure to remember your medicine, stay away from alcohol and stress-provoking situations as much as possible, but in the same way that I'll probably always have migraine headaches when I put too much pressure on myself, you'll have an occasional seizure or seizure equivalent."

Rusty sat up and crossed her legs underneath her. Then she reached for her cigarettes on the end table and lit one. She seemed to be listening, so I went on, "All that stuff they laid on you about your seizures not being real because you didn't wet yourself or bite your tongue, every time they doubted you when your EEG's came back normal, was because of ignorance on their part. Pure bullshit! Blaming the victim is what it's called. And the truth is, even though I don't believe they did it to be malicious, I do believe they don't know enough about epilepsy to be as certain as they pretend to be. So I figure, in order to cover their ignorance and impotence, they had to somehow make what was happening your fault."

"I don't think I get it," Rusty said, frowning.

"Well, let's see if I can make this clearer. Mental illness is a catch-all now for everything that happens to fall outside their realm of knowledge," I explained. "It goes something like this: epilepsy can't be fit into a clean little box because no one knows yet exactly where it comes from or what really happens. Oh, they know about some kinds of epilepsy and they understand some of the causes, but there's too much yet that's unexplained. Therefore, because all of the symptoms are not always recognizable, they can't always see it. If they can't see it, it must not exist. If it doesn't exist and you say it does, you must be crazy. That gives them the label for the thing that can't be seen. Get it?"

"God," Rusty said, laughing, "you mean it was them, not me? And all the time they made me feel like such a failure. I couldn't even have a seizure right."

"But that's why I wanted you to read some stuff," I said. "It will be such a kick for you to know just how right you were.

Rusty made a funny face. "Small victory," she said, "when my brain is shorting out on me all the time."

"I think I understand what you're feeling," I said.

I thought about how I would feel knowing that my life was constantly affected by something outside my control, how uncomfortable and frightened I would be not knowing whether or not I could even make it across a street. Then I decided that I probably would never make it out of bed in the morning. I'd probably just lie around waiting for it to happen. But then, I didn't have Rusty's courage.

CHAPTER 23

Since Rusty had been home, each week she went to see her mom a couple of times. As she drove over to the house, she'd stop at the store and buy Nona groceries. Usually she relented and bought her a six-pack of beer as well. "What else has she got?" Rusty had asked when I questioned her about it. " She's lonely and she needs to pass the time."

"But she could get drunk, fall and hurt herself," I said.

"Then in the morning she'll pick herself up," Rusty explained, "and she'll have gotten through another night."

Before she went now, she drove up to the drugstore to pick up a couple of crossword-puzzle books to take with her. She wanted to bring her mother something, and she knew Nona enjoyed games. When she got back she handed me a card with a beautiful girl on the cover, leaning over in a field of daisies, one hand on the stems, pulling them out of the ground. The outside read, "YOU REMIND ME OF A GARDEN." When I opened the card, all it said was, "PICK. PICK, PICK!"

I started to laugh. "I guess that's how it must seem to you," I said.

"I was kidding, Carol," she said. "Honestly."

"Well, be careful," I told her, "and try not to get home too late." Rusty was whistling when she left.

Not more than a half-hour later, the phone rang. "Carol," Rusty said, and I could hear she was upset. "Could you come and pick me up? There's been a car accident."

"Where are you?" I asked. "Are you okay?"

Rusty gave me directions but hung up without giving me any details. What had happened, I wondered. Had she had a blackout? I couldn't afford even to consider that. I grabbed my keys and ran out to my car.

As I pulled up to the corner, I could see her standing on the sidewalk, blood running down her neck. Her car was nowhere around; apparently it had been towed away. Rusty smiled and held out her thumb. Instantly I was reassured. If she could kid around, she must be fine.

I stopped and she pulled open the car door. Her movements were stiff as she bent toward the seat of the car, a slow-moving marionette, and I asked, concerned, "What hurts? What's broken?"

She sat absolutely straight. Then she turned her head carefully toward me. "My spirit. And I have a lot of glass in my bra." She made a face.

"I was being serious," I told her. I started to drive home.

"So was I," Rusty went on.

I could see slivers of glass glittering in her blond hair. And she assured me that glass was hiding in every crease of her clothing.

When we stopped at a red light, Rusty asked, "Can I borrow your lighter?"

"Sure," I said, rummaging with one hand through the pocketbook that lay beside me on the front seat. "Did you lose yours?"

"No," she said, "but if I shove my hand into my pocket to get it, I'm bound to slit my wrist and someone will insist on taking me to the hospital, which is too dangerous for me."

We were almost home when I finally pulled over to the side of the road and asked, "What happened? I'm not moving until I find out."

"It wasn't my fault," she said quickly. "It really wasn't. When I saw that other car coming at me, I even managed to jump the curb and get up on the sidewalk. But it didn't help. I got hit anyway."

"Who hit you?" I asked.

"God," she said. There was a small splinter of glass like an icicle stuck in her neck where it was still bleeding.

"You'd better take a shower, not a bath, to get all that glass off you," I told her.

"If you were a real friend," she said, "you'd vacuum me first."

I laughed. "Do you want to tell me, or don't you?"

"Okay," she said. "Just some poor woman who was coming home from waitressing. She had been working overtime and she fell asleep at the wheel. When she woke up covered in glass, she was devastated."

"I'll bet you were surprised," I said, thinking about how I would feel if I saw another car coming right at me.

"Not really," she replied matter-of-factly. "All this stuff is becoming ordinary. In fact when the cops arrived, one of them came right over to me and said, 'Hi, Rusty, can I see your license?' "

At home, after Rusty took her shower and washed her hair, she came out and sat on the couch. As she unwrapped the large white towel that she had wound around her hair, I noticed a large raised bruise on her forehead.

When I questioned her about it, she looked at me sheepishly and admitted, "My head went through the windshield. That's why I was sprinkled with so much glass."

"Maybe you should get an X-ray." I was worried about a fractured skull again.

"You mean voluntarily go to an emergency room?" she asked, shocked. "No way, Carol. Can't do it."

"Well, how do you feel?" I asked. "I mean, does it hurt?"

Rusty got up and walked into the bathroom.

"Rusty?" I shouted. "I said, does it hurt?"

But she didn't answer.

That night Rusty wasn't right again. And I was almost in as big a fog as she. It had been four months without a seizure, and now this. Not again, God, I pleaded. Uncle, I give up. Let's try something else, a different kind of game. I'm humbled, I swear. I don't have the guts of Job, and I sure as hell am no Solomon. I know my limitations. Really.

It was late at night and I couldn't get through Rusty's dreamy state to get her up to bed. When Jeremy came downstairs to go to the bathroom, he looked at her sitting on the couch and asked, "Rusty's being sick again, right, Mom?"

"I don't know, honey," I told him, "but it sure looks that way." The expression on his face was as forlorn as I felt.

"Who can help her now, Mom?" he asked.

"I'm not sure, honey," I told him, "but I'll think of something."

"Good," he said, reassured, "because I sure like Rusty." After he went upstairs again, Rusty started to seize. Bad seizures. Long seizures. And I sat across from her just watching for a while, afraid that if I did anything, the whole cycle would start again. I thought about what she had said, "Just put me in a closet," and wondered why I couldn't just leave her alone and let whatever was going to happen, happen. But I couldn't.

"Should I call emergency?" Jeremy was standing at the foot of the stairs again. His voice had startled me.

"No, honey," I said, his question making my decision. "I will."

After twenty minutes had passed, Rusty was still going from one convulsion to another. Jeremy stood by the couch and I called the police for the rescue ambulance.

Suddenly I realized that I still believed in doctors and medicine more than I thought I did. Just one more try. Straight to the top. To one of the biggest neurological centers in the city. Where top dollar was paid to its doctors, where government research money was sent, where many of the brightest and the best went to study. Certainly an entire medical complex that people came to from all over the world would have an answer. They had large research grants. And they'd have to take Rusty as a patient. I just wouldn't accept no for an answer any longer. I quickly dialed the phone again and said a silent prayer that Rusty would forgive me.

When the operator at Calvary Neuro Center answered, I asked, "What's the name of the chief resident on neurology tonight?" When she told me "Dr. Michael Louden," I thanked her and hung up.

Then as Jeremy opened the door to let the police inside, I called Calvary back and asked the same operator, in a disguised voice, "Can I speak to Dr. Louden?"

"Dr. Louden is busy," she informed me in the standard nasal institutional voice that is required of hospital operators, "but if this is an emergency, I can give him a message. Who will I say is calling?"

"Tell him this is his wife and I'm leaving him," I said quickly.

And just as quickly she said, "Hold on one minute, please. He's accepting personal calls." From then on whenever I needed a doctor, instead of saying it was an emergency, I said it was a personal call.

When Dr. Louden answered, I immediately went into a ten-minute diatribe about Rusty which rendered him speechless. He probably would have given his right arm to have his wife calling rather than me, even if she was threatening to leave him. And as the ambulance crew arrived in my living room, I told him, "We're keeping eighty-year-old people alive who don't want to be alive, and yet we're letting a twenty-year-old girl who wants to live, die."

"How can I help?" Dr. Louden asked.

"I don't know," I told him, "but you must be able to. Otherwise why are you a doctor?"

"You can have our first open bed," he told me. "Admissions will call you in the next few days."

The police, the ambulance crew and the sound of the walkie-talkies made my living room sound like the scene of some gory TV crime. Lynn had stayed upstairs but Jeremy was standing by the door as the men placed Rusty on the stretcher. They began to carry her out. "Bring her right back," Jeremy told them as they walked past him, "as soon as she wakes up, or she'll be scared." The white-uniformed attendant nodded and smiled.

"Remember," I warned, "don't turn on the siren."

The other technician nodded and said, "We know, ma'am."

Thank God, I thought, because during one of Rusty's bad seizure periods, some lunatic ambulance technician kept pushing the siren during the whole ride to the hospital. I had been riding in the back with Rusty at the time, and each time the siren went off, so did she. I had asked the tech to stop. He wouldn't. Then I had pleaded for him to stop. But still he wouldn't. Finally, when he laughed at me, and Rusty was in a particularly bad seizure, I was so enraged at his obvious prejudice and sadism that I had pulled out my scissors and threatened to plant it in his back. He stopped. The next day, I went to the police station and reported him. They were kind enough to see he never rode with us again.

Now, as I followed them outside into the gravel driveway, Rusty started to seize again and they were having great difficulty handling the stretcher.

"Jesus," I heard one of them say, "if she keeps this up, she'll have mush for brains."

I wanted to ride with them now, but I had promised Rusty months before that I would try not to sacrifice the kids anymore for her epilepsy.

It had been a particularly good day that day. We had all gone to the beach and out to dinner like in the old days. And when the kids were safely asleep, we had been sitting talking. Rusty's eyes were bright and clear but she looked troubled when she had said, "A lot of times, I don't want you coming to emergency rooms or visiting me in the hospital. Not because I don't want you around, I really do. When I don't feel good, it makes me feel safer. But with my guilt over the kids, it gets too expensive for me. It costs too much."

"That's funny," I had said, smiling at her. "I don't feel much guilt over my kids."

Rusty raised her eyebrows. "We're not talking about your guilts," she reminded me. "The easiest time for me was when I was in Brighton Hall and we had no contact. It was awful but it was better because I had no guilt over the kids. And honestly, that was worth more than having you there."

"How can you accept guilt for my choices, for the things I choose to do?" I asked. "And why didn't you ever tell me before?"

"I couldn't always put into words what I was feeling," she told me, "and when I could, when I started to tell you, you'd reassure me by saying it was no problem. You'd reason with me, but that didn't make the feelings go away. I would have had to scream at you, 'Go away!' or physically push you away. Many times when I looked angry, it wasn't at you. It was at me and our situation. Instead of being able to do things as friends, instead of being able to visit museums, walk through the city, take the kids to the beach, where were we? In a hospital room. Our friendship had become a nurse-patient relationship. That infuriated me. I was always afraid that instead of getting angry verbally because of the guilt, I'd get angry inwardly and turn it on myself." Rusty took a deep breath and asked softly, smiling, "Could you spare us both from your virtue? Could you stay home with the kids and let me work things out for myself next time?"

"I'll try," I had promised. "I'll really try."

Three hours later, Rusty was home again, a little groggy but not at all confused. She had signed herself out of the emergency room and one of the policemen who had called the ambulance gave her a ride home. She had managed it alone and she was pleased.

"Are you okay?" I asked, shocked that she was back so soon.

"They gave me a couple of shots of Valium," she said, "but other than that I'm fine."

I was surprised that she wasn't sleepier; with two shots of Valium, I'd be embalmed. I had almost forgotten about Dr. Louden when Rusty asked, "Do you want me to move out again?"

"No, I don't," Then I told her. "Let's give it one more chance. Maybe it was just the clunk on the head from the accident. Maybe it won't happen again." I told her then about Calvary and the offer of their first bed. We had tried to get her in before, without success, because they always had a long waiting list, especially for people who couldn't pay.

"I'll call them back in a few days if everything's okay," I added.

"And if I'm sick, I'll go there until I'm well again. At least it's not the nuthouse."

The following afternoon Rusty had another seizure. She hadn't fully regained consciousness when the woman from admissions at Calvary called to say they had a bed. "Bring her right in," the woman said jubilantly. "We'll be waiting for her."

I called Creede and asked if she'd drive. The ride in was especially awful because Rusty was in and out of consciousness and I couldn't really explain to her what was happening. I felt as though I was deceiving her again. Once we had reached the city, several ambulances passed us with screaming sirens and I nearly had a heart attack each time, although Rusty never had a grand-mal seizure.

Walking through the emergency room was a blur; the only things I could see were rows and rows of poor, raggedy people covered with dirt and poverty and pain. I was glad I didn't work in a city hospital. Calvary was one of the best hospitals, so it had to handle some of the worst cases.

The neurological intern, Dr. Sutter, examined Rusty in one of the small ER cubicles and quickly called for a stretcher to take her up to a room. "From the signs," he said wisely, "it looks like a lesion of the brain." I was stunned until I remembered that in even the most sophisticated hospitals an intern is a person in training. Even a brilliant young doctor still in training doesn't have the benefit of experience and has to make mistakes as he learns. I was certain Dr. Sutter was looking at the obvious clues of Rusty's brain dysfunction caused by her seizures: the lowered level of consciousness, the inability to respond properly to his questions, the decrease in reflex response. All things that could also be caused by a lesion. Without testing he couldn't know.

Upstairs on the ward, she was left in the hall on the stretcher. A tall immaculate-looking male nurse explained, "The aides are cleaning up a bed for her. In the meantime, she's just as well off here where I can keep an eye on her." He tightened the straps around her waist so she wouldn't fall and said, "The doctor has ordered some medication that will probably put her to sleep, so it might be better if you leave now and come back tomorrow."

I thought again about the deal Rusty and I had made. And so as I looked at Rusty lying on the stretcher in the hall at Calvary, I knew I had to go. "Okay," I told the nurse. "If she wakes up, please tell her I'll see her tomorrow."

CHAPTER 24

The long neurological ward at Calvary seemed crammed, seemed filled with poor and desperate people dressed in drab worn clothes and hopelessness, their different voices raised in one sad and anxious common tongue.

I stood in the doorway looking for Rusty. There were several small clusters of visitors, and within each cluster there lay a thin pale patient in a chipped white metal hospital bed. Like cribs, side rails up. Each patient wore a white gauze cap and some had black eyes from surgery. They looked as though they had been beaten. Even for me, a nurse, the sight was appalling. I could only imagine what these other people were feeling.

One lady in the corner of the room had a cloudy white tubing inserted into her nostril, the end of which was taped to her cheek.

Her head hung to the side as though her neck was broken, and her mouth drooped so badly that when she tried to speak, her tongue fell forward, making her speech unintelligible.

I walked quickly to the far side of the room to a cubicle made by closed tan curtains. I pulled them back and looked in. There, in a metal crib just like the rest, Rusty lay asleep.

I bent down to kiss her. "Hi, kiddo, how are you feeling today?"

Rusty's blond hair was separated into thick spaghetti strands around her pale face. She looked drawn and tired when she turned toward me, her eyes dazed and cloudy. Then she slowly turned away.

"Hey, Rusty, it's me," I said, teasing. "What kind of greeting is this?"

She tried to hoist herself up in bed but her hands just kept slipping on the sheets and soon she fell backward. Then she tried to shake her head back and forth to clear it. "I can't, Carol," she whispered. "I just can't . . ." Her voice sounded hoarse. Her eyes closed again as she ran her tongue over her parched cracked lips.

"What the hell happened to you?" I asked, but she was already asleep again. I couldn't believe this whole cycle was about to begin again. But at least now Rusty wasn't labeled mentally ill, she was in one of the best available medical-surgical hospitals and she would have the best options of the sane. That was something.

I walked quickly out of the room and down the dreary beige hall to the nurses' station. There were metal charts, some open with pens stuck in them, scattered all over the white Formica desks. The station looked deserted. I stood for what seemed a very long time, seeing no one, before a young nurse came out of one of the other rooms and started down the hall toward me. She was tall, with straight waist-length brown hair that she wore tied back with a yellow ribbon.

"An emergency?" I asked, smiling at her.

"No," she said kindly, "just routine. One of the patients came back from the OR." When she shook her head and sighed, I knew she wasn't pleased with whatever had been done.

"I'm a nurse too," I told her, "and Barbara Russell's roommate. Can you tell me why she's so sleepy today?"

Her green eyes were bright with intelligence. "Are you Carol?"

she asked.

When I nodded, she offered me a seat on the small aluminum chair behind the desk. "She had a seizure this morning and one of the guys medicated her. Gave her an ox dose because he was afraid of Status."

"Do you know what he gave her?" I asked.

"Amytal," she said, and then quickly added, "See if you can get up to see Dr. Pento before you leave. He's the chief, and a nice man. Besides, you don't want to mess with the interns and residents."

Then she held out her hand. "My name is Rosemary Parks, and I'll be taking care of Barbara, as her primary nurse."

I liked her and was pleased Rusty would have someone to help her when I wasn't around. "She likes to be called Rusty," I told Rosemary, "and when she's feeling well, she's a riot. I think you'll like having her as a patient."

"I'd like it better if she wasn't in here at all," she told me gently. "Hospitals are the one place nice people should stay away from. Especially neurological floors in teaching hospitals. And especially if they're bright nice young people."

"I know," I said, "but Rusty has a long history of uncontrolled seizures . . ."

Rosemary nodded. "I read her history. And it reads like a nightmare for a girl her age. So I'm hoping that Dr. Pento can help. That's why I suggested avoiding the interns and residents."

It was impossible for me to get to see Dr. Pento. His waiting room was filled to overflowing with patients with obvious neurological problems. Crossed eyes, weaving gaits, and shaved heads told me more than any words.

Dr. Sutter ran interference. That day when I talked to him, Rusty's diagnosis had been changed. By now he believed things weren't as clear as he originally thought they were. I told him I understood. I was glad it wasn't a brain lesion. He told me until we tested, we couldn't be certain. I thought he was odd.

That night I called Rusty and she sounded fine again. She understood why I had brought her in, even though she didn't really believe in it. "I'll be up to see you tomorrow," I told her.

"Don't, Carol, please," she said. "Let's just see if I can get through this by myself. Otherwise it's no better than keeping me home. Let me try to handle it until I find I can't. Then I promise I'll call for help."

"But why not? Just for a visit?" I asked. "I won't even talk to anyone important, I promise. I won't interfere."

Rusty laughed. "Be serious, Carol," she said. "You know you won't help yourself." She was quiet for a minute before she explained, "There may come a time when you can't be around. I have to be able to trust myself enough to know that I can make it on my own if I need to."

Calvary made Rusty feel paranoid. She was certain that if anything could scare the epilepsy out of her, the terror she felt here could. Each time she saw another patient with a white-gauze-wrapped head and a large clear plastic tubing or an intravenous line coming out of his neck, she'd tuck her own neck deep down into her hospital gown like a turtle. Rusty was sure that if she ever got out of this place she'd never be able to move her head the same way she had before. Each time a new patient arrived, it seemed to her that they'd be taken upstairs to the operating room and then returned to the floor bad, bald and bandaged.

Dr. Pento, the chief of neurology, came to see her. He explained that he was waiting for her to get her period, since her history showed that her seizures were worse at that time. Once they were able to see her in active convulsions again, they would be better able to diagnose her. Rusty wanted to cooperate, so she did all she could to trigger a seizure. Each time she heard a police car or a fire engine, she'd race to the window and stare at the flashing red lights. Nothing happened. She stood outside the nurses' station each time they put on water for tea and strained to listen to the kettle shriek and screech. Still nothing happened. At night she lay in bed and tried to dig up all sorts of painful anxiety-provoking thoughts and feelings to try to worry herself into a seizure. And again, nothing happened.

Rusty called me most mornings, and I called her each night. Though I was more comfortable having her in a neurological hospital, it was slowly beginning to dawn on me that there might not be a solution in medicine. I began wandering around the house trying to adjust to that conclusion. What would we do? Could Rusty live her life having to deal with these episodes forever? Could I have her live with us and accept that? What about the kids?

I called Dr. Nelson to ask him if we could get Rusty off some more of her medication while she was in a protected environment and could be observed. She was still getting ten pills a day.

Dr. Nelson called Dr. Pento and Dr. Pento ordered blood work. Each morning before Rusty's eyes were open more than a slit, a white-coated lab tech would come in like a vampire and, with a smile, draw another tube of blood. When the blood levels for medication toxicity came back, Dr. Pento was appalled. They were much too high.

Dr. Pento called Jeff Lamberta. "Doctor," he said, "if this young woman is ever to be controlled, we must begin again. Understanding the possibility and danger of Status, I'd still like to withdraw all of her medication and start from the beginning."

❖ ❖ ❖

The following week Rusty pulled the curtains around her bed and kept them drawn. She explained to the nurse, Rosemary, that she was tired of community living. None of the other patients was healthy enough to relate to, and she found that watching their suffering depressed her. Also, she was beginning to have trouble sleeping at night. Often she slept upside down in bed. When Rosemary asked her why, she said, "This way, if someone gets a little too enthusiastic about operating, they can only cut my toe-nails." She joked about it but it really frightened her. What if she was "out of it" and they decided to operate? She really couldn't stop them. She was sure she was getting paranoid. Her hands shook badly and even her eyelids had tremors. She was so jittery that at every night noise she was up and pacing around the room. She tried to decide what was happening. As far as she was concerned, she was an active healthy person who had been sitting around for too long doing nothing but waiting to get sick. She figured maybe she was just getting stir-crazy. Or maybe it had finally happened and she was really going mad.

"I think I'm getting nuttier and nuttier," Rusty told me when she called one morning. "I'm so jittery, every part of my body is jumping around without my consent. I can't stand it."

"It's probably withdrawal from the meds you've been taking all these years," I said. I'd been reading my Merk Manual and everything Rusty described was a symptom of barbiturate withdrawal.

Rusty was quiet for a long time. "Why didn't anyone tell me?" she asked. "Why did they let me think I was going crazy or getting sick again?"

"I guess they never thought about it," I said weakly, aware that I was making excuses because, as a nurse, I was one of "them."

Dr. Pento ordered a shot of progesterone for Rusty, which he hoped would bring on her period. Nothing happened. So Rusty spent her days impatiently waiting, reading a ton of books, and then decided on a plan of her own. As long as nothing was happening when everyone wanted it to, and as long as there was any possibility that something unconscious inside her was causing her seizures when she least wanted them, she knew there was one more avenue left to explore. In all the years in mental institutions, she had never had therapy. She asked for a psychiatric consultation.

Rosemary, having worked on this particular ward a long time, and knowing the Chief of Psychiatry, tried to discourage her. "You're not crazy," she told Rusty; and then, seeing Rusty's concern, she asked, "Do you think you are?"

"No," Rusty answered seriously, "but maybe the seizures are my way of acting out. And if that's so, I'd really like to stop it."

"What have you been reading?" the nurse asked her as she helped her wash her hair in the sink. "Where did you get the idea that you were causing them?"

"Oh, I don't know. Over the years I guess it's been suggested several times and I thought maybe I should just make sure. The other day, in fact, I heard Dr. Sutter say something that sounded as though he believed it." Rusty sputtered through the water running off her hair and into her face.

Rosemary made a face. "Dr. Sutter is only an intern, and not a very good one at that. He's the one who said you had a brain lesion on admission, isn't he? Don't pay any attention to him. He's really book smart but he doesn't know anything."

"Does that mean you won't get me a consult?" Rusty asked as Rosemary dried her hair.

"No," Rosemary said, "I'll get you one. With our top man. The Chief of Psychiatry himself, if that's what you want." Then she laughed as she tossed Rusty a dry clean towel. "And I'll even wish you luck."

Dr. Germaine, the Chief of Psychiatry, came the next morning. With him came his assistant, carrying a paper-stacked clipboard. Dr. Germaine was a short burly man with dark skin and a soft voice. Rusty thought the young man who was with him was too pale and insipid-looking. They both pulled up chairs, in tandem, and Dr. Germaine asked Rusty, "Could we have your history, please, dear?" The assistant, with pen poised, looked expectant.

"Couldn't you just send for my records?" Rusty asked. "I've already told several people the same thing. It could save hours."

The assistant looked confused as he cast a glance at Dr. Germaine, who said, "Please cooperate, dear, we want to hear it in your own words."

Rusty laughed. "They are my own words. All of them. Never translated. All original. I was the one who told the woman in admissions. I told the resident. I told the intern. I told the social worker. I told the head nurse."

Dr. Germaine smiled. He said patiently, "We want to make sure there are no discrepancies. That nothing is left out."

Rusty sat up straight in bed. She thought about why she was giving this doctor a hard time. But then she knew. This all reminded her of Rambling Woods. Here she had expected that the doctor would have at least taken enough interest in her to have read her history before he came to see her. She was only twenty years old and she had already given her history at least two hundred times. At twenty, even with the kind of life she'd lived, there can't be that much history. And besides, he was being condescending and the idiot who was his assistant was studying her as though she were a bug, not a human being with a problem. "Dr. Germaine, if you keep asking the same history from the same person, there are bound to be discrepancies. Each time I retell it, I'm so bored with it that I edit it. So certainly things will be added or left out."

"We can't help you if you won't cooperate," he said again sadly.

And so Rusty repeated for the next two hours all she could remember. When they had finished, Dr. Germaine smiled and promised to return the following day so that together they could explore in detail some of the problems that concerned her. His assistant hadn't said a word. The thin young man stood when Dr. Germaine stood, smiled when he smiled, nodded when he nodded. He reminded Rusty of a mechanized robot, a reflection of his mentor. He had never given his name and he wore no badge, so when she said, "Bye, Dr. Germaine," she added, "Bye . . ." to see if the other could act on his own. But he hesitated until Dr. Germaine turned and waved. Then so did his assistant. Rusty got the creeps. They're going to help me? she wondered.

Dr. Germaine didn't return the following day; in fact, he never showed up the following week. But Rusty didn't really mind. She had done what she had set out to do, explore all the angles, and having approached the doctor, she felt content.

She had made up her mind that no one was getting her under anesthesia, but other than that, she was open to suggestions. She was even willing to undergo lengthy analysis if that's what it took, but no more invasive techniques. When Dr. Germaine didn't show up, she figured he was working out some special plan of attack for her so that the therapy would be really effective.

When he did come back, Rusty was surprised to see that he wore a neck brace. She was in bed working out a crossword puzzle when he approached. The first thing he did was apologize for not keeping their appointment.

Rusty noticed his mannequin alongside him, but the young man didn't greet her so she felt no need to speak to him. "That's okay," she told Dr. Germaine. "I'm just sorry you hurt yourself."

"Are you upset with me?" he asked then, coming closer to her bed.

"No," she said; then, teasing: "I didn't even miss you."

"I didn't mean not to make it," he said, and his assistant stood behind him looking as though he was about to cry.

"It's okay, really," Rusty said, when she saw how upset they both were, but she had to interrupt him because his apology went on and on. Suddenly Rusty had had it. She held up her hand and said, annoyed, "Wait a minute. Could we talk about me for a while?"

"I know you're angry with me," Dr. Germaine insisted, "and I want you to know I understand. It happens . . ."

"Get out, please," Rusty said quietly. "Go, before I have a fit."

Only when Dr. Germaine and his assistant looked horrified did Rusty realize what she had said. Then she started to laugh.

Rosemary, who had been changing the patient in the next bed, turned to Rusty with mock seriousness. "You shouldn't use the word 'fit,' "she said. "It's 'seizure.' "

"Why?" Rusty asked, smiling. "Who in this room am I going to offend?"

They moved Rusty to a private room and began giving her sleeping pills when she couldn't sleep. She told Rosemary, "I want out. I can't spend the rest of my life sitting around here waiting for something to happen."

Rosemary encouraged, "Give it another couple of days. The guys want to do another EEG."

"Okay," Rusty told her, "I'll consent to any test where they don't have to blow air or dye into my body. But nothing else. And nobody's putting a knife to my head. I'll never let them do that."

Another couple of weeks had passed, and each time I had talked to Rusty, she sounded better than before. I was beginning to think we were wasting Rusty's precious healthy time, having her stuck in the hospital. Once I had begun to get it through my thick head that maybe nothing could be done, it all seemed so absurd. And I began to feel foolish for insisting she subject herself to testing again. She was handling it better than I. I figured it was because once she got it all out of the way, she'd never go through it again.

The grinning monkeys looked grotesque. One wore a rubber cap with wires coming through; the other's head was shaved. Rusty turned the page in the magazine and stared at the pictures of more monkeys. These monkeys were snarling, their teeth bared, they were hanging by their torn fingers to the sides of a cage. They looked enraged.

Dr. Sutter was sitting beside Rusty's bed, explaining another option in case her seizures went out of control again. It seemed, he told her, that scientists had been having great success implanting electrodes into monkeys' brains. Originally the researchers were able to evoke several different emotional reactions, as the pictures showed. Sometimes rage, sometimes pleasure, according to where the electrode had been planted. Now they had discovered that in special cases, seizures could be stopped by electrode implantation. And it had been shown to be effective even in human beings. The person just had to carry a small box on his belt, and whenever he felt a seizure coming on, all he had to do was press a button on this box. That would interrupt the electrical charge which caused the seizure. Of course, the box was attached by wires to the electrode planted in the brain.

Rusty was horrified. It was like being a machine, wires and all.

That night when I called, Rusty told me about it, saying, "God knows what could happen. They could hook me up to a Muzak station and play whatever songs they wanted. I'd really have no mind of my own."

"Maybe they could give you a choice of channels," I teased, but then, more serious, I added softly, "Medical research is great, if we don't spend a lot of time considering people's feelings or the ethics involved."

❖❖ ❖❖ ❖❖

The EEG came back normal. Dr. Pento came up to talk to Rusty. He asked if she would consent to other tests. She said no. Then he asked if she would consider an operation; if they found anything on a repeat EEG, any particular focus, they could possibly do a resection, remove a small portion of the brain that was causing the problem. She said no.

That choice Dr. Pento had just given Rusty was one of the most abhorrent to me. To remove a portion of someone's brain when eighty percent of that brain was uncharted territory seemed barbaric. Especially Rusty's brain, which was, as we knew, not only the site of her illness but also the tool of her healing. That could never be allowed.

Afterward, Rusty was worried again. She wasn't sure, having been a former psychiatric patient, whether she had any right to refuse. At Rambling Woods she had been told that once she was committed, she would lose all her constitutional rights. Now that she had thrown the Chief of Psychiatry out of her room and refused the treatment that the Chief of Neurology offered, she wondered how long it would be before someone got two physicians to sign so that they could again do whatever they wanted to her.

That night when Rusty called and told me about her conversation with Dr. Pento and her concerns, I was outraged. I hollered at her as though I was talking to someone else. "Just think of that," I shouted. "Externally you have to worry about loss of control from the seizures, internally you have to worry about not behaving well enough because then people might say you're crazy and lock you up again. This is horrible." When I remembered who I was talking to, I tried to reassure her. "Don't worry about it. We won't let it happen again." But this time I said it softly, I didn't swear. I sort of asked it like a favor.

CHAPTER 25

Rosemary called me at home. She told me that she thought Rusty was doing well. Then she added, "Mr. Crosley from Social Services wants you to stop in to see him sometime this week."

"Who's he?" I asked, "What does he want?"

"He's a social worker here, and he probably wants to talk to you about manipulating Rusty's environment," Rosemary said sarcastically.

"You don't like social workers?"

"On the contrary," she said seriously, "most of them here are terrific. It's just that I find him a bit strange. She hesitated a moment before she added, "I shouldn't influence you by saying the things I have, it's just that I'd like you not to have to go through more than you have to."

I drove into the city the following day. It took me an hour to find a parking place and another half-hour to find Mr. Crosley's office in one of the dark lonely alleys of the hospital basement. I finally discovered his name etched on a small gold nameplate glued to the front of a dark wooden door.

I knocked.

Mr. Crosley was impeccably dressed in a three-piece gray tweed suit. His thinning brown hair was combed over his bald spot and pasted down. His teeth were perfectly straight and only slightly yellowed from the pipe he now held in them. The whole place smelled of vanilla tobacco.

After he greeted me and introduced himself, he led me over to a straight-backed oak chair. He sat at his desk directly across from me and pulled a manila folder from one of the drawers. He looked over it quietly for a few minutes and then put it back into one of the side drawers. Then he sat up straight, took a deep breath and smiled at me. He said nothing.

I waited, smiling uncomfortably. After what seemed like a very long time, he finally leaned forward and whispered conspiratorially, "I want you to tell me all about it, Carol. Everything. I don't want you to worry about what you say, because everything said in this room will be kept confidential."

I was immediately wary. I had worked in hospitals for years and I knew that what he said was just not true. Social work records are as accessible to all other health disciplines as any other medical records. The information shared with one is shared with all, under the assumption that it will be used for the patient's good. The only person medical records are usually kept from is any layperson, and of course, the patient.

Mr. Crosley smiled, a store-bought smile, and said with studied sincerity, "I'm not here to judge, you understand. Never to judge, only to help."

Now I was puzzled. Mr. Crosley was acting as though I had voluntarily sought out his services for my own private therapy. Some little gnome from deep down in my belly shouted, "Watch it!" But as usual, I overruled him with my logic and decided to get past what I thought of as my prejudice. I wanted to help him help Rusty.

"Now, dear, try to remember when you first felt that this was a problem," he said with a quiet intensity. "When did you first find yourself wanting to sacrifice yourself for Barbara Russell?"

"You're making it sound like martyrdom," I told him, "and it's not."

"What is it, dear," he asked, "that you've chosen to get so involved in her life?"

I was tired of defending myself "Social conscience," I said sarcastically.

"There's a difference between social conscience and martyrdom," he explained patiently.

"Well, then, I'm not sure what it is," I told him. "And I didn't call it martyrdom. I just understand that she could as easily be me. She's not in a particularly good position to help herself right now." I stopped for a minute, just thinking. Then I added, "Besides, in essence I'm not sure there is a difference truly between those two. Except that social conscience is an intellectual concept and martyrdom has spirituality as its base. But in a highly technological and scientific culture, maybe social conscience is a cover for the same feeling. Calling it social conscience makes it seem more acceptable today because lots of people who value intellect above all else see spirituality as dopey."

"One of the big differences . . ." Mr. Crosley almost drawled with condescension, "is that martyrs expect some reward in an after-life–something that exists purely in the imagination."

Maybe I should hit him, I thought, but then I reconsidered. His arrogance and his feigned humility drove me crazy. "Mr. Crosley, many people in society today pay social security and have retirement funds," I said testily. "That appears to be the same thing to me. Not one of us knows whether he will live until he is old enough to collect. Any of us could die anytime. Still, we plan for retirement just in case. As near as I can tell, the only difference in the two concepts is the time a person's imagination can span."

I couldn't get a fix on him. His questions seemed inappropriate. But it never occurred to me that he was being irrational. I thought maybe it was some sophisticated psychological approach that I hadn't heard about. Nevertheless, I felt as though I had missed the first two acts. I began to toy with my pocketbook as I started to rattle on about meeting Rusty while she was working as an aide in Salvation Nursing Home. When I told him how impressed I was with Rusty's ability and compassion while she was taking care of the old people, he folded his hands on the desk in front of him and shook his head sympathetically.

Then he leaned back in his chair with his eyes narrowed and said, "You really love her, don't you?"

He looked so perverse he almost drooled, and put so much emphasis on "love" that I was afraid I was going to get the giggles, as I did in church when I was nervous as a kid. I began to drum my fingers on the side of the chair to take my mind off him. We were supposed to be concerned about Rusty.

He stared at me for a long time. I tried to look him in the eye but it was just too embarrassing. After several minutes he asked, "Is there a man in your life?"

I laughed. "Oh God!" I said. "That's all I'd need now."

And he just stared at me again.

I was tapping my feet on the floor in front of me, trying to decide how to exit. I realized I should have listened to the gnome.

"Would you like to go out for a drink?" he asked then, and when I frowned, he quickly added, "You look as though you could use some light relaxation."

"No," I said, really puzzled now, "no, I haven't any time."

Suddenly Mr. Crosley got up, walked quickly around his desk and stood directly in front of me. He towered over me. Then in a very soft, seductive voice he asked, "What would you say if I told you that right now I know you want to go to bed with me?"

That did it. I stood up like a madwoman. "I would say you were an egotistical son of a bitch," I shouted. "I would say you were a delusional nut. And I would probably gag, throw up, get sick and . . ." But I never finished. I was so disappointed, felt so betrayed, felt so exploited that I wondered how Rusty had stayed sane in a system where so many of the people who were supposed to help laid all their problems on you. It could make you crazy.

I ran from the office to the closest ladies' room. I hid in one of the stalls. There I leaned against the cold metal partition and cried. It was so long since all this had started. We had gone to three neurologists, several doctors, a psychiatrist; Rusty had been in four hospitals, undergone tons of tests both psychological and physical, and still there were no answers. During the time between hospital admissions when I had taken her home, there hadn't been three nights in a row that either of us slept through. Most of the time I could just lie next to her holding a tongue blade between her teeth until the seizure had passed. But the other times, when the police and ambulances had to be called, it had been a mess. All that fighting so they wouldn't turn on the sirens, all the struggling to get her released from the emergency room, and the hospitals, all the long-winded discussions with all the doctors, the explaining to the kids, and the money problems.

In the twentieth century, with all the hallowed scientific discoveries of medicine, we couldn't stop one twenty-year-old girl's brain from shorting out long enough to allow her to even try living. There seemed no answers, even here in one of the largest, most progressive medical centers in the world. And yet nobody would even admit that.

Instead, labels and categories and boxes were invented to provide the illusion of progress and truth. First came the diagnosis. Like epilepsy, or mental illness, which frightened people. Once someone is diagnosed as crazy, everything becomes a symptom. What for a normal person is need for privacy for a person diagnosed as mentally ill becomes withdrawal. Anger becomes agitation. Refusal to submit to the will of others becomes passive aggression. Disagreeing with others' perception of reality becomes loss of contact or thought disorder. Real fear over what the people in control can do becomes paranoia. And so with labels stronger than iron bars, the people who claim to want to help build cages from which there's no escape.

What was worse was that the choices for the sane weren't much better if you happened to have epilepsy and your seizures suddenly went out of control. Those choices were medication with often intolerable side effects, or surgery with a permanent alteration of some part of your brain. What the hell were we going to do?

Suddenly all the fury and frustration I had felt for all those months came sweeping up from the center of my body, threatening to blow my head off, when in a flash I heard myself say: "No! No! He's not going to do this to me or anyone else ever again."

Before I knew it I was flying down the hall, pushing open Mr. Crosley's door, and like a madwoman I was pacing right in front of him. He started to stand, but he sat right back when he knew I wouldn't have thought for a minute before I pushed him down in his chair. "You're an idiot," I hollered, with tears falling and nose running. "But because you're an idiot who works in one of the finest hospitals and treats some of the sickest patients, I'm going to try to explain something to you . . . just once."

I turned and looked at him, sitting there, eyes narrowed, confused–but there was no stopping me now. "You see, Rusty's my friend–my very best friend, at that. And for a while there, she and I were . . . Let's see if I can explain this simply. We were walking along a cliff together. Well, you see, Mr. Crosley, Rusty fell off. . .

but I managed to grab her hand." I took a deep breath and almost choked on my tears. "From the beginning, I was just hanging on waiting for help to come. After a while she started slipping but I kept hoping somebody would notice and help me pull her up again. We waited a long time. Finally she was the one who let go. She fell to a smaller cliff down below, and seeing her there, I tried to find a rope, a lifeline of some sort. But nobody had one. I frantically ran to enough people, God knows. But instead of admitting they had no lifeline, all of them asked, 'Why did she fall? What had she done?' And now, 'Why do I want to help her?'

"It's simple, you ass. She's my friend and she's going to fall off that cliff into the great black abyss if somebody doesn't do something. She has epilepsy, granted, that's no one's fault, but all the rest is. First, because they needed answers and there weren't any, they misdiagnosed her and put her in a nuthouse. Then they overmedicated her. Then she had to go through all those harrowing tests just so they could find something to blame.

"When they couldn't find that, they tried to blame her, and now, goddammit, you're trying to blame me. What the hell is wrong with everyone?

"There are no social services that offer enough help. There's no sheltered or supervised place to stay until her seizures pass. There is no understanding of how her life has to stop while everyone looks for answers. Instead there's ignorance and prejudice and rejection. And yet instead of doing something about all the things we can, you turn to me and ask me what I'm doing. I'm hanging onto my friend, you jerk, because I can't let go because no help has come."

Mr. Crosley looked upset by my tirade. "I was trying to help," he said.

I shook my head as I walked away. "I know," I said. "That's what makes it so much sadder."

CHAPTER 26

Jeremy stayed home from school because when he woke up he had a fever. He had been limp and listless for days and I wanted to watch him.

After Lynn left to catch the bus, I made breakfast and brought it upstairs to Jeremy. I set it on a tray over him in bed and then I turned on his favorite cartoons. His skin was whiter than usual, with only the pink cheek flush of fever. As I was about to leave, I saw him shiver.

"Jer," I said, walking back to sit on his bed, "how about taking that heavy sleeper off and putting on something lighter?" Whenever he ran a temperature, it usually skyrocketed to above 105 degrees within a few hours, and wearing heavy clothing always made it worse.

He looked at me through heavy-lidded eyes and shook his head. "I can't," he said solemnly. "Rusty gave this one to me."

I didn't want to upset him, so I said, "Okay, we'll decide later, but right now I'll get you some Tylenol and you can take it like a big boy. Okay?"

Jeremy dozed on and off throughout the morning while I vacuumed and did laundry. Then I made him lunch and asked him to come downstairs. We sat at the kitchen table silently, he with his head in his hand, picking at his sandwich, and me wondering how long he would be sick, when in a squeaky voice he asked. "Am I smart, Mom?"

"I think so," I told him, tousling his damp hair.

He looked pensive for a few moments and then with six-year-old sincerity he said, "Know what I'm gonna do? I'm gonna read books day and night, night and day, without any stopping, and I'll be a doctor."

"Well," I said, laughing, "you'll have to get some rest, or as a doctor you won't be able to treat people well."

"I'll get enough sleep, don't worry," he reassured me.

"Because you have to take care of you first," I reminded. "Remember, you're the most important. Before you can take care of other people, you have to care about yourself."

Jeremy was deep in concentration, hardly listening to me. He took a small bite of his jelly sandwich and then turned in the chair to face me more directly. "I will care about me," he said matter-of-factly, and then with renewed fervor, "But even if I have to work for years, I want to help people like Rusty. I'll help every sick person in the world."

Oh brother, I thought, and immediately felt guilty about setting a bad example in Jeremy's formative years. I didn't believe people should live a life of self-sacrifice and not consider their own needs. I didn't want Jeremy to misinterpret my motives. Because despite what it looked like from the outside, I did consider my needs. And I had learned that often behaviors look different from the outside than they feel on the inside.

"Why do you want to help people, Jer?" I asked.

Jeremy thought for a minute. "So they get better and the people who love them don't worry about them. Cause if you love someone who's sick, you worry a lot."

I reached over and touched Jeremy's cheek. He spoke more slowly and more deliberately when he added, "So I'm gonna cure them, if there's a cure."

"You know, Jer," I said gently, "there is no cure for what Rusty has."

He looked straight at me. "Then I'll find a cure," he said simply.

I wondered how much these last months had cost him. All the emergencies, the chaos, the focus so often being taken off the children and placed on Rusty. My being worried and preoccupied much of the time. I was certain there must be some resentment, but the kids had never voiced any. "Do you love Rusty?" I asked him softly.

He cocked his small head to the side and made a funny face. "Tsk," he said. "Do I love Rusty? Mommy, you answer that."

"No," I laughed, "you answer it."

He took a deep breath. "Yes, I do love Rusty–very, very much. More than anything in the world, I do love Rusty."

"Why?" I asked him.

He was using his small index finger to slide some crumbs along the slick white tabletop. "I don't know . . ." Then for the first time that day his sad little face brightened. "Rusty taught me the Godfather prayer," he said excitedly. "I know almost the whole thing."

"The Godfather prayer?" I said, puzzled. "What's that?"

"Mommy," he said, frowning, "don't tease me."

I tried not to laugh. "Could you start it for me?" I asked. "And then maybe I'll remember."

He bit his bottom lip and frowned. He concentrated hard, and resting his head on his hands, he started: "Our Father, who are in heaven–"

"Oh, that prayer!" I said, relieved. "That's called the Lord's Prayer or the Our Father."

"See, I told you you know it!" he said, pleased with both of us now.

That afternoon, after Lynn came home and we were sitting in Jeremy's room playing Monopoly, I asked, "Lynn, do you love Rusty?"

"Yes, Mom, I do," she said seriously.

Then Jeremy asked, "Why can't they let Rusty come home for just one day, so she can get used to us again?" He looked upset again.

We were all lying on the floor with the game board between us. "Your move, Mom," Lynn said. Sure is, I thought.

"Can't we call Rusty?" Jeremy persisted.

"Not today, honey," I told him. "The doctors are doing some tests."

"Rusty's going to be real anxious to come home when she hears my voice," Jeremy added.

"Jer, pay attention," Lynn ordered. "It's your turn."

"I would like to have Rusty back," Jeremy said, his voice cracking. "I would really like to have her back."

"Me too, Mom," Lynn added. "I'd like that too."

I sat up. "Kids," I said, "when Rusty has seizures, does it cause you all kinds of chaos?"

Both kids looked puzzled, but it was Jeremy who answered again. "No, no, Mom," he said earnestly, "I don't feel anything bad. I just get mad if anybody else is here and they try to make me go upstairs so I can't help Rusty."

Lynn shook her head and said, "And I don't feel anything bad as long as everybody lets me stay upstairs."

I laughed. "Lynn, you never told me why you love Rusty."

She looked up at me and smiled. "Remember, Mom, it was Rusty who taught me to dance?"

We all played Monopoly for another hour before Lynn went to her room to do her homework and left Jeremy and me alone in his room. He climbed into bed as I gathered up the game pieces and put them back in the box.

The sun was setting and a bright orange light came through Jeremy's window and fell across his bed. "Look, Jer," I said, pointing to his wall. "It's Mr. Bibble."

"Mom, is Rusty coming home?" he asked, ignoring me.

"Jer," I said, "didn't you hear me? There's Mr. Bibble."

Jeremy started to cry. "That's not Mr. Bibble, Mom," he said. "That's my shadow. Is Rusty coming home?"

CHAPTER 27

I'd heard it before, of course, from others, and I'd read it, about the solution to a baffling problem that comes in sleep. But I had no idea of the feeling until it happened to me.

In the dream, I was running down the corridor of a new hospital complex dragging Rusty along behind me. She was pulling back against me and it took all my strength to move us forward. Both of us were wearing long white hospital gowns and suddenly they were radiant white robes and we were shepherds following a luminous star. I was pointing up to it, the star in the East, the Star of Bethlehem, of course. Rusty shook her head and pulled us to a halt. "That's not the Star," she said softly, "it's only the reflection of the Star."

I was frowning. "Of course it's the Star," I insisted. "Can't you see the cross in the middle?" I looked up at the brilliant star and where I had seen a cross only a minute ago, now there was a caduceus.

Rusty smiled sweetly and pulled open the front of her robe. A star! A shining star . . . a spectacular glow–right in the middle of her body. The golden light surrounded a child in the manger. "Here's the star, Carol," she said gently. "The other is only a reflection."

I didn't believe her. "Open your robe," she urged. "Look at your star."

To my amazement, my body was starless. No glow in the middle. I looked up the corridor again. I pointed to the star.

"Take it down and put it in your mouth," she said.

And I thought she was being crazy, sacrilegious. "It's really all the same," she insisted.

Tentatively I reached up, pulled down the Star, carefully put it in my mouth and swallowed it. Then as both Rusty and I watched, my middle began to glow. And I smiled. But when I looked up and the Star was gone, I got frightened.

"Stop looking up," Rusty instructed. "Look down, look in, look at you. Look at me. *We're* the Star."

Acceptance doesn't come easy for me. It occurred to me and God only knows how long it took–that my journey with Rusty from the first visit to Dr. Lamberta until we reached Calvary Neuro Center was my trip to Tibet for enlightenment or my Indian Vision Quest.

Everything I considered power until then had been focused outside myself I thought everything that could help Rusty, my patients or me existed in an outer world. All authority and knowledge came from someone or someplace external and could only be absorbed by me through my intellect. And if it wasn't known by them, if I couldn't read it or find it, if it wasn't documented as science or verified by statistics, I doubted it was "real."

When I finally could understand that none of the doctors, psychiatrists, psychologists and social workers were being particularly incompetent, particularly uncaring, that they just didn't know more than I did, I finally could see that there was something I hadn't figured into the equation.

And I began to understand that there was knowledge and power that wasn't written down, that came from someplace else–someplace internal. I knew what I had to do.

❖❖ ❖❖ ❖❖

The next time I saw Rusty, she was feeding an old woman in one of the large wards. She looked good. Her blond hair was shiny and clean, carefully blown dry with no out-of-the-way wisps. Her skin was rosy, her movements quick and easy. When she saw me she ran over and kissed me hello. "How are the kids?" was the first thing she asked.

"Jeremy misses you terribly," I told her, "and Lynn says to tell you that she hasn't danced since you left." I smiled when I added, "I called Jeff Lamberta. He called Dr. Pento. They'll discharge you tomorrow."

Rusty looked concerned. "Do you want me back home again?"

I hugged her. "How much trouble is a girl who only needs an empty closet?" I said.

She looked at me, puzzled. "You mean even if I have a seizure, I don't have to check into a hospital again?" she asked, and with that she broke my heart.

I put my arm around her shoulder. "Rusty, you've been dusted, cleaned, tested and treated until there's practically no part of you that hasn't been examined under a microscope, literally or figuratively. I have finally realized that the part of you they're trying to find is outside their vision. Unable to be measured by medical tools, or even neatly cataloged. Given that they can't find it, they can't treat it. Which makes you the expert on your body as near as I can figure. So I have decided to honor your wishes, and the next time you get sick, I'll just throw you in a closet."

"And if I don't only have one seizure, if I have ten?" she asked.

"Still I throw you in a closet," I said.

"And if I have twenty?" She was smiling now.

"The old closet routine!"

"And hundreds?" she asked, her eyes lighting up.

"I'll check with you again," I told her, hesitating for the first time.

"And if I'm so out of it I can't decide?" she asked, really enjoying herself.

"Still I'll honor your wishes and keep you in the closet," I said, shaking my head.

"Come on, Carol," she said, laughing now, "give a girl a chance. What kind of life is life in the closet?"

And then we both laughed until we were in tears.

"Well, what the hell do you want me to do?" I asked, smiling but more serious.

"Use your own judgment," she said. "I trust you."

"Oh, shit," I said, "we're back to square one."

"Not until I have over a hundred seizures," she reminded. And so we added another amendment to the Buddy Doctrine.

The next day. Early morning. Rusty was barely awake when she heard Rosemary's voice.

"Knock, knock," the nurse said as she walked into the room and stood at the bottom of the bed. "How would you like to help with the patients today?"

Rusty laughed. "What brought on this sudden concern for my need for productive activity?"

"Necessity, my dear girl," Rosemary answered. "One of our girls called in sick. Besides, I heard that Dr. Pento is discharging you today. I want to get some work out of you before you go."

Rusty smiled. "Thanks, Rosemary, for everything."

Rosemary walked closer. "I'm glad you're getting out. I'm really glad that they didn't find anything. It's great to see somebody go home in as good or better condition than they came in."

Creede and I picked Rusty up and brought her home. Jeremy ran out to greet us wearing Rusty's gold helmet. "Hope it's okay," he said, jumping up to kiss her. She nodded, then bent down on one knee and whispered something in Jeremy's ear. His smile made me jealous to know what it was.

"Where's Lynn?" she asked Jeremy as she took his hand. He pointed to the house.

"Want to eat over?" I asked Creede.

"Sure," she said, "but first I want to run and get a cake, to celebrate."

Once inside the house, "Rusty's home!" Jeremy called upstairs. Lynn was in her room. I heard the door open slowly.

Rusty was sitting on the couch and as I stood at the foot of the stairs I watched Lynn walk down slowly.

And then she was in the living room just looking at Rusty. When Rusty said, "Lynn. . ." and stood up, Lynn could see she was fine. And so she ran, fast, to hug her. When she moved away, I could see she was crying.

Rusty put her arms around Lynn, and then, holding her away to look in her eyes, she said, "I missed you."

"And I missed you," Lynn said, sniffing. "As much as Jeremy did."

"I know that," Rusty said.

"Really, Rusty?" Lynn said. "Really, you know even if I can't help you, I love you?"

Rusty nodded.

Later, upstairs, I helped Rusty get settled in again.

"I'm sorry I put you through all that and still we have no

answers," I said. "We don't know where your epilepsy comes from. We don't know what causes your seizures. We don't really know how to stop them and we don't know when they'll hit again. But at least we've stopped pretending we do."

"That's part of what we learned," Rusty said, smiling at me.

"I'm not sure I understand what you mean," I said.

"Your being there really helped me. You gave me encouragement. Your family, Creede and the kids made me feel normal. And when my perceptions were off, I still knew you believed in me, in my ability to be well. Because I believed in you, I could believe in me," she said. "You gave me credit for all the little things I did and so you made me feel good about myself. By acknowledging my strengths when I wasn't sick, you made me feel important. You convinced me that the more accomplishments I had, the more little victories, the stronger I'd be when I had to take on the big challenges. And it worked. You gave me the courage not to rush myself, you taught me to be patient with myself, and because we believed it would work out, it did."

I smiled at her. "I couldn't have done it without you. I couldn't do it myself."

"You could if you had to," she explained. "None of us know why we're born. We don't know what we're doing here, or if we're doing anything. Any of us can get sick anytime. None of us knows when we'll die. All of us live with hundreds of questions every day. This is just a different question. Nobody else waits around to find the answers, we all just live."

As we unpacked Rusty's suitcase, Creede ran upstairs and handed a piece of paper to Rusty. On it was a poem in her handwriting.

"What's that?" I asked.

Creede shrugged and smiled. "Just something I jotted down while I was doing a lot of thinking," she said.

It read:

> *We're each a note in the same song*
> *And each of us knows our own key*
> *But we couldn't all be the same note*
> *Or there would be no melody*

I looked up at her and laughed. Then I looked at Rusty. "What note are you?" I asked.

Rusty threw herself down on the floor. "B-flat, obviously," she said, smiling.

It was late afternoon, and the sun was still shining when Jeremy and Rusty walked down to the canal. They were happy and excited, talking in animated gestures as they finally sat on the dock.

Later, when I looked out the window, I could see Jeremy crouched down in front of Rusty while Mr. Bibble, Sebastian and Pokey danced on the shed by the canal. I laughed. Suddenly I thought I saw another small figure but he quickly disappeared. I looked closer. It was then that I noticed Lynn. She was kneeling next to Rusty, her hands raised–and as I watched, another little elf began to play.

It was my father, of course, who originally told me about the difference between doctors and nurses and healers. But it was my grandmother who was the inspiration.

"What's better, Daddy," I asked him, "a doctor or a nurse?" I was young and it was bedtime. He had tucked me in and was sitting next to me.

He smiled and brushed my hair off my face. "Neither is better," he had said, "and either can be a healer."

I had wrinkled my nose and asked, "A healer? What's a healer?"

He smiled. "There have always been healers, from the earliest civilizations and throughout all the world. In each culture, in each time, he is called something different. The Indians think of him as a holy man, a combination of doctor and priest. For them he's called a shaman or a medicine man."

"What does he do?" I had asked.

"He can see past the concrete world, past current knowledge to a special kind of truth by looking deeply inside himself. He understands the connections between human beings, nature, the spirits and the animals and he uses that truth and that understanding to help heal his people."

"How?" I asked, not really getting it.

"In different ways," my father explained reverently. "But many times by taking on the pain of the person he's trying to heal–by putting himself in the other's place. But also by bringing back, from a time of testing and chaos the special visions he has, to the other people in his tribe. Information that can make the community better."

"What makes him want to be a shaman?" I asked.

My father tousled my hair. "It's a calling. A gift from the Great Spirit," he said, smiling. "And it's usually passed on from one shaman to another. The older teaches the younger."

"Are spirits like God?" I had asked.

"Very much like what we call God," my father explained, "except that the Indians see 'God' in all things."

"Can girls be shamans?" I asked. "Are there medicine women?"

My father laughed. "Girls can be anything boys can be," he said. "How many times have I told you that, baby?" Then he hesitated and looked sad for a moment before he added quietly, "Your grandmother was a healer. Her diploma said she was a nurse and a midwife, but everyone who knew her knew she was a healer."

"Can I be like Grandma?" I asked:

My father bent down to kiss me good night. "You can be whatever you want to be, if you want it badly enough," he said. "But to be a healer involves sacrifice. There's pain and a lot of responsibility. And you have to pay attention to your visions . . . and listen for the calling."

"But what does a calling feel like, Daddy?" I wanted to know.

"A gentle kiss on the lips from God," he whispered.

A healer heals, my father had said, by taking on the pain of another. What my father forgot to tell me was that hunting for visions to bring back was a lot trickier and a lot more difficult than hunting for deer or buffalo. Indians knew that. I didn't.

Finally I understood that the way we practiced modern medicine provided only half the answer to healing. That it functioned almost solely on a "masculine" or "aggressive" principle. I'm not talking about men or women here. I'm talking about masculine and feminine aspects of a psyche. The destroyer and the creator in each of us.

Both exist in men and women in varying degrees. All labels have limits.

The masculine principle, I could see now, was a throwback to our primitive beginnings, where for survival the hunter had to carry a stick, track and find the enemy–then beat him to destroy the danger. Of course, we don't use sticks anymore. We use lab tests, scalpels, needles, respirators and other high-technology weapons. And we dress in animal skins any longer; we dress in fine clothes. In order to track, then find, then destroy–whether it be bacteria, cancer or any other known enemy. And that's good and that's fine some of the time.

But when the enemy is unknown or unconquerable, outside the reach of our understanding, the track/hunt/destroy/masculine principle is an abuse of power, a mindless aggression that at its best is ineffective.

It's the "feminine" or creative principle which knows that too much pain impairs survival–and it's that principle, whether in men or in women, which understands that life is power. And that sometimes in order not to destroy that life, we must yield, not fight. And in chronic illness, not only epilepsy, but cerebral palsy, multiple sclerosis, senility, mental illness and all the others for which we have no cure. . . there remains the unmet need for sanctuary, nurturance and compassion. In many cases only the feminine principle, protect, nurture and create should be used. Only that has the chance to renew health and ensure survival. If we can't beat the disease, then we have to remember to do no harm.

Until Rusty, my definition of heroism was one of activity. Heroes fought . . . and conquered. As a nurse working in the system, I had been aggressive in my fight for power over sickness and death. And often because I had worked with acutely ill patients, I succeeded. But in all my years of nursing, never before had I reached the limits of my endurance or really tested my power. Never before was I forced to acknowledge there was something bigger than me, bigger than medicine. Never before did I have to use *more* than I had. But with Rusty, all my activity, all the force I'd used, all my intelligence, did me little good. I could have walked around whistling and twirling my spear for those times she was sick. With

Rusty, Fate grabbed me by my hair and pulled me to my knees . . . and then it held me there.

I had to acknowledge my impotence. I had to surrender.

With the destroyer destroyed, the creator appeared. With the masculine defeated, the feminine began to surface. Then the woman in me, the mother in me, quietly, insistently, intuitively helped to heal. By loving, by caring, by being a friend. And finally I could see that the woman in me had real hero power ... different from the male heroes I had grown up with, but not less powerful.

Nothing I had done seemed to have worked. And yet we had found the answer. Rusty was well again. We never had to call an ambulance again. She never had a period of uncontrolled seizures again. She was never hospitalized again.

And as for me, I was a better nurse after my experience with Rusty. My priorities had changed. Doctor's orders came second to patient's orders from then on. I had finally learned who the experts were. Even more than all that, while I had been paying attention to Rusty, I had discovered another part of myself. And so, the debt is mine.

Epilogue

The years since Rusty was discharged from Calvary have been good. Maybe better than good. She worked to pay the rent while I went to college. She helped me study for my nursing finals and brought the kids to my graduation. When I remarried, she helped me and the kids move to our new house.

It was a beautiful day, the sun was glistening off her hair, and I was gloomy.

"I feel so bad leaving you here," I had said.

But Rusty reassured me with a huge smile. "Stop making such a big deal of it. I've always wanted a place of my own and now I've got it. Packed full of great times and laughing.

She was walking alongside me, helping me carry some cartons to the car. "Besides, you're just moving around the corner. We'll still practically be living together."

"Are you afraid to live alone?" I had asked.

"A little," she said, grinning. "Are you afraid to live with someone else?"

"A little," I had said.

She had hugged me. "You've got the key. If it ever gets too rough, you and the kids can come back," she said, laughing.

"And if you ever need me, I can let myself in," I said crying.

During those years, each of us had made the trip around the corner many times: I'd call, she'd call . . . the kids would call. And we had continued to do things together. Rusty was more excited than I at Jeremy's graduation, and more nervous than I at Lynn's wedding.

Rusty signed up for college. She took courses that could be applied to a nursing program. She got all A's. She was promoted at work. The golden oldies still loved her madly, and now she was in charge of her floor. She furnished her house with things of her own that she'd managed to buy with the money she earned by working each day. And she ran through the grass with the wind in her hair and stayed on her feet most days. I really felt like a fairy godmother.

As an added bonus, last year, when we no longer expected it, Fate even threw in a couple of small miracles.

Miracle Number 1:
>   We met a man who used no labels
>   Wanted no records
>   Took the time—to listen.
>   He said, "Tell me your story."
>   And Rusty did.

The man was a doctor, a neurologist at that. He was intelligent, compassionate and—to Rusty and me—a hero. I had gotten Dr. Gary Gerard's name from both the Epilepsy Foundation of America and the Epilepsy Institute. Those groups were now effectively organized to help people with epilepsy.

After Rusty finished talking, Dr. Gerard shook his head, looked sad and said, "I'm sorry. How can I help?"

I told him, "Rusty hasn't had any grand-mal seizures for several years. But she still does have night terrors and sometimes sensory distortions." I had been reading about a pill which seemed perfect for this kind of seizure. "We need some Tegretol," I said, "but we can't get a doctor to prescribe it without doing all kinds of tests again."

"You've got it," he said, smiling.

"No tests," Rusty insisted.

"No diagnostic tests," the doctor agreed. "But periodic blood tests are a necessity to prevent toxicity."

Rusty agreed.

"Why would the epilepsy have caused such behavioral changes? Why would it make me cut myself?" Rusty asked. She was still bothered by the lack of answers after all these years.

Dr. Gerard kindly explained, "The other day my wife was holding a cup of coffee and a bee landed on her hand. She jumped, spilled the coffee, and burned herself. Anyone who hadn't seen the bee would have thought her actions inappropriate."

"So you think Rusty's actions were appropriate for the perceptions she was having?" I asked.

He smiled. "I do."

Then he asked Rusty, "Are you certain you'd like to try this new pill?"

And she smiled happily—because it seemed important to this man to finally include her in her treatment. "More than I wanted a promotion at work and more than I wanted my new car," she said.

Outside his office, while we stood waiting for the elevator, Rusty asked, "Wouldn't it be wonderful if when you had to hear you had epilepsy, a doctor like Dr. Gerard could tell you?"

Rusty began taking Tegretol. She went faithfully for her lab tests.

The medicine was working. No more night terrors, no more wind that smelled like bananas—and still no grand mal seizures.

Often, Gary Gerard called her at home to see how she was feeling.

"Any side effects from the medication?" he asked.

"Only that I feel taller," Rusty answered.

Miracle Number 2:

Rusty must have run, because when I opened the front door, her cheeks were flushed and her blond hair curled and wet.

"Close your eyes," she told me. "And don't open them until I tell you to . . ."

I covered my eyes with my hands and waited.

"Okay," she said, happily. "Get this! Check the name."

And there it was! A credit card—American Express!

In bold black letters on the green card BARBARA RUSSELL was shining like a brightly lit marquee.

The Doctor's Note

Misunderstanding about epilepsy is unequaled by any other physical condition. It is surprising that a condition as common and prevalent would be surrounded by so much mystery. Over 2,000,000 people in this country have epilepsy and 1 person in 20 has a seizure during his life. This is certainly an underestimate, society's attitude toward epilepsy causes many more to deny having seizures.

The social attitude toward epilepsy is, at times, more difficult for the person with epilepsy to overcome than is the medical problem. If it were not for books like Rusty's Story and tireless efforts by volunteer organizations such as the Epilepsy Foundation of America, few lay people would have any information on epilepsy.

As Rusty's Story vividly illustrates, many people with epilepsy struggle with the attitudes of family, friends, physicians, society, and their own identity. Fear, prejudice, and ignorance continue to harm and undermine self esteem. Many people like Rusty are fortunate to be blessed with indomitable personalities and caring, enlightened people around them, but others are not; their seizures are frightening and mystifying to the people around them.

Many people, including physicians, do not recognize the various forms of seizures other than grand mal. Adults who have behavioral attacks (complex partial seizures), like Rusty, are often mislabeled as psychiatric and never receive the appropriate help. This can have tragic results since the "reality" of seizure episodes is largely dependent on the reactions of others: Suddenly, without warning, someone finds herself on the ground . Her speech is slurred and incoherent, and she is unable to convince bystanders that she will be all right in a few minutes before she is put in an ambulance heading for the hospital. In the emergency room, back to normal, she is informed that she must be admitted and is put in a bed, side rails up, lined with padding. It is not hard to imagine how this person begins to think of herself as "different."

The most significant development in the understanding of epilepsy was the electroencephalogram in the 1930s. Since then there have been many advances. Long term simultaneous EEG and video recording has increased the accuracy of diagnosis. Computerized tomography and now magnetic resonance imaging allow detection of structural brain abnormalities without discomfort, risk, or hospital admission. Positron Emission Tomography(PET) as well as Single Photon Emmision(SPECT) imaging helps to identify patients who would most benefit from surgical removal of a seizure focus.

New concepts of antiepileptic drug therapy have developed. Increased knowledge about old antiepileptic drugs have better defined their usefulness. New effective drugs have been introduced. Determination of blood levels of anti epileptic drugs is now widely available allowing better control with less risk of toxicity. Wide variations exist from one patient to another on the same dose. Much has been learned about the way drugs are handled by the body since the time Rusty's symptoms of drug toxicity baffled her physicians. The National Institute of Neurology and Communicative Disorders and Stroke (NINCDS) has implemented comprehensive epilepsy centers nationwide for the purpose of getting research results to the patients who need them.

Since the time Rusty developed epilepsy, the care of people with epilepsy has improved. The Epilepsy Foundation of America is reaching more people each year and eradicating ignorance concerning epilepsy, and Rusty's Story has been shared with thousands of people. Rusty's courage will serve as an inspiration to us all and her story will greatly increase our knowledge of people with epilepsy.

GARY GERARD, M.D.
Director-Neurology Center of Ohio
1000 Regency Court
Toledo, Ohio 43623

Update on Rusty 1997

Since the release of "Rusty's Story," we have received many calls and letters wanting to know how she is doing now. So in this edition, we want to update all of you.

Rusty has managed to stay healthy through making a conscious decision to try to balance her life by getting proper rest, eating well, meditating and respecting the needs of her body/mind/spirit. She still has occasional "visionary" experiences but has learned from them and has integrated them as part of who she is.

A few years ago Rusty began to see all efforts toward healing as part of a "recovery" process. She went to school and graduated as an alcohol and addictions counselor and is now enrolled in college to obtain her Bachelor's Degree. She is working as a counselor to help develop new programs which will honor the experiences of those who consciousness is altered by either drugs, alcohol or illness.

Rusty has taken her experiences and has brought them into the world with added wisdom and compassion, hoping to effect a change in the Health Care System so others won't have to experience what she did. She has moved from victim to victory. We're still best friends. And she still lives around the block.

With hope for all healing,

Carol Gino

Available in bookstores
in November
by Kensington Books

It happened in a single moment. Their lives were changed. Their souls shaken. And then, when they were most vulnerable, their hearts opened to the miraculous . . .

They were a three generation Italian-American family steeped in traditional values. Carol Gino's old-world father was a stern disciplinarian who loved opera and polka; her mother, a shy housewife who lived for her family, while Carol herself had made a spiritual journey away from her Catholic roots. But nothing in the Gino family's past could ever have prepared them for the tragedy that would change all their lives forever.

On Wings of Truth

Janith, an Archangel, lives in the Light. She's compassionate, witty, wise. Her focus is on helping us create a more loving planet by helping each of us create a lighter more loving and less fearful individual.

Janith's simple and practical information is given from an unlimited viewpoint:

- *Why should we explore our past lives?*
- *Why is there so much suffering in the world?*
- *Why are human beings frightened of the unknown?*
- *What is death?*
- *What is the difference between channeling and schizophrenia?*
- *What is the purpose of addictions?*
- *What are the basic truths?*
- *What is free will?*

224 pgs - $12.95
Questions and answers.
Beautiful original illustrations.

This book was compiled by Teri Griswold, who is the channel for Janith.

Star Water Press, Ltd.
(516) 598-8842 • Fax (516) 691-1357
PO Box 488 • 12 Virginia Ct • Amityville, NY 11701
Visit Our Web Site at http://www.starwater.com